# DAYS OF HONOR AND HONESTY

A MEMOIR

# DAYS OF HONOR AND HONESTY

MARY ITA MALONE

Copyright © 2018 Mary Ita Malone.

All rights reserved. No part of this book may be used or reproduced by any means, graphic, electronic, or mechanical, including photocopying, recording, taping or by any information storage retrieval system without the written permission of the author except in the case of brief quotations embodied in critical articles and reviews.

Will Parkes, Marketing /Rights and Permissions/eBooks/Audio books.
Darton, Longman and Todd.Ltd to quote from the Jerusalem Bible.

Professor Miriam Were to quote the Forward to the book

Professor David Nyamwaya to quote from his Ph.D. thesis, *The Management of illness in an East African Society: A study of choice and constraint in Health Care among the Pokot*, Cambridge, 1982

Keith Drew to copy the map of *The Kerio Valley and the Cherangani Hills* out of *The Rough Guide to Kenya*, 2016 edition, page 242

Father Leo Staples to use photos of people, scenery and projects from West Pokot during the 1960s and 1970s

Kelly Galiszewski of *Spirit Led Photos* for permission to use studio pictures of author

Scripture taken from THE JERUSALEM BIBLE, copyright (c) 1966 by Darton, Longman & Todd, Ltd. and Doubleday, a division of Random House/Penguin, Inc. Reprinted by Permission.

Scripture quotations are from the ESV® Bible (The Holy Bible, English Standard Version®), copyright © 2001 by Crossway, a publishing ministry of Good News Publishers. Used by permission. All rights reserved.

Archway Publishing books may be ordered through booksellers or by contacting:

Archway Publishing
1663 Liberty Drive
Bloomington, IN 47403
www.archwaypublishing.com
1 (888) 242-5904

Because of the dynamic nature of the Internet, any web addresses or links contained in this book may have changed since publication and may no longer be valid. The views expressed in this work are solely those of the author and do not necessarily reflect the views of the publisher, and the publisher hereby disclaims any responsibility for them.

Any people depicted in stock imagery provided by Getty Images are models, and such images are being used for illustrative purposes only.
Certain stock imagery © Getty Images.

ISBN: 978-1-4808-6151-0 (sc)
ISBN: 978-1-4808-6150-3 (hc)
ISBN: 978-1-4808-6152-7 (e)

Library of Congress Control Number: 2018907497

Print information available on the last page.

Archway Publishing rev. date: 12/31/2018

# CONTENTS

| | | |
|---|---|---|
| FOREWORD | | vii |
| AUTHOR'S NOTE | | ix |
| PROLOGUE | | xi |
| CHAPTER 1 | Memories Lane | 1 |
| CHAPTER 2 | Childhood | 13 |
| CHAPTER 3 | Worlds Shift | 45 |
| CHAPTER 4 | Joining the Holy Rosary Sisters | 85 |
| CHAPTER 5 | In Training Incognito | 123 |
| CHAPTER 6 | Africa, Finally | 155 |
| CHAPTER 7 | First Tour of Duty | 189 |
| CHAPTER 8 | Vows Put to the Test | 241 |
| CHAPTER 9 | Formation of a Larger Vision | 275 |
| CHAPTER 10 | Great Accomplishment, Great Heartache | 329 |
| CHAPTER 11 | A Turn to Teaching | 359 |
| CHAPTER 12 | Global Soul Searching | 385 |
| CHAPTER 13 | Rehabilitation | 421 |
| CHAPTER 14 | The Real World | 437 |
| CHAPTER 15 | Musings | 459 |
| EPILOGUE | | 473 |
| ACKNOWLEDGEMENTS | | 475 |

# FOREWORD

The life story of Dr. Mary Ita Malone begins with her visit to the area of Kenya where she had worked some forty years back. This points to the commitment and love that she had for my country and its people. It is even more revealing when one realizes that the place where she practiced for twelve years was in one of the most underdeveloped parts of Kenya, specifically, the District of West Pokot, centered in an obscure village called Ortum.

Her childhood was steeped in love of family, church and country which prepared her to follow the promise and dream of her- eight- year self: - she would devote her life to help the neglected children of Africa.

Growing up she envisaged herself as a teacher. Instead she was chosen by the superiors of the missionary congregation she had joined, to study medicine at University College Dublin (UCD), Ireland. She survived this rigorous medical training and embraced the challenges of practicing in a remote area that had neither the laboratory nor technical support of modern medicine. This, by itself, reveals her tenacity, capabilities and conscientiousness.

Dr. Malone recognizes that her independent spirit caused

some conflicts in her life as a nun. As an example, in her role as medical doctor, she had the overall responsibility in the hospital setting. Yet there were situations when a nurse whom she professionally supervised was her superior in religious lines of authority.

The climax came following her studies at the prestigious Johns Hopkins University in Baltimore, Maryland, USA. As part of a requirement to obtain a Master's in Public Health degree, (MPH), she developed a Maternal and Child Health Program to be based in Ortum and extending into the surrounding territory. However, this project never came to fruition,

Consequently, Dr. Malone ended up teaching in the Department of Community Health in the Nairobi University Medical School where she and I were colleagues for six years. The duties involved teaching medical students both in Nairobi and in the rural areas. She also contributed valuable research into improving primary health care services. Dr. Malone's love for the people of Kenya shone through all.

When her teaching responsibility at the Nairobi Medical School ended, Dr. Malone embarked on a journey exploring where her future lay, not only in her professional career but if she would continue to be a nun. Her decisions led her to the USA where she eventually settled and from where she writes this most interesting and inspiring book.

It is a read I highly recommend.

Professor Miriam K. Were, MB ChB (Nairobi), Dr PH (Johns Hopkins), EBS, IOM.
Chancellor, Moi University, Eldoret, Kenya

# AUTHOR'S NOTE

The people, places and things contained within these pages are not fictitious.

I have tried to remember the conversations and events contained herein as accurately as I could.

I have changed the names of some of the people to maintain their right to privacy.

# PROLOGUE

Picture the scenario. It's a beautiful autumnal afternoon in Florida, with low humidity, temperatures in the mid-seventies Fahrenheit, a mild breeze blowing. The room is filled with ladies, all recently retired, seated at card tables in teams of four or five, playing either the original Chinese game of mah-jongg or the card game of canasta. The chatter is at a tolerable decibel as it accompanies the concentration and camaraderie of the sixty-something participants. The ladies are all American and Jewish except one, an Irish woman by birth but a United States citizen by adoption.

Five good friends are enjoying their game, when Tobi, the nurse, jubilantly exclaims, "This is paradise! I never envisaged myself retired and playing mah-jongg midafternoon—and in such good company."

"How much more so for me!" says the Irishwoman. Everyone in the bunch agreed that this is a unique and unlikely situation that deserved further telling, even if it never reached the history books.

So began my saga down memory lane recalling how I (Marita) got connected to F (Florida) and how this might never have occurred if I'd followed other what-ifs along the way.

In life's journey, there are times when reality can be stranger than fiction, and following the star can take us through undreamed-of and uncharted waterways. In my youth, should a fortune-teller have read my palm and foretold the above scenario, in today's jargon, I would have laughed out loud (LOL). Even still, I have to pinch myself to realize it is reality. Hopefully you, the reader, will feel the same as you follow me on life's circuitous journey.

The title, as strange as it seems, was prompted by the following episode. My father was a hardworking man—a farmer at heart—but because he was not the firstborn son in his family, he did not inherit the family farm. To provide for us, his family, he became a psychiatric nurse at a hospital for the mentally ill in our hometown. While I never felt close to him, I always knew he was there to nurture and support not only me but my five siblings. As they say in Ireland, he died at the good age of ninety-two years. After his funeral one of my cousins shared some fond memories he had of my father, one of which left a lasting impression.

For several years before his retirement, Father had been the night superintendent at the hospital, which involved control of the main and other entrance and exit doors as well as other supervisory tasks during the night shift. One day in the staff dining room, long after Father had retired, my cousin John, who worked there, overheard a conversation among senior members lamenting how, in recent times, hospital affairs appeared to have changed for the worse at all levels of the administration.

One of them summed up their sentiments by proclaiming, "God be with the good old days, the days of honor and honesty of John Malone." The person who said this had no idea that John was my father's nephew. That remark made me feel proud, and to this day, it resonates with me as summing up not only my father's legacy but also that of my mother and, in many ways, most of the people I knew of their generation. Not only did they serve their country with honor, but there was a sense of honesty that permeated their whole way of living. I've titled and dedicated this memoir as a tribute to their memory.

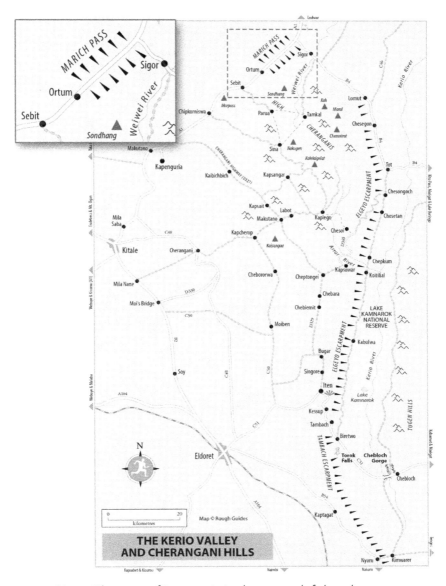

Note: The area of interest is in the upper left hand corner. This map is courtesy of the publisher of The Rough Guide to Kenya—2016 version.

# CHAPTER 1

# MEMORIES LANE

After four decades, I returned to a place that was dear to my heart and where I had spent twelve of the best years of my life. That place, Ortum, lies on the floor of the aptly named Forbidden Valley, amid the Cherangani Hills of northwestern Kenya.

When I left Ortum in 1972, I was a medical doctor and a member of the religious order of the Missionary Sisters of the Holy Rosary (MSHR). I was on my way to the United States to study for a master's in public health at the prestigious Johns Hopkins School of Public Health in Baltimore, Maryland.

After a dozen somewhat frustrating years of acting as a general doctor for the indigenous people of the Pokot tribe, who had scarce knowledge of and little interest in Western medicine, I had hatched an ambitious plan to organize community-based health services for the area around Ortum and to expand into a neighboring territory that was also isolated and in dire need of primary health services.

I had no inkling that I would never return to implement the program.

In January 2013, about two weeks after my eighty-second birthday, I met up in Kitale, Kenya, with Father Leo Staples, the priest who had founded the missionary church in Ortum in 1952. Although he knew nothing of it, Leo had played a critical role in the trajectory of my life.

At almost eighty-eight, Father Leo was still working in the Rift Valley as an associate to a Kenyan pastor while overseeing the building of his latest project, a home for neglected children challenged with physical disabilities. Our life paths had certainly diverged since we'd soldiered together so many years ago. Like Leo, I had been born in Ireland, but I was now a US citizen living in Florida, content and comfortable in retirement, except for the part time volunteering of my services in primary care at a local clinic.

I had stayed in touch with Father Leo after we both moved on from Ortum, he to another remote mission and I to the capital of Nairobi. After I left Kenya, we exchanged occasional letters and got together a few times when we were both visiting Ireland. Yet in 2013, despite our long friendship, it took some persuasion to get him to leave his parish and charity work to escort me back to Ortum.

Riding the newly paved road to Ortum was nothing like being jostled on the deeply rutted one-lane dirt track I vividly remembered. Chokingly dusty in the dry season and a viscous red slop in the wet season, the road had barely clung to a steep mountainside as it descended in a series of hairpin bends three thousand feet to the valley floor.

Before Kenya transitioned from a British colonial government to independence on December 12, 1963, certain remote territories were closed to people who did not have official permission to enter. In those days, to get to Ortum, at the entrance to the district, we had to stop at a police barrier and be checked out—our religious habits served as our IDs—before we could continue down into the Forbidden Valley. In 2013, of course, the barrier and *askaris* (the Kiswahili word for uniformed guards, police, or soldiers) were long since gone and forgotten.

As I looked out the window of Leo's Toyota SUV at the mountain peaks I'd often longed to climb, I was transported back to the times when I would find solace and peace in contemplating their beauty after a long, hot, trying day of treating patients at one of the outstations.

As we came into Ortum finally, I was mesmerized by the lights. Rural electrification had arrived in this center a few years earlier, thanks to the influence of a local politician. This was incalculable progress from the days when our old geezer of a generator could only provide a few hours of electricity each evening. If we had to perform surgeries or emergency procedures later in the night, we relied on the light from kerosene-fueled lanterns.

Until I arrived at the convent in Ortum, I was unaware that this was the end of an era for the Holy Rosary Sisters, the familiar name by which we were known. The congregation, which had served there since 1956, was soon to be replaced by one of Kenyan sisters. In a way, we had come full circle. This congregation had been founded by the late Bishop Joseph Houlihan, who had established the Ortum mission in the first place.

Everywhere, we saw evidence of the indigenization of the mission facilities, which had always been our goal. Even the two pastors stationed in Ortum were Kenyans.

The outgoing sisters in the Ortum convent were Nigerian, something I could never have envisioned forty years ago. Nigeria was the Holy Rosary Sisters' first destination in Africa, and these nuns were proof that those labors had borne fruit. The MSHR still took the word *missionary* literally, meaning that each sister was sent to work in a different country from her native one, even if she was originally from a country where there was a Holy Rosary presence.

Father Leo and I spent that evening, to the excitement of the resident sisters, watching on television a live soccer match between Nigeria and South Africa. Needless to say, we had no TV during my tenure there.

The next morning, Father Leo declined a visit to the hospital, so alone I walked down the hill by treading the dusty path I'd once known so well. I felt nervous anticipation and excitement as I approached the entrance. On the way I noticed some familiar sights, but mostly nothing was the same as I remembered.

The hospital compound was fenced in, with uniformed askaris on duty. At the center of the circular driveway that now graced the entrance was a large plot of flowering shrubs. This beautification obviously had not just gotten there but bore evidence of the fruits of much sweat and many green thumbs reaching back through the years. I couldn't help but reflect back on the simple hospital, church, convent, and outbuildings

I remembered, all huddled together on the open hillside, surrounded by a few hardy native plants and thorn bushes.

I was amused more than amazed by the large notice boards that proclaimed the range of services rendered at Ortum Mission Hospital, all proclaimed in English, a language unknown to the illiterate Pokot in the 1960s. The Pokot language was mainly an unwritten one, necessitating that Father Leo not only learn to speak it but also translate the catechism and other religious documents as his first order of business after his arrival in the early '50s.

The most amusing signs were the details of visiting hours and the indicator to the parking area.

The phrase at the bottom of the sign, "Security is at high alert," reminded me of another change, this one sad. On this recent visit, everywhere I went, from Nairobi onward, I saw walls topped with loops of razor wire or, where resources were scarcer, jagged glass inset into the mortar at the top of the wall. Askaris stood watch beside the entrances to hospitals, government buildings, housing complexes, the tonier homes, and even sisters' convents.

The gap between the rich and poor in Kenya is probably smaller today than in colonial times or the early years of independence, but the high crime rate probably comes from the fact that Kenyans are more aware of their disadvantages on a global scale, thanks to television and the Internet. Everyone had a mobile,(a cell phone)—incredible!

As I approached the reception window of the hospital, cheerful Pokot ladies in contemporary Western dress welcomed me.

They were speaking impeccable English and were graduates of the local girls' secondary school.

My mind immediately flashed back to the Pokot women draped in long skirts of cured animal skins, naked above the waist except for their traditional collars of blue, red, and white beads strung on ever-widening circumferences of copper wire. Traditionally, the women kept the hair on the lower half of their heads closely shorn and twisted the hair at the top of their heads in a braid-like fashion, infusing it with a blend of the local castor oil and charcoal. To my unaccustomed nose, the acrid smell took some time to get used to.

I was happy to see that the women had embraced education in the decades since I'd left. In the 1960s, the Pokot had had no use for the missionary school, especially the one established for girls. "Who will mind the goats?" was the refrain we always heard.

The next experience will demonstrate progress from those tentative early days.

Upon my arrival in Kitale, the northernmost town of the famous Rift Valley and, in the days of yore, our lifeline to the civilized world, one of the first sights that caught my peripheral vision was a beautiful motor coach parked on the side of the road. Inscribed in large letters on its side were the words: *Fr. Leo Staples Girls Sec. School.* Having pulled over to admire the spectacle, we were greeted not only by the driver in his impeccable white uniform but also by a group of the most beautiful-looking, healthy Pokot teenage girls, pupils of the school in Sigor, where my friend had been pastor for many years after I left.

In their smart uniforms of green pleated skirts topped by white shirts, over which they wore green sleeveless pullovers with the motto of the school, "Foundation of Excellence," embroidered into the school crest, they were a sight to behold. With the most cordial of greetings, they informed us that they were just in town to shop and admire the sights. Tears filled my eyes, and emotions of wonderment and gratitude washed over me as I witnessed a scene I could never have imagined, much less experienced.

The matron of the hospital was a Pokot lady; unfortunately, she was off duty and away. Her assistant, Mrs. Lucy Githoni, a registered nurse from the Kikuyu tribe who hailed from hundreds of miles away, escorted me around the various departments. As we toured, she explained that she had been stationed in Ortum for five years, leaving her children in the care of her mother. Needless to say, she was anxious to be nearer to her young family.

During my tenure, either we had to recruit staff from outside the area because none of the local people had been trained or, later, the local people who had been educated fled to the larger towns and cities, where they would get higher pay and enjoy more modern facilities and amenities.

It was exciting to see the well-equipped laboratory and modern x-ray department. Outpatients, I discovered, were being treated by an indigenous certified medical officer. More exciting still was to see the Maternal Child Health Clinic abuzz with activity as mothers waited patiently to have their young children weighed, checked for health problems, and given scheduled immunizations. All was taking place in a welcoming environment replete with relevant health-education props, including a television screen—a wild dream I'd had that I'd never thought I would see become reality.

Even though the sponsorship and administration of the hospital were still under the auspices of the local diocese, the two Kenyan doctors on staff were appointees of the Ministry of Health (MOH), who paid their salaries. It represented the good working relationship between the two. Both of the doctors were graduates of Nairobi Medical School, where I was an associate professor after returning to Kenya with my master's in public health. Of course, that was long before they were students in this exalted institution.

As we entered the neonatal unit (for premature and sick newborns), I could hardly contain myself when I saw the two incubators, each holding a premature infant. I greeted the proud and conscientious mamas, who were hovering near the cribs. My mind reverted to the inventive ways we'd been forced to devise to protect these tiny tots.

Because nights in the hot, dry valley could be chilly, we'd used a crude charcoal brazier for heat, over which we'd kept a kettle of boiling water to provide the needed humidity, making sure there was plenty of ventilation in the room. When the newborns could not breastfeed, drip by drip by pipette, we'd fed them the mothers' expressed milk. Even with those primitive conditions, it was amazing to see how many of the preemies, some with birth weights of just two pounds (one kilo), had survived and flourished.

One of these preemies who lived to tell the tale—and whom I accidently met during my travels—was an aspiring member of Parliament for the district. As I conversed with Mr. Stephen Kalimuk, he informed me that he had been born in Ortum Hospital in early 1972 and that his mother still talked with gratitude about the *Musungu* (European) sister doctor who'd delivered him and allowed him to thrive and prosper. Neither of us could believe the coincidence that we were now meeting forty years later and in such unusual circumstances. He was anxious for me to meet his mother, who was still well and hearty, but unfortunately, our schedules did not allow that encounter.

When I'd arrived in Ortum in 1960, the infant and maternal mortality rate had been extremely high—although we don't know the extent of it because countless Pokot mothers and babies died without coming near the hospital. Childbirth had been extremely perilous for Pokot women because of their traditional practice of female genital mutilation (FGM) and other practices of the traditional midwives.

Over the tenure of my stay, we had solved some of the problems militating against women being able to have safe delivery of their babies. It was not unheard of for a woman to have ten pregnancies and have no living child to show for the effort. Through trial and error, bearing in mind the centuries-old traditions regarding childbirth, we had made progress in assuring a woman that she would have a living child and hopefully learn to care for it while she was in the hospital.

One such innovation was to construct a basic building on the campus, which we christened the Ladies in Waiting, so that women in the advanced stages of pregnancy could live there until the onset of labor. Then they would be admitted to the labor unit, and under the vigilant care of the nursing staff, have the whole process supervised until they delivered healthy babies and the mothers were safe and well.

I was surprised to learn that this idea had flourished and that the old building had been replaced by a new permanent hostel funded by USAID. This agency was so impressed at how well the idea was functioning that they plan to use the approach to encourage safe labor and delivery in isolated, remote areas of the developing world.

Another source of joy and pride was learning that the Enrolled Community Nurse Training School that had opened before I'd left had now been replaced by a higher level of training, a Registered Community Nurse Training School. On the day I was visiting, the sister tutor and the hospital administrator were involved in supervising the final examination for twenty-nine students from all over Kenya, who were completing their training at the hospital. In my wildest dreams, I could never have imagined that progress.

Feeling gratified and proud of the progress I'd witnessed at my former hospital, I climbed back to the Ortum Convent to resume my journey with Father Leo. Although I really wanted to visit one of the outstations, he was anxious to get back to his regular responsibilities. I got the sense that this was an emotional issue for him; his heart was still very much with the Pokot people, and perhaps it was not of his doing that he was no longer their pastor. To witness the cheers of "Lokomul, Lokomul!" from the surprised men and women who recognized him and to see how he reacted and spoke in kPokot was inspiring. The name had been conferred on him years prior when he had been inducted into the tribe. It was of the highest honor to be called after a prized bull of their herd.

We settled for a drive through the Marich Pass, a ruggedly beautiful area with awesome views across the valley toward Mount Sekerr. I recalled some scary experiences on the old one-lane road, with a drop of several thousand feet to the fast-flowing river below. There was no room for maneuvering or faulty driving. We traveled that road at least twice monthly to reach the thriving center of Lomut at the floor of the valley, where we ran a medical outstation. Although we could see remnants of the old road, I was able to relax as we cruised the new one at the foot of the incline, including a well-maintained bridge crossing the river.

I glanced over the side of the bridge to see local women washing their clothes in the pristine waters of the river. That was an unfamiliar sight because Pokot women did not wash the animal skins they traditionally wore. Even without soap and water, the skins resisted dirt much better than the fabrics of today.

Another thrill for me was stopping at the town center of Ortum and seeing a market in full swing. As soon as the car stopped, we were swamped by local women, all colorfully dressed, with bags of onions, oranges, mangoes, and bananas on their heads. Traditionally, it was a woman's job to do the farming, not only among the Pokot but among all Kenyan tribes. As I gazed down on the area of the fertile river basin, I could see the rows and rows of neatly cultivated crops. I could never have envisaged such a social change for this traditional pastoral people.

In earlier days, the small local shops, called *dukas*, were mostly run by foreigners. The one shop in Ortum when I arrived was run by a family from India. Today the Kenyans have embraced entrepreneurship, and major thoroughfares are lined with Kenya's version of mini-malls, essentially long mud-and-wattle buildings with verandas in front. Brightly painted, they are mostly one-room establishments. One row included a Supermatt Food Store, a Titanic Investment Agency, the Tomani Hotel, and the Lomut Hardware Store, all of them a hive of activity. The whole setup tickled my fancy.

I spent another week in Kenya, spending time with some other friends from days gone by. When I returned home, it took me some time to return to earth from my emotional high. I will treasure both the old and new experiences in Kenya for the rest of my days.

The trip jolted me at a deep level and gave me the emotional energy I needed to sit down and write this memoir. Like the tiny mustard seed of the Bible parable (see Matthew 13:31–32 in the Jerusalem Bible), I played a very small part in something that grew and flourished enormously: independent, modern Kenya.

But I also lived a life before and after my twenty years in Kenya. After eight decades on earth, I want to share my struggles and challenges, my what-ifs, and a Deo Gratias to let the record show that I ended up happy.

CHAPTER 2

# CHILDHOOD

I was the first of six children born within a seven-year span to John and Mary Malone. I was delivered by the local midwife in a one-bedroom rented apartment on Centaur Street in Carlow. The house was owned by Miss Davis, a member of one of the two Jewish families in town. The town, situated about halfway along the main thoroughfare between Dublin and Waterford, is the local government headquarters for County Carlow, one of the smallest of the thirty-two counties in Ireland, six of which are still under British rule.

As a doctor, I sometimes reflected on what it was like for my mother to deliver me. Was labor prolonged? Was it painful? Was it frightening? It wasn't until my retirement years that I learned from my sister Eilish, herself a nurse and midwife, that Mother was alone in the apartment when she went into labor and had a difficult time getting the message to my father, who was at work. The midwife, Mrs. Hickson, lived at the far end of town, a distance of some miles, so I can imagine my father riding his bicycle with urgency to advise her that the baby was about to be born. Later, when we youngsters would encounter this kind lady wearing her uniform of a navy-blue coat and veil and carrying a little black suitcase, she would remind us that she had brought all of us into the world.

I was given the first name Mary after my paternal grandmother and the middle name Ita after an Irish saint, patroness of Munster and godmother of St. Brendan. My birthday coincided with her feast day in the Irish Church's calendar. At the suggestion of a cousin of my mother, the two words of my name were combined to form Marita, the name I answered to for the rest of my life.

Sometime during my first year, my parents and I took up residence in what was to be our permanent home on St. Killian's Crescent. The house was an end unit attached to approximately eight others at the crest of a row of houses that curved around to form a half-moon shape. From the living room window, our location afforded a good view of the entire street, with visitors coming into view as soon as they turned the corner from the main road.

Built by the Urban Council, the two-story unit was rented for something like five shillings per month. Few newly married working-class couples could afford to purchase homes, and mortgages, if they were conceived by the banks, were not an option. Years later, the Urban Council decided to allow long-term renters to buy their houses for a modest sum, and my parents eventually became homeowners.

Our home had three bedrooms upstairs. Downstairs was a kitchen and living room with a stove that could burn either coal or turf. In a small room off the kitchen called a scullery, we had running water, which ran into a large laundry-style porcelain sink called the George tub. I have no clue as to the origin of that name. There was no indoor bathroom. A door side by side with the back door led into a toilet that was flushed by pulling on a wire chain to empty the water cistern high on the wall.

My brother Thomas was born on St. Killian's Crescent five days before my first birthday, making him my Irish twin, as siblings born within the same year were known. Because of my parents' strong patriotic spirit, they wanted to call their children by the Irish versions of their names. In Gaelic, Thomas is Tomas, pronounced as Toe-maus (like the *a* sound in *awful*), with emphasis on the last syllable. When I began to talk, I couldn't quite manage the first half of my brother's name, so I started calling him Mausie, a name that stuck to him for the rest of his days, poor guy.

My first sister, christened Bridget and known as Breed, was born fourteen months after Thomas.

When I was almost four, I remember Mrs. Hickson arriving at our home, her little black bag in hand, and hastening up the stairs. My father followed with a basin of boiling water. Later, we were told we had a new baby sister. Of course, I confidently assumed the nurse had brought the baby in her bag! The newest member of the family was named Bernadette for St. Bernadette of Lourdes.

It was almost a year and a half before Mrs. Hickson came back to the house to welcome baby Elizabeth, whom we called by the Irish version of her name, Eilish. My sixth and final sibling, Henry, was born in August of the following year, when I was six years and seven months old.

In retrospect, it is amazing we all survived. Prenatal care, if it were sought, consisted of one visit to the general practitioner. There wouldn't be any further follow-up unless the midwife called the doctor to handle complications during the delivery process. Of the two hospitals in the town, only one provided maternity services, and that one charged fees, which most young couples couldn't afford. Infant and maternal mortality was high, with most women dying from uncontrollable hemorrhaging. On more than one occasion, I overheard Mother lament the death during childbirth of one of her friends or acquaintances, which often left a large family motherless.

## LIFE IN THE CRESCENT

Nearly all the residents on our horseshoe-shaped block were like our parents, married couples with young and ever-enlarging families. That meant we had plenty of other children to play with. This we did mainly on the street, playing hopscotch when the weather was mild and sliding on the frosty ground in winter. Carlow County is one of the two counties in Ireland that has no coastline. Needless to say, there was no such thing as a public swimming pool. The only safe place to go swimming, which was done only in the heat of summer, was in the Burren, a tributary of the River Barrow. Hence some of us, including me, never learned to swim in our youth. Any attempts as an adult led to panic attacks.

The word *bullying* wasn't a household term, but in retrospect, I recall at least one bully during those days.

When I was at most four years old, I repeated something uncomplimentary I had overhead my mother say about one of our neighbors. I don't remember what I said; it was probably nothing more than "Mrs. X wears lipstick," which Mother, like many of her contemporaries, regarded as being worn only by loose women. A playmate about two years older than I seized on the remark and taunted me that she was going to tell the lady concerned what my mother had said. For years following the incident, this girl continued to threaten me, even during school hours. I was scared, but I kept it all bundled up inside me. I was convinced that if I told Mother, she would only scold me for eavesdropping and especially for telling tales from home. I don't remember how this was settled. I believe the girl concerned eventually decided she had caused me enough upset to drop it.

The main railway line ran just to the rear of our row of houses, and at least twice per day, the whistle blew, and the train passed on its way either south to Waterford or north to Dublin. The ease of access to the railway line was a source of anxiety to our parents, who forbad us from playing in the vicinity. That didn't deter us, even though we had to cross a field belonging to a farmer whose two grown sons frequently chased us for trespassing. On one occasion, one of them followed a group of us to the railway, but I was the only one he captured. He threatened to call the Garda, the Irish name for the police. When he saw my ashen, anxious face, he realized he had scared me sufficiently and let me go. The railway line was out of bounds for me after that.

We had a wraparound garden larger than our neighbors', which my father kept cultivated, and it supplied the family with fresh vegetables for most of the year. He used to take such pride in the potatoes, which earned the high praise of being "flowery," when they burst through their skins as they were boiled.

Initially, no one on our street and little of the town of Carlow were connected to the electricity mains. We lit our homes at night with kerosene lamps. These beautiful table centerpieces of colored glass and brass fittings were often heirlooms given as wedding presents and passed on from one generation to the next.

Our house eventually got hooked up to the electric grid, and there was great rejoicing as a little electric bulb, invariably hanging solitary from the midpoint of the ceiling, scattered the darkness. After that milestone, other conveniences gradually came into the home, such as radios, electric irons, stoves, and toasters. In later years, with great publicity came the scheme for rural electrification, which brought power out to the farms. It was one of greatest boons to Irish agriculture since the creation of the steam engine.

Neither our family nor any of our acquaintances owned or had access to a telephone during the 1930s and 1940s. In fact, our household was one of the first on the block to have a phone installed sometime in the late fifties. My sister Eilish, who was practicing midwifery in town, was given priority to have one. Subsequently, there was quite a procession of neighbors requesting the courtesy of using our phone to call family or friends when urgent communication was necessary. This is just one example of the spirit of neighborliness that pervaded our street. There would have been reciprocity if one of the neighbors had had a phone and we hadn't.

At least during the war years, few businesses in town had access to a telephone. Even if they had one, unless the person or business they wished to communicate with had one, it was of no use. The main means of domestic and commercial communication was by the postal service. The cost of mailing a letter was just one half penny. Mother, every week, did the crossword puzzle published in the Sunday *Independent* newspaper, and it was my task on Thursday afternoon to go post it for her. Unfortunately, she never won a prize. Urgent communications were achieved by telegrams, often delivered from the post office by teenage messengers on bicycles.

The concept of television hadn't entered the conversation or for that matter, our shores. . I was at least ten years old before we had a radio which kept us amused and up to date with news. Every evening, we knelt around the kitchen fire, propped up by the seats of the dining chairs, and recited the Rosary, some of it in the Irish language. We each took our turn in proclaiming the title of one of the five decades and then saying the first half of the Our Father, Hail Mary, and Glory Be. The rest of us would complete the latter half of the prayers. Mother would pray with the utmost fervor. This was a time for antics among us siblings, either hair pulling or back kicks, which produced a good swipe of the *ciotóg* (kitt-oogh), the Gaelic for "left hand," from Mother.

Only once, when I was a preteen, do I remember my father giving me a good spanking. With the short leather belt he used to sharpen his razor, he gave me a few wallops on my posterior. I had been in a major fistfight, including hair pulling, with my sisters. This lesson, well deserved, was never repeated.

My brother Mausie was always in trouble. My parents feared he was keeping company with friends who were having a bad influence on him. He frequently disobeyed orders to return home at an appointed time. Once, when Mother was really angry with him, I was so distressed that I came between them and saved him from the lashes.

"Spare the rod and spoil the child" was the belief of the time. The usual punishment meted when children misbehaved was a few strokes of the cane, either on the palm of the hand or on the rear end. Boys especially were inclined to earn their licks on the derrière, often a naked one. There were horror stories of boys coming home from school with welts on their hands or legs, inflicted by a teacher. In my experience, the nuns only slapped children on the palm of the hand. I remember only getting one series on the palm of my right hand. It left a welt, and it hurt.

It was unusual for a parent to intervene on behalf of a child when it came to so-called discipline in school. Rather, children would come home to be greeted by their parents with a "Well, how many slaps did you get in school today?" Or when a pupil complained of being punished in school for bad behavior, parents usually reacted with a "You deserved it."

## EARLY SCHOOL DAYS

I was three and a half when I first attended the Presentation Convent National School on Tullow Street. The first two years of schooling were the equivalent of kindergarten or nursery school in the United States' educational system. I couldn't be registered as a pupil in the school until I was four. That was the beginning of a long road into the realms of intellectual stimulation.

Because my mother didn't have a babysitter, on that first day, she was unable to take me to school, so I was sent along with Maura Dooley, an older girl and one of our neighbors. I guess I wasn't unique as a three-year-old to cry my heart out when, for the first time, I found myself in such a strange environment. Then, as I was enveloped in the comforting arms of Sister Rosario, I could relax and know I was safe. This dear sister was legendary as the mistress of the infants' class. Actually, she doesn't deserve the title of mistress. Her motherly, caring ways endeared her to generations of four- and five-year-old girls as they experienced separation-anxiety syndrome for the first time.

We did the usual fun things that first graders do, of which I remember best playing around the maypole and learning the alphabet with the help of rhymes and songs. The latter had long-term effects on my vocal abilities. I still have vivid memories of Sister moving from child to child, listening with her hand held to her ear, which was invisible under her black veil, and singling out those of us who were not singing in tune. I was one of them, and she asked me to keep quiet during singing lessons.

That began a long, sad history of my feeling left out and becoming something of a wallflower. I remember Mother not being happy, but like most Irish mothers of her day, she did not question the nuns' decisions.

Preparing for our First Communion and the Sacrament of Penance was a major focus the second year of school. We had to show that we had reached the use of reason, meaning that we knew right from wrong—at least in theory. We also had to be able to answer most of the questions in the short Penny Catechism, including concepts beyond our understanding, such as theatrical representations and coveting a neighbor's wife.

I, with my classmates and with boys of the same vintage, made First Communion on Saturday, May 22, 1937.

Mother made my white dress. I had a veil and wreath that encircled most of my head right down over my ears. The unflattering photo is still in an album somewhere. That morning, we met in a school classroom, where we were paired off two by two and sent in a procession to the Cathedral of the Assumption next door. After the Mass and solemn reception of Communion, back in the school, we were treated to a breakfast of tea and cake. Relatives and family friends would deposit a few pennies or, at most, a shilling—a fortune in our eyes—into the little white bags we carried. That was the height of the celebrations.

After I had been officially photographed at Mr. Beard's studio, Mother took me to visit her grandaunt, Sister Dymphna, a Sister of Mercy, who was in poor health and mostly bedridden. We were allowed visit her in her cell, an unusual dispensation, as one did not visit nuns in their private quarters. Her room was on the ground floor of the convent and had a French door opening onto the landscaped garden. It was a beautiful setting, at least in late springtime.

After we'd exchanged the usual greetings and Sister had admired my outfit, she suggested I open the door of her bedside locker and choose a gift for myself. Within were delicately wrapped chocolate Easter eggs and a celluloid fish with a sailor boy riding on its back. I hesitated for a moment. The lure of the chocolates was tempting, but I settled for the fish as a more lasting memento, which it was, on display through the glass door of the cabinet in the living room at home for many a year afterward—a harbinger to wise choices later in life.

Prior to receiving Jesus for the first time in the Eucharist we had to go through our first confession. There was a lot of discussion among us children and our parents about the sins we were going to tell. Besides, there were many other important details that were challenging for a six-year-old to remember. We had to rehearse the words of two prayers of penance, the Confiteor and Act of Contrition; enter a dark box; and kneel in front of a wire screen to wait for a little sliding door to open before the priest's profile appeared through the dimness.

I don't specifically remember that first confession, but an experience that happened shortly afterward colors my view of the Sacrament of Penance to this day.

I was spending the summer at our grandmother's, as usual, so it must have been the first Friday of July or August. There were special devotions on first Fridays, so there was always a good turnout and a full congregation in the church. Holy Cross Church in Killeshin had no resident priest. The priest assigned that day was Father Campion, who was well known for his speedy ways both in saying Mass and in hearing confessions.

When it came my turn to enter the confessional, in my conscientious way, I followed the routine I had been taught, and I was still saying my Act of Contrition, when Father opened the sliding door again, having already heard a confession on the other side. Next thing I knew, the priest opened the door of his cubicle, and his voice echoed out into the church, calling my grandmother to "remove this child" from the confessional. I was mortified!

I always did well in school and was usually ranked near the top of my class. Being the best wasn't the most important thing in my family, though, as one incident taught me. It was the end of the first-class (first-grade) school year, and I had come in third in my class on the final test, with a score of 97 out of 100. Each of the three top students was given the opportunity to choose a small gift from the sister teacher.

The girl who had the highest score soon realized she did not like the prize she had chosen, a child's prayer book, and asked me to trade with her. I cannot remember my prize, but I agreed to the exchange. While walking home that day, a thought hit me: *I am holding the first prize, so I am going to pretend to Mother that I came in first in the class.* It was meant as a prank with the reasoning of a six-year-old, and I intended to tell the full truth after a minute or two. However, my mother must have expressed such pride in my accomplishment that I did not have the heart to tell her the real story.

I spent the summer vacation at my grandmother's farm and never thought again about the lie I had told Mother. I wasn't even concerned that she might find out. But find out she did, although she never mentioned it to me. Soon after school reopened, she one day appeared in my new classroom, and I was called up to the top of the class. I am not sure if my classmates overheard Mother detailing my transgression, nor do I recall Sister Ita, my teacher and also the school's headmistress, giving any reprimand or even what she said to me. I only know that in front of my peers, I froze all over and was humiliated.

I still find it hard to understand the way Mother handled that affair. I like to give her the benefit of the doubt and believe she was concerned that I was becoming deceitful and that her reaction was the best way she knew to nip it in the bud.

One of my proudest accomplishments was that I had perfect school attendance from my first day up to Christmas of seventh class, a total of almost nine years. My record was shattered, however, when there was an outbreak of mumps in the school. I was hoping that at least I would not contract the contagious disease until after the school closed for the Christmas holidays, but I developed the telltale swelling of my parotid glands just two days before the end of the term. I did not feel particularly sick. I wanted so much to go to school, but my parents would not allow it. The disappointment I experienced on breaking my record reflected my love of school and learning and, in hindsight, my desire for perfection.

We had drama lessons, and invariably, I had parts in the annual school plays, most of which were in the Irish language. Since Irish independence in 1922, the Irish language was compulsory in both spoken and written form. Although I was not a natural polyglot, I did well in Gaelic, helped no doubt by my family's patriotism and emphasis on Irish traditions.

On one occasion, when I was performing in the town hall in conjunction with other schools and artists, the experience's significance to me had nothing to do with the play. In the printed program, my name appeared as Movita instead of Marita. My parents were annoyed by the mistake because a vaudeville act of questionable repute with artists Movita and Jack Doyle had recently come to town. The lady who'd typed the program was well known to the family, which made it all the harder for Mother to understand the faux pas. She held on to that peeve for many a day.

Each year, the Feis was held in town, a traditional Gaelic arts and culture festival, when competitions were held for Irish dancing, language, and history. My parents were always so proud of me when I won prizes, not in dancing but in speaking the language and recalling Irish history. In preparation for one feis, my dancing teacher decided at the last minute that I should not participate. While I had mastered the steps well, I was unable to keep time with the music. My mother thought I was just stubborn when she could not get me to enter the competition. I was too ashamed to admit to failure. Instead, I took the blame for my stubbornness. It's amazing how instances like these are seared in our memories.

At home, I was a bossy older sister. I loved playing the schoolmarm, and especially on rainy days, my younger siblings were subjected to many hours of my "teaching." On the other hand, I wasn't inclined to be motherly. That distinction fell to my sister Breed, who enjoyed being the babysitter in the neighborhood. It was a familiar sight to see her wheel the pram (baby carriage) of a neighbor's child up and down the street for hours at a time.

One incident demonstrative of my stubborn bent is sealed in my memory. Mother was busy and asked me to take my then-two-year-old brother Henry outside to play so she could get on with the housework. I hesitated, if I did not outright refuse. The next thing I knew, he reached up to the table and pulled down a basin of nearly boiling water onto his head and body.

There was panic all around, and Mother called for help from a nurse who lived across the street. I disappeared to my parents' bedroom; I don't recall whether I was sent there or went on my own recognizance. I was convinced that Henry was about to die, so I took to standing on the bed and prayed fervently before the pious pictures of Jesus and Mary on the walls: "Please, God, don't let my baby brother die."

Remarkably, Henry got through the incident without hospitalization or even a scar to show for it. The scare I got was punishment in itself. I don't remember any other.

My image of my mother from my early years is of her always being busy and always having a baby to care for. As a stay-at-home mom, she dedicated herself to caring for the children, cooking, housekeeping, and handling finances. Fortunately for her emotional health, there was great comradery among the women in the neighborhood, and they would not hesitate to ask one another for help. If someone got sick, my mother was often called to give an opinion or suggest a remedy. She was a font of kindness and had such a deep concern for others that people felt they could call on her in their time of need.

Mother and Father had a cordial relationship. We children never saw them arguing, but as was the mode of the day, they did not outwardly show many signs of affection. Mother appeared to defer to Father, but she also made decisions on her own without necessarily consulting with him. I never heard my father mutter a bad word about anyone. If, on occasion, Mother was inclined to say something derogatory about an acquaintance, Father would immediately interrupt her with "Now, Mary." That was enough to seal her lips. How I wish I had followed his example.

Alcohol was rarely served in our home. Father could take the occasional Guinness at Christmastime when it was offered to guests. Mother was a teetotaler all her life; she had taken the pioneer pledge (a promise to God to abstain from imbibing alcohol for life), and she kept that promise till the day she died. She would have liked her children to have followed her example.

Earlier in life, Mother felt called to join the contemplative religious congregation of the Poor Claires. This was at the same time my father was courting her. When she discussed the possibility of becoming a nun with Father Dunny, the parish priest of the time, he remarked, "What will poor John do then?" This seemed to confirm for her that her path was to be a wife and mother rather than a nun.

Yet Mother kept a special place in her heart for the contemplative nuns who lived their lives completely enclosed. Their only contact with outsiders was from behind a grille at the entrance door. They lived on donations, and there was a legend in the area that they would ring a bell if they were in need, so the local community could come to their aid. It was a source of community pride that they never rang the bell.

My father was an attendant, equivalent to a male nurse, in the mental hospital. He worked long and difficult hours, toiling from early morning till ten o'clock at night, interspersed with an occasional month at a time of doing night duty. Those months were particularly difficult because we children had to stay quiet during the day while he slept. We had no idea what his job entailed, as he never discussed it. In fact, he did little talking. It just wasn't in his nature.

When Father wasn't at work in the hospital, he was either cultivating our garden or up the hill at his mother-in-law's farm. Nana, as we called our mother's mother, was a widow. Her eldest son, Willie, spent a lot of his time involved in politics and the younger one, Dan, had a job outside the farm, so my father saw a need to help out—an activity he clearly enjoyed.

The hospital where Father worked was often referred to as an asylum, a common term at the time. Mental illness still had a stigma attached, and even to work there was considered infra dig by some of our contemporaries. Occasionally, our schoolmates would taunt us that our father worked in the asylum.

It was common practice that patients who developed psychiatric illnesses, once they were admitted to a mental hospital, never left the institution. They were frequently abandoned by their families. People with bipolar disorder and schizophrenia would be treated with straitjackets and isolation; depressed patients might receive convulsion therapy.

Our parents always referred to the place as the mental

hospital and never used the derogatory term *asylum*. For years, a permanent resident of the hospital, Mr. Flanagan, occasionally came to our house as a handyman. He was always dressed in the same gray flannel suit, which was issued by the hospital. He was pleasant and friendly, and Mother received him with the utmost respect.

The mental hospital, which was later called Saint Dymphna's, is now closed. A chapel that was on the grounds has become a military museum. On a recent visit to Carlow, as I was walking through that hallowed spot, my mind reverted to the days long since gone, when after our Christmas dinner, the whole family would be taken for a walk, at least three miles long, to admire and pay homage in front of the life-size crib on display there. It always seemed more beautiful than the one in the cathedral. I think that was the only time of the year when the grounds of the hospital were open to the public. I had a special affinity for those yearly visits due to their association with my father.

As I look back on the Carlow town of my youth, I am struck by how simple life was. For many years, there was only one cinema in town. Because it was a popular spot in town for dating, my parents weren't keen on us going there. I can count on the fingers of my right hand how many pictures (what we called movies) I saw in my preteen years. Two were on the lives of saints, those of Therese and Bernadette, and then I may have seen one or two with the cute young Shirley Temple as principal character. How we wanted to emulate her!

After household electrification, most families had a radio, which we called the wireless. Outside the active gossip network in town—everyone seemed to know everyone else's business—the radio was our main source of news and entertainment. People would request songs or music to be played for birthdays and other celebrations.

Many requests were to greet and cheer patients in special hospitals, called sanatoriums, which were set up to treat those infected with tuberculosis. There being no antibiotics to cure this disease, these patients were submitted to various long-term treatments, mainly bed rest, fresh air, and often, as a last resort, removal of part or a complete lung. Those with the skeletal form of the disease were put in casts, including full-body ones, and kept immobile for long periods, sometimes more than one year. Besides, these patients were isolated to the extent that family could not visit, on the understanding that if they had contact with the patient, they would develop or transmit the disease. Listening to the names of patients being greeted by their families had a salutary effect on my young mind. Little could I have guessed how much in future life I would have to deal with the ravages of this infection.

I am often struck by the amazing advances that transformed medical care in my lifetime. One particular incident illustrates this.

Long before the development of antibiotics capable of combating bacterial infections, my mother developed a severe infection of her right index finger. Her first course of action was a folk remedy: using a poultice of hot linseed oil to try to draw out the infection. Next, she went to the doctor, who, without a local anesthetic, used a scalpel to lance the infected part to allow discharge and drainage. It was sobering to watch Mother cry out in severe pain. She kept holding the finger over her head, telling us how much it was throbbing. Then, one day, the pain was gone, but she was left with the bony tip of her finger loose in the dressing. In medical terms, she had had osteomyelitis, infection of the bone itself, which she was lucky healed in due time. Otherwise, she could have lost her finger, hand, arm, or even life from sepsis, a not-uncommon result.

## TRAVELS UP THE HILL

Both my parents had grown up in County Laois (pronounced "Leash"), in the countryside adjacent to Carlow. My mother's family, the Boltons, owned a farm named Keelogue, derived from the Irish *Cill og*, meaning "Young Woods." It was in the townland of Killeshin, part of a hill range separating the two counties of Laois and Carlow. The farm encompassed a good slice of the Hill, which is what we affectionately called it and the surrounding area. From that vantage point, there was a magnificent view of the town of Carlow and beyond. Climbing the hill to get to the farmhouse, by foot or bicycle, was a challenge, especially the ascent up the final steep mile on the dirt road.

Frequently, on Sundays, especially the days my father was working, Mother would get us all dolled up, and with the two youngest accommodated in the pram, we would trek the three and a half miles to the farm. Those of us walking did our share of the grunting and groaning along the way. The anticipation of visiting Nana and Mother's younger sister, Aunt Lil, kept us going. We were always welcome and couldn't wait to enjoy the feast of freshly baked scones and apple tart (pie in other jargon) Aunt Lil had prepared. Most times, one of our uncles would give us a ride in the horse and cart for the journey back home in the evening. The descent was so steep that at times, the poor mare would lose her footing and fall to her knees, with Mother's audible prayers pressing my panic button. The mare always recovered without being seriously hurt, though, and all of us made it home safely but exhausted.

On special occasions, our parents would hire a hackney car (taxi) to take us up the hill. I can still visualize Mr. Hunt, the owner, cranking the engine and mouthing some choice expletives as he tried to get a croak out of a machine that was well past its expected life span.

Our grandfather Henry Bolton had died years before we were born, so we only knew Grandmother Bridget as a widow. True to custom, at home, she always wore a long black skirt and blouse, topped by a blue-and-white checked apron when performing household duties. For going to church or market, she was again dressed in black head to toe, which created a somber atmosphere and an aura of sadness around her. In spite of that, she was gentle and kind and showered us with love and affection at all times.

Father grew up on a farm in Rossmore, a townland on the same hill range. The land was not particularly fertile. Some of it was a peat bog from which valuable turf could be harvested. Peat is the result of years of vegetation decaying and being compressed in soggy ground. During the early summer, men used a slán, a tool like a machete, to cut thick strips of peat, and then they stacked it to dry in the sun. Somewhat akin to charcoal briquettes, turf burns much longer than wood logs, and it was a common source of fuel for heating homes and cooking in Ireland when I was growing up.

Grandmother Mary Malone had died prior to my birth. In her later years, she suffered from diabetes. She had to have part of her right arm amputated due to a severe infection and gangrene. I can only imagine how painful it was to undergo that surgery in the days of limited anesthesia and painkillers.

Rather than dividing up a farm among all the children in a typical large Irish family, farms were passed down intact to the eldest son. My father was the seventh child and third son in his family of eight siblings, so the homestead had gone to his eldest brother, Uncle Michael "Mick" Malone. He and his wife, Anastasia, had a large family, and most of the cousins were older than I. Grandfather lived with them.

We rarely saw Grandfather Thomas Malone except in the summers, when we were staying up the hill with Nana. He walked alone across several fields and miles of road to attend Sunday morning Mass in Killeshin. I never understood why Uncle Mick and family did not attend the same church. They apparently went to one situated on the crest of the hill, called Mayo, not to be confused with the county in the west of Ireland of the same name.

We never saw him in church either, because there was separation of the sexes. The men stayed on the right aisle, and women and children stayed on the left. After Mass, Grandfather invariably got a ride in a pony and trap as far as the spring well on the Bolton land, where he would rest prior to hiking the remainder of the way back home. That was where we would meet and greet him.

Grandfather had a rounded, oval face with a white beard. He walked with a moderately forward stoop, his hands clasped behind his back. While he recognized us as his grandchildren, I do not recollect him being overly inquisitive about our welfare or in any way demonstrative.

I vividly remember attending Grandfather's wake after he died in 1940, when I was nine. I recall entering the home, which was dimly lit by candles and the turf fire in the hearth. As was the custom in the rural areas, Grandfather's body was dressed in a brown shroud resembling a Franciscan friar's habit and laid out on the table in the main kitchen and living room combination. The table was covered in white sheets and enclosed in a canopy of similar white sheets. Adult family members stayed with the corpse all night, but there were no other activities suggestive of the much publicized Irish wake.

The night before the funeral, there was a procession to the church around seven o'clock in the evening. All the able men walked behind the hearse, and the women followed in horse-drawn carts and a few motor cars. Mother and we children followed the cortege in Mr. Hunt's hackney car. Once we got to the church, the coffin was brought to the mortuary chapel, a small room at the rear of the main transept, where the rosary was recited, after which everyone dispersed.

By the time we arrived in church the next morning, the coffin was on the catafalque, draped in a black pall in front of the altar rails. Everything and everybody looked somber, dark, and dismal. The priests, five of them, emerged in black cassocks and white surplices; took their seats in the sanctuary; and, in a high-pitched, dirge-like tone, started chanting psalms and antiphons in Latin, all of which were double Dutch to us. It was called the Office for the Dead. After what seemed like an eternity, the priests went back to the vestry, and only the parish priest returned in black vestments to say the Requiem Mass—in Latin, of course—which was another mournful and incomprehensible ritual for the congregation.

Immediately after the funeral Mass, burial took place in the graveyard that surrounded the church. Seeing my father shed tears at the graveside touched me deeply. Big men weren't supposed to cry.

Speaking for myself, the overall experience was spooky and depressing. Thank God the church of today makes funeral rites a more meaningful, comforting experience.

School closed for six weeks during the summer months, and we couldn't wait to get to Grandmother's for the duration. It gave Mother a well-earned respite from caring for her ever-enlarging family and gave us a freedom and many memorable experiences we would never have had in town.

We liked to help Aunt Lil with the farm chores, including milking the cows. At least we thought we were helping. In reality, we just watched as she moved her three-legged stool from cow to cow and, with great dexterity, squeezed the milk from the tits of the cows' udders into the pail she held between her legs. Now and again, especially if we were being obstreperous, she would jovially send a squirt of milk in the direction of one of us. With glee, we would duck to avoid the deluge.

Unlike many farms in the area, my grandmother's farm had a modern milk separator that mechanically skimmed the cream off the still-warm milk. Knowing friends who had lost fingers while working this machine, Aunt Lil monitored us with increased vigilance when she had it in action.

The separated cream was stored in large vats until churning day, which happened once weekly. Taking turns, we would delight in somersaulting the churn until we could see through the peephole that little balls of butter had formed.

Grandmother used to rear turkeys as a source of pocket money, and she'd give them to the extended family as gifts for Christmas. In addition to feeding skimmed milk to the calves and baby goats, we delighted in helping her feed the turkey chicks. It was a risky job, though, because the turkey cock could be ferocious in protecting them. Getting chased and followed by the unruly gander was even more precarious.

Uncle Willie kept pedigree bulls, and neighbors would bring their cows in heat for their services. If we were in the vicinity when a mating was to take place, Uncle would yell at us in not-too-refined language to get lost. Invariably, we just ran behind the bushes and caught a peek at the activity, which we didn't connect with the birth of a new calf nine months later because we were never told anything about the mechanics of procreation, whether animal or human.

On rainy days, which are frequent in Ireland, we amused ourselves by playing records over and over again on the His Master's Voice gramophone, a lot of patriotic ballads and some songs of the great John McCormack. We also played board and card games, all simple and innocent activities that carried us through the whole summer vacation from school.

## INDELIBLE IMPRINT

Although I treasure many memories from summers at Nana's, there was one painful incident that I have kept to myself for nearly eighty years. It is still difficult to write about.

This incident occurred when I was either eight or, at the most, nine years old. While I don't remember the exact year it happened, I remember every other detail as if it were yesterday. I was sexually assaulted by a male relative who was then in his middle to late teens. It started when he inappropriately touched me while we were tumbling in the hay. He then maneuvered me into a secret place where he easily overpowered me, and it happened.

Although I had no knowledge of sexual behavior, afterwards I was deeply disturbed and ashamed. I am not sure if the perpetrator warned me not to tell anyone about the incident, my instincts told me not to. I didn't share my secret with my grandmother, aunt, or mother—not with anyone. When my innocence was stolen from me that summer, my personality also changed. I became more private with my thoughts and feelings, more introspective, and secretly anxious someone would find out.

It was years before I became aware that I was a victim of a criminal act. I never received any counseling regarding the matter, not even in later life, when I sought this for another reason. While I could convince myself intellectually that I was totally innocent, that deep sense of shame and self-blame had already left its mark. I can testify that the emotional burden on a child of carrying a secret of such magnitude is detrimental, possibly for the rest of an individual's life. I can also vouch that sharing this secret, even after such a long interval of time, is liberating.

Characteristic of the times, no one told me about menstruation before I got my first period a few years later. The bleeding in that area convinced me that I was being punished by God for "the bad thing" that had happened. It was a relief when Mother explained that menstruation was normal. Appearing not sure how to handle the situation, in veiled language, she tried explaining what people euphemistically called "the facts of life."

I was equally embarrassed and made the encounter short, asking no questions. One strange piece of advice stuck with me: that I should not wash my hair during those days. That seemed ominous, but I didn't question why. If you Google that myth today, you'll realize this was a widely held old wives' tale with no scientific basis. One opinion held that one would lose one's curls if hair was washed during menstruation!

In this era when nothing is held sacred or secret, it is easy to look back with a critical eye as to how we were prepared to enter the adult world. Adults prepared children with the best of intentions and according to the mores of the day. I recognize that my parents—like those of my peers—were still following a script from the previous century, in which children were seen and not heard. Our parents showered us with care, love, and the solicitude that we do well in life, but there wasn't a relationship where we felt free to confide in them our inner thoughts, worries, and sexual awakenings—a relationship where a teenage girl could call her mother her BFF (best friend forever).

# INDEPENDENCE IN MY BLOOD

Ireland obtained independence from Britain nine years before my birth. Because politics and nationalism played such an important role in the lives of my parents, relatives, and family friends, this cultural inheritance is deeply imbedded in my life too.

Near the end of the nineteenth century, a group of poets and intellectuals led an effort to revive the Irish language, which was fast fading from use because English had long been the official language in Ireland, and speaking Irish had been actively discouraged. The Gaelic League, founded in 1893, set out to make Irish a living language once again by holding classes all around the country and codifying a written version of the language. The League also supported other Irish cultural traditions, particularly music and dancing.

A branch of the Gaelic League was started in Carlow in 1899 and quickly became popular. My father was born in 1894, and my mother was born in 1899, so my parents and their siblings were reared in the midst of this patriotic cultural revival.

Gatherings of the Gaelic League became recruiting grounds for the Irish Volunteers, a paramilitary group founded in 1913 with the intention of declaring an Irish Republic by force if necessary. My mother's two brothers, William "Willie" and Daniel "Dan" Bolton, answered this call, as did our father and at least two of his brothers, Edward "Ned" and Thomas "Tommie." After the Declaration of the Irish Republic in 1918, the Irish Volunteers became the Irish Republican Army (IRA).

Not unlike patriots in the American Revolution, the Irish

waged a guerrilla-style war against the highly organized and well-armed British forces. Units of just ten men, known as Flying Columns, would serve under a brigade captain.

Mother joined Cumann na mBan ("Organization of the Women" in Irish), which was formed as a support system for the IRA volunteers; one of their chief duties was to relay messages to the Flying Columns. In his 1978 book *My Kilkenny IRA Days 1916–22*, James Comeford devotes a chapter to the women of this organization and gives a glowing account of the work our mother did from her base in Killeshin, where she was captain of the branch, a fact I did not learn until decades later.

Mother often recalled one poignant story from that time. In the spring of 1921, an informant alerted the authorities that she was holding a meeting of her Cumann na mBan company on a Sunday afternoon. Separately, two IRA men on the run had come to the house for a meal. When they saw the soldiers approaching, they hid their guns in oats in the loft and disappeared. The soldiers, who were actually my family's neighbors recruited by the British, started searching the property. My grandfather Henry Bolton, who was close to death, was taken out of his bed, and the bed was torn apart in the search. The thatched roof of the house was riddled with bullets.

The guns that had just been left by the two runners were found, and Uncle Dan Bolton and his cousin Dan Pender were taken prisoner. Grandfather died soon after that incident. A sad reminder of "the terrible times," as Mother often referred to them, was that neither of his two sons was able to attend his funeral; Dan was in prison, and Willie was involved in "maneuvers" and on the run.

Shortly afterward, in December 1921, the unity of the IRA was shattered by a treaty with the British that partitioned Ireland, with the twenty-six-county Irish Free State separated from the six counties of Northern Ireland, which remained under British control. A civil war broke out between the pro-treaty and antitreaty groups, and my family aligned with the Republicans, also known as nationalists, who wanted to continue fighting until one united Ireland became free and independent.

After the signing of the treaty, Uncle Dan was offered release from prison, but he refused to go unless some of the other prisoners claiming nonpolitical status were also released. Then, for reasons that the history books do not make clear, Uncle Dan and a well-known Carlow patriot, Padraig Mac Gamhna, went on a hunger strike. The strike lasted for several months until the protest was settled. On their release and return to Carlow, they received a tumultuous welcome from the residents of the town.

Uncle Willie served time in prison sometime during those years, the timing of which I was unable to verify. But more tragically, he was arrested again by detectives of the Civic Guards under the Irish Free State in September 1925, when, by all accounts, due to the work of an informer, the house and farm in Keelogue were raided. The guards found a gun in a loft of the house and a dump of ammunition in a ditch of one of the fields. He was sentenced to six months of hard labor. It is heart-wrenching to read the account of the trial, which took place at Carlow District Sessions, when the judge, an Irishman by the name of J. J. Molloy, proclaimed that "to have such people as the accused going around the country was a menace to security. The rule of the gun must be stamped out of the country altogether"  [1]

Uncle Willie (who preferred to be known as Liam), served his time. In a letter only recently discovered, he wrote to his mother from Mountjoy Prison on October 14, 1926. It is sad reading. Willie was a true patriot and not a criminal. There was no evidence that he was engaged in any military activities at the time of his arrest. Over the years, he refused to recognize the Irish Free State government, even refusing to accept a small stipend offered to participants in the War of Independence.

The saddest part about that time in Irish history was that it was brother against brother, friend against friend, and neighbor against neighbor. They betrayed each other when they supported opposing sides of the conflict. This was particularly applicable in Willie's case, an opinion that bothered Mother to the end of her days.

When Mother died in 1997, she was given a patriot's funeral, including a twenty-one-gun salute at her grave. Her casket was draped with a flag of the Cumann na mBan, a version of the Irish tricolor with the initials of the organization embroidered in the center. Two of Mother's comrades, Breed Brophy and Essie Snoddy, had sewn it by hand while they were prisoners for the cause in 1922. Michael Purcell, Essie's son, had donated it to the Kilmainham Museum to add to the artifacts of that time, on condition that it be used to drape Mother's casket at her

---

[1] Weekly Irish Times (1921–1941); September 5, 1925: ProQuest Historical Newspapers: The Irish Times (1859–2011) and the Weekly Irish Times (1976–1958), pg. 20: "Jail for Possession of Ammunition"

funeral. The museum formerly had been the notorious prison by the same name, where many of our patriots, both men and women, suffered and died for the cause of Irish freedom. In spite of our grief, it was a proud moment to see our dear mother so honored.

CHAPTER 3

# WORLDS SHIFT

On September 4, 1939, World War II began when Germany invaded Poland. Mother was concerned and described to me the horrors of war. The time was obviously a flashback to her years of personally participating in the struggle for Irish freedom as well as what she'd heard as she lived through the First World War. Ireland was part of Great Britain at the time, and some two hundred thousand Irish volunteers fought in the war.

I remember being so convinced that airplanes would come over our house and bomb us all that I would lie awake waiting for it to happen.

As an independent republic, Ireland remained neutral throughout the war, but we suffered economic side effects. In spite of the shortages, though, I do not remember ever being without heat or going hungry, thanks to my resourceful and hardworking parents.

Certain foodstuffs that used to be imported, such as tea and tropical fruits, were in short supply, but people were creative in devising substitutes.

With precious tea leaves severely rationed to one half ounce per person per month, we learned to drink a beverage with roasted and finely grated carrots instead. On the whole, this did not satisfy the desire of most adults for a good cup of tea. Instead of fruit fillings for sponge cakes, we used a substitute made of mashed parsnips, which are sweet, believe it or not, with sugar and banana essence added.

Most of the coal used both for cooking and heating homes was previously imported from Britain, so we had to devise other alternatives during the war.

Sawdust was used for cooking on an improvised stove outside the house. These stoves were constructed out of forty-gallon oil drums filled with sawdust. The drum was placed on three or four stones or bricks to allow air to circulate under the drum for combustion purposes.

With a dousing of kerosene, the sawdust was set on fire—at least that was the plan. It did not always work. Even if the sawdust started burning, it took forever to boil a kettle of water, let alone cook a meal.

Without coal, turf became essential for home heating, but even it was hard to get. Fortunately for us, my father had access to the peat bog at his childhood home, where he cut and dried peat to make turf. To transport the turf to our home in town, my father procured a donkey named Dolly and a cart. Dolly Donkey was a sensation in the Crescent. She stayed around for a long time and became not only a family pet but also a favorite attraction for the neighborhood children.

At one time, Mother had a cow that grazed on no-man's-land out back and that she milked each day. For years, she also kept hens in our small backyard, which kept us supplied with fresh eggs. I don't remember any of the hens ending up in a pot or roasting pan. Perhaps they did, unbeknownst to us.

Some in the neighborhood frowned upon these agrarian ways, but it was characteristic of my parents not to care what the neighbors thought. As for myself, I rarely acknowledged or spoke about our little farm on St. Killian's Crescent. Rightly or not, living as a townie was seen as a social upgrade, at least to our school friends, and I greatly wanted to fit in.

We got our news of the war from the radio. A German newscaster with the assumed name of Haw-Haw gave us, in all probability, a biased, one-sided account of the progress of the war in Europe and the Far East. I think my parents and their friends avoided English broadcasters because they had no great love for Britain or its interests after its centuries-old treatment of Ireland. One thing I can say with conviction is that neither our parents nor their acquaintances had any idea of the extent of the atrocities being perpetrated by Hitler and his minions against the Jewish people and others.

We had cousins on Mother's side who lived in Belfast, Northern Ireland, which was still part of Great Britain. Some goods were easier to procure there than south of the border, where we lived. On one occasion, a customs official at the border checkpoint asked our cousin Mollie O'Reilly, who was on her way to visit us, if she was transporting any unlawful goods. She responded in the negative. Luckily, she wasn't body-searched, as some passengers were, because she had a bicycle inner tube wrapped around her waist. My father greatly appreciated the tube, as the bicycle was an essential mode of transport for him.

As the war progressed, the German Luftwaffe bombed cities in England nightly. Belfast in Northern Ireland, long known as a center for building ships, including the *Titanic*, became a target. To help the Allies win the war, manufacturers in the city were concentrating on making war necessities, including bomber airplanes, so it was anticipated that Belfast could easily become a target for the enemy.

This prediction was realized after the Nazis invaded France in mid-1940 and were able to set up air bases in that country. The first bombing raid of what would later be known as the Belfast Blitz hit during the night of April 7 and early morning of April 8, 1941.

A telegram arrived from one of my mother's first cousins, "Uncle" Pat Pender, on April 9. Worried about his wife and children, he asked if they could take refuge in our house. A reply was prepaid, and Mother, without hesitation, appended just two words: "Most welcome."

The next day, which was the Thursday of Holy Week, "Aunt" Mollie Pender and her five children arrived by train at Carlow station. In my mind's eye, I can still see Father coming up the street with at least two suitcases strung over the crossbar of his bike and the whole family walking beside him. In retrospect, I wonder what his feelings were as he realized a family as large as his own was about to descend on our humble home and our meager resources. Mother had no opportunity to consult with him before she sent back the affirmative telegram, so he could not assert his authority. That he probably had a positive attitude toward the situation shows the priority that hospitality held in the culture of his day, a *cead mile failte* (a hundred thousand welcomes) to friend and stranger alike.

I am certain neither he nor my mother had any idea that the sojourn would last two years, until almost the end of World War II. This gesture of hospitality was to have far-reaching effects on the trajectory of my life and the lives of my siblings.

Mother had made arrangements for the two oldest Pender children, Rosemary, who was about thirteen years old, and Jackie, a boy a year younger, to stay with neighbors. The rest set up house in our home.

Having four additional people living in the house was stressful for our family, but I never heard any complaints from either my father or my mother. No doubt it was uncomfortable for our cousins also. To add to the strain of the situation, Aunt Mollie gave birth to her sixth child while living with us, a son named Patrick.

Our four oldest cousins attended local schools. Teresa, who was nine days younger than I, was in my class. That was a big transition for her—not only fitting in but also speaking and writing the Irish language, which was compulsory in our curriculum at the time but not in that of British Northern Ireland.

Shortly afterward, Uncle Pat's brother James arranged for his wife and two children to leave Belfast for refuge in the Irish Republic. They joined with Nana and her three adult children on the farm in Keelogue. In that household, the accommodations were even more meager than at our house. The three older children of that family, who were already in boarding school, stayed behind and continued with their education.

"Aunt" Norah arrived at Nana's with her daughter Loretto and son Dennis. The latter was ten years old and had a severe cardiac condition resulting from a bout of rheumatic fever. Dennis was a sick child, needed a lot of care, and had no energy to walk even minimal distances. It was a pitiful sight to see his mother take him outside for fresh air, carrying him on her back. Dennis died sometime after their return to Belfast.

At age ten, I was old enough to feel the effects of the overcrowding and the disruption of our family unit. I especially resented how "Aunt" Mollie appeared to put the needs of her family before ours. One example etched in my memory is of the Pender family sitting down to the evening meal while my siblings and I watched and waited.

## A NEW ERA FOR ME

After about a year of our cousins living with us, I was suddenly given the chance to take up residence with two spinster sisters, the Misses Maher (pronounced "Mar" as in *far*). These two ladies had been friends with Mother since they all served together in the Cumann na Mban.

They continued that friendship after Mother was married and had children. In fact, we saw them as extensions of our family. At least once per week, they came to visit, and as they turned the corner from the main road onto the Crescent, we would alert our mother with "Here comes Miss Maher and more Miss Maher." Social mores of the time did not allow children to call adults by their first names, so no matter how often they visited, we always called them miss, and so did our parents in speaking of them. The same applied to adult male friends or acquaintances; they were always called mister.

Sarah and Annie "Nan" Maher were each at least twenty years older than my mother, which would have put them in their early sixties when I went to live with them in the spring of 1942.

My sojourn with these good ladies began when Nan was taken by ambulance to Dublin for emergency surgery. Sarah asked Mother to allow me to stay with her while Nan was recuperating in the hospital. I was given the best room in the house, directly over the shop, with one half set up as a sitting room and the other half as a bedroom. For the first time in my life, I had not only a bed to myself but my own magnificent bedroom suite. I was in heaven!

Sarah and Nan owned a shop in Carlow town. On the right side of the doorway was the general grocery store, and on the left was the drapery shop. (In the vernacular of the day, a drapery shop sold clothing, not window curtains.) Sarah ran the grocery store, which was where Mother bought all her groceries. The drapery side, run by Nan, carried clothing accessories, such as underwear; lisle stockings, which were the precursors of nylons; white handkerchiefs for men; and smaller lacy, embroidered handkerchiefs for women. Larger items of clothing, such as dresses and skirts, were not part of the inventory. I guess in today's jargon, we would call it a haberdashery store.

After Nan returned home from the hospital, both ladies

suggested I continue to live with them. One probable reason for the invitation was to ease the crowded situation at our home, although that was never discussed. Whatever the logic, it was fine with me.

I was allowed to serve in the shop, which I relished because it made me feel all grown up. As another bonus, my school was just a few hundred yards down the street. I could be there in less than two minutes.

I loved my palatial bedroom, which faced south and had two large windows. I recall sitting in an armchair on the window side of the bed in the sun-filled room, where I could observe whatever was going on in the street below. I had a beautiful washstand and a chamber pot under the bed. In that room, I read, in secret, my first romantic novel, which, if I recall correctly, was entitled *Carina*. Therein I learned the scenario of two people falling in love. I found it on the bookshelf, along with two volumes of *Butler's Lives of the Saints*. I even dipped into those tomes on occasion.

The outhouse, a simple shed with a galvanized roof and cement floor, was in the yard and had neither heat nor light. It held the flush toilet and nothing else, and it was not easy to visit at night. Hence the need for the chamber pot under the bed, the contents of which the good ladies disposed of daily.

Sarah, the older sister, was the dominant one. She was articulate and could be argumentative and crotchety at times. Nan, the more motherly of the two, was comfortable allowing Sarah to own the spotlight. On occasion, they would have a difference of opinion, but on the whole, they got along well.

It was a peaceful, if too old maid–ish, environment for a girl entering her teenage years.

While they were both diminutive in stature, Sarah was probably the more attractive looking. They were fastidious in how they groomed and dressed. However, as with most of their compatriots, wearing facial makeup, including lipstick, was not a choice.

I think some people found the sisters a little bit snobbish, more so Sarah, but they were also renowned for their generosity. People were expected to pay cash in the shop, but the sisters allowed many customers, including my mother, to pay for groceries on tick (on credit) until the end of the month, when the paycheck arrived. When times were hard, I think they were owed a lot—and they also forgave many of the debts.

The Misses Maher, who never married, were devout Catholics who attended Mass every morning, and they soon had inveigled me to accompany them. In the cathedral, they had preferred seating, so to speak, which might have contributed to their snobby reputations. They sat with the town's elite and business leaders in the side aisle, which was separated by a railing from the main transept of the cathedral and had its own side entrance. Like the others in that special section, the Mahers paid an extra fee to be there.

They dressed in full regalia—ankle-length coats, hats, and gloves—even to attend daily Mass. Afterward, there was a routine of putting everything away neatly in the chest of drawers or hanging items on a hook behind the bedroom door. Some of this routine and tidiness rubbed off on me and might explain why I am a neat freak even to this day.

The sisters had a clear demarcation of duties between them and a fairly rigid schedule. In addition to managing the business side of the shop, Sarah did the house cleaning on Thursday afternoon, when the shop was closed for the half day, as were all businesses in town. She also took care of the garden.

They had a wonderful garden at the back of the house. It was a large, oblong stretch of land the width of the house, and it extended at least one hundred feet to the boundary wall of St. Patrick's Seminary. It was separated from Mr. Bowe, the bachelor neighbor on the left, by a twenty-foot-long wall. He was an odd bod, had a long white beard, and was cantankerous by nature. I was acutely scared of him. Luckily, he kept to himself and did not bother us. On the right side were Mrs. Hanlon and her daughter, Mollie, who were friendly neighbors. Except for about twenty feet of a low fence near the house, the only separation between the gardens of the Mahers and the Hanlons was a central pathway extending the length of the garden, which made it easy to access for working.

The lower half of the garden was given over to the cultivation and growth of vegetables, including potatoes, cabbage, carrots, and parsnips, to name a few. In between this and the proximate flower garden, there flourished many varieties of fruit bushes, especially gooseberries and black currants, and one or two apple trees. Of course, there were also the ubiquitous rhubarb stalks.

The summer garden was a joy to behold. There was a profusion of flowers, including pansies, sweet pea, roses, phlox, and a plant called honesty. In autumn, the honesty produced translucent silver seed pods the size of half dollars, so it was called the money plant.

I can still see myself doing my homework at the little table in the window alcove that overlooked this panorama of color, imbibing the beauty of it all. No doubt it had an influence on my nascent love of flowers and gardening.

Nan did most of the cooking and kitchen work. She would make the most delicious jams and jellies, using gooseberries, black currants, rhubarb, and apples all harvested from the garden. It was my job to top and tail gooseberries, a boring exercise. My sisters Breed and Bernadette were often roped in to help. The home-made preserves, presented in glass jars, were sold in the shop, where they disappeared like hot cakes.

Nan had trained as a tailoress (the feminized word for *tailor*). Soon after my arrival, she resurrected her well-used Singer sewing machine, one that could penetrate heavy fabrics, and started making dresses and even a coat for me. She didn't use store-bought patterns; she simply followed my bodily measurements for the cutouts. I realized that the clothes were often out of fashion for my age group, but I guess I was too beholden to object or refuse to wear them.

I was in my late teens when Nan made a green woolen coat for me. I cannot recall if I had a say in the selection of the fabric. I only remember that as I wore it and saw my reflection in the mirror, I was convinced that both shoulder widths were asymmetrical. This bothered me, but I never had the guts to voice my concern. I continued to wear it, even though I hated it. Actually, my sister Bernadette wore that coat as a hand-me-down for several seasons afterward, and she says she never noticed a defect. Maybe it was a fantasy of my imagination.

On Sundays, the shop was closed in observance of the Lord's Day. After church and the customary roast beef dinner, I would visit my family in the Crescent. I hate to admit it now, but I only visited my real home about once a week. This was even after the Pender family had returned to Belfast. As a consequence, my sisters began to call me Marita Maher. I became more and more estranged from my siblings.

My father frequently asked when I was coming home, but he never insisted. How I wish he had. My relationship with Mother was also becoming more remote. She often visited in the shop and even socially when it was closed, but we rarely had a one-on-one conversation with each other.

A few times each year, I accompanied the good ladies to visit their brother, his wife, and their two eligible single sons at their farm about ten miles distant. Anywhere they went, they took me with them—to visit relatives nearby or even as far as Tramore, a popular seaside resort on the south coast. I accompanied them to social events in town, such as whist drives. (Whist is a card game similar to bridge.) While I played the game like everyone else, I was the only person in my age group at the event. Yes, I was de facto their adopted daughter.

They insisted I should hone my social skills. Seeing that singing was not my forte, although I was good at recitations, they arranged for me to take piano lessons. I started learning scales and tunes, including the "Blue Danube," under the tutelage of Miss Noude, a retired teacher. As neither they nor our family owned a piano, I got permission to go to the school after hours to practice.

Years later, especially when I attended gatherings with my sisters and brothers and their children, I realized how much I had distanced myself from my family in those formative years. I didn't share in the everyday details of their lives, and I missed taking part in the fun things young people would ordinarily do.

I didn't form close friendships with any of my school peers either. I encountered them in school, but as soon as classes were over, I returned to my little nest, did my homework, and helped in the shop. I was in the company of adults all the time and assimilated many of their prim and proper characteristics. At their house, my lifestyle was comfortable and familiar, and it fit my personality. I always understood that Mother and Father would want me home in a heartbeat. It was my choice to stay where I was treated so specially. For their part, the good ladies were never possessive of me. They always recognized that any big decisions regarding my welfare rested with my parents.

During those years, I was first exposed to local and national politics. Living with the Misses Maher as a lodger, the colloquial name for a tenant, was Padraig Mac Gamhna, the well-acclaimed Carlow patriot and labor trade unionist. Without going into details, I'll just say that the good ladies hosted frequent meetings with aspiring members for elected national and local offices, meetings at which I was a focused observer. The discussions helped awaken my social consciousness and concern for the needs of the wider community, especially those of the working man and woman.

## A MOVE FARTHER AFIELD

At the end of sixth class, we sat for the primary certificate examination. Most students were between the ages of thirteen and fourteen years at that stage, and for many, perhaps the majority, it was the end of their formal education. A minority of us went forward to seventh class, which was voluntary. Sister Brigid, our teacher that year, suggested that a few of us do extracurricular studies to prepare to take an examination for scholarships to secondary school.

Among the subjects were drawing and still-life painting, which appealed to me and in which I showed some talent. There seems to be an artistic bent in our family, as two of my sisters and several of my nieces and nephews have aptitude in painting and drawing.

There was rejoicing all around when I was awarded one of the two county scholarships. It was for the sum of ten pounds per year for four years. The amount would have covered the full yearly fees to attend the local secondary school, St. Leo's, as a day pupil.

However, on Sister Brigid's suggestion, I applied and was accepted to attend Brigidine Convent Secondary School in Tullow, approximately ten miles away. Although Tullow was also within the county of Carlow, there was no public transport linking the two towns. As a consequence, people from our town had little contact for trade or otherwise with Tullow.

The mother superior at the Brigidine agreed to have me as a boarder at no extra expense other than the amount of my scholarship. This was a welcome relief for my parents, who had five other children needing to be educated.

I should add that primary education at that time was not only compulsory but also free. Secondary education was not subsidized to the same extent, so there were fees attached. Mother valued further education and was determined we would get it. She always regretted that further education was not available, at least for girls, under the British system of her day.

In September, Uncle Willie escorted Mother and me to the school in his pony and cart. The school and convent shared an entrance, and the convent was physically attached to the parish church. This was a strange arrangement, and it gave us a greater sense of being trapped than a freestanding school building might have.

My mother and uncle were happy to meet and greet a neighbor and contemporary from their young days in Killeshin. The former May Dooley had joined the Brigidine Sisters and was known by the religious name of Mother Cataldus. Yes, in that congregation, all the sisters were called Mother, even if they were not the superior. She promised to take good care of me. When my mother and uncle took their leave and the big, heavy door of the convent closed behind them, I felt a rush of loneliness and abandonment that is still fresh in my memory.

By any standards, it was a small school, with only about thirty boarders and an equal number of day pupils. The three-story school building was compact, adjoining and perpendicular to the convent, where the nuns resided. On the ground floor were the classrooms that, when the divider was opened, served as our evening study. There were extensions for the refectory on one end, and on the other were classrooms and a great hall, which was mostly the domain of the day girls.

The dormitories, large rooms reminiscent of hospital wards of their day, were situated on two floors over the study hall and dining room. Each dorm was named after a saint and had two rows of eight to ten beds arranged head to head. White curtain panels placed between the beds were drawn at night but tied back, each dorm with a distinctive colored band, during the day. We were, on the whole, assigned to dormitories according to class year. Assigned to each dorm was a head girl, whose role was to maintain discipline. This included a rule of silence once we retired for the night. Of course, we did not always obey this rule. The password *Knicks* voiced by the lookout girl proclaimed the imminent approach of the sister in charge. Then—presto—one could hear the silence as we became as good as gold!

In each of the dormitories, one of the nuns slept in a tiny cubicle in the corner near the entrance door. This eight-by-eight-foot space was cordoned off by white curtains, which were always drawn closed. It seemed too sacred a place for any of us, even if curiosity got the better of us, to take a peep behind the curtains. As I reflect on it now, I marvel at how these women were subjected to and accepted such lack of privacy and comfort.

Study, followed by a period of recreation, ended at nine o'clock. Then it was bedtime. After we had partially undressed and donned our dressing gowns, we proceeded to the communal washroom. There, each girl was assigned a personal enamel basin. The basins sat on a long white table with attached cubbyholes to hold personal items. There was space for about eight girls at each table, and the tables were placed in rows, one after another, filling the room. If I recall correctly, there was only one row of mirrors, in front of the first table. There was little opportunity to assuage our emerging feminine vanities.

Once we had filled our basins with warm water, we proceeded with the ablutions, which only encompassed washing our faces, forearms, and hands and, of course, brushing our teeth.

At a signal from the sister on duty, we commenced to comb and brush our hair for what appeared to be an eternity. All the while, the sister recited prayers and litanies, and we responded, "Pray for us. Pray for us," in a singsong fashion. Finally, we emptied our basins and refilled them for the morning ablution.

Before lights-out, it was the task of the sister assigned to our dorm to ensure that all her charges were in bed and accounted for, bless each with holy water, and commit each of us to the care of her guardian angel.

Whether by design or chance, during my first year, I was assigned to the dormitory that Mother Cataldus supervised. On her nightly rounds, in her raspy voice—for which she earned the pseudonym *Whispers*—she talked to me of home and helped allay my loneliness.

The morning routine was the same, minus the prayers. As we exited, we individually had to approach the sister on duty with both our arms extended, palms facing up and fingers bent so that she could inspect our nails for cleanliness. The use of nail polish or any form of facial makeup was forbidden. It wasn't a big deal, as I don't believe that even as seniors, we were interested.

One year, we had several snowstorms and exceptionally cold weather, and we had to break the ice in our basins before performing our morning ablutions. I can still feel the sharp sting of the water on my face.

Once a week, usually during study time, we took turns taking hot baths, a welcome respite from the persistent chill that came from living in a damp northern European country, where, due to the wartime scarcity of fuel, central heating was curtailed and conserved.

Certain items were forbidden to be stored in the dormitory, and occasionally, our beds were searched, especially beneath the mattresses. The worst contraband was cigarettes, not that I am aware that any of the girls smoked. The sisters did sometimes find packets of sweets (or candy, in American jargon) and some seedy romance novels. The offending culprit was reprimanded in public.

From the first day of the term until we arrived home, we wore our uniforms. While wearing a uniform was boring, at least it had the advantage that there wasn't competition to know who was best dressed or wearing the latest fashion. My Irish readers will know what I mean when I say our everyday uniform consisted of a tunic, called a gym slip, with three box pleats front and back attached to a square yoke, underneath which we wore a navy woolen jumper in the cold months and a white blouse in the warm ones. This translates into American semantics as a navy jumper with three box pleats front and back, underneath which we wore a navy woolen sweater in the cold months and a white shirt in the warm ones.

There was no such thing as modern gym attire.

The tunic fell well below our knees. It was tied at the waist by a striped cincture. Our legs were covered with black full-length stockings, and we wore black laced shoes.

In order to keep the pleats looking sharp, we frequently placed our gym slips under our mattresses before retiring, with the weight of our bodies simulating a good press from a hot iron.

We had a special uniform for Sundays and feast days: a princess-style navy woolen dress complete with a detachable white collar.

The ensemble was completed by a trench-style coat called a Burberry. I hasten to add this was before that word entered the designer category. In summer, a navy blazer replaced the coat. On our heads, we wore either a classical navy beret bearing the school crest or a wide-brimmed felt hat adorned with a one-inch white ribbon band.

To any fashionista, we must have looked a dowdy lot as we processed two by two either to the parish church or, occasionally, as a treat, to the edge of the town to admire the scenic area near the River Slaney.

One of the rules that I never understood and that I have since regretted complying with, was that except for sitting in the same class with them, we never associated with the day pupils. They even wore a distinguishing uniform: a cerulean-blue jumper instead of our navy one. They must have regarded the boarders as snobs, even though I believe the raison d'être was to prevent us from using them to get contraband. I think we might have had a friendly game of camogie (a type of hurling game played by women) once per season between the two groups. Otherwise, the segregation was complete and reprehensible.

My background gave me no grounds for being a snob. I was occasionally reminded of this when one of my peers would remark how she could not be awarded a county scholarship, as her parents were too well-to-do. Yes, even at that level, there was opportunity for making one feel inferior. This had a negative effect on my self-image and made me maintain an arm's-length approach to some of my schoolmates.

Any bad behavior was reported to Mother Aloysius, whom we nicknamed *Switches*, the mistress of discipline. Her method of punishment was usually to revoke a privilege, such as making us take our meals in silence or denying extra recreation on a school holiday. Depending on the situation, one girl might be punished, but often, we were penalized collectively.

On the whole, I did not get into trouble. However, one occasion stands out, when I felt I was unfairly punished.

It was in my final year, during the height of winter, and it was bitterly cold outside. Because we, for some reason long since forgotten, had been deprived of a free afternoon of recreation, the whole school decided to go on strike. We decided not to answer the bell announcing the end of camogie practice but to defiantly stay out in the field in protest. Inwardly, I didn't agree with the decision, but I felt peer pressure not to voice my objection or to break rank.

When at last, order was restored and we were all assembled in the great hall, Switches gave us a good dressing down. I believe we were put on silence at meals for at least a week. She picked on some of the leaders of the revolt, who received extra punishment. Then it was my turn to be singled out and, in front of the whole school, proclaimed a hypocrite. Why I deserved that title, I have no idea, except that over the previous four years, I had been regarded as exemplary for keeping the rules and staying out of trouble. That experience hurt deeply.

It was a source of pride for me and my parents that I was fluent in the Irish language. My family heritage of patriotism most likely played a key role in that regard. I had no problem writing several pages of an essay in Gaelic, and I still have the gold *faine* (ring) I earned for proficiency in speaking the language.

English and Irish were compulsory, but I had a choice whether I would take French or Latin as a third language. My hunch was to study Latin, but on the recommendation of the headmistress, I agreed to take French. Reminiscent of my trials in learning to sing as a young child, I had a hard time speaking the French language, which, although it has a beautiful cadence, is not pronounced as it is written. I could learn the grammar and write essays in it with ease. One essay I wrote, titled "Mon Hero Favorie," was a tribute to the Irish patriot Padraig Pearse.

Math was my favorite subject, and I would spend a good part of the study time working out geometry, trigonometry, or algebra problems.

In each of the four years I spent in school, I took one of the national qualifying examinations, and I studied hard in preparation. When the results of the honors intermediate examination were posted, I was proud of myself for achieving almost a perfect score in mathematics.

That led to a secret ambition to study at the highest level

in mathematics for the final certificate examination, which I would take in two years. As strange as it might seem today, this ambition remained a secret. In the mores of the day, I could never have imagined approaching our math teacher with such a request.

Taking the honors math course in preparation for the leaving certificate was almost exclusively the domain of boys. It would have involved my having to take extracurricular courses, including calculus, which none of the other students were taking. So in spite of my ambition, I settled for sitting for the leaving certificate examination in 1948 at the pass level in mathematics, as all the other girls of my class did. I did have the satisfaction of Mother Therese telling me in the days before I left school that she appreciated my analytical prowess and had considered tutoring me for the higher level but feared it would be overwhelming, or some words to that effect.

I was always confused by European history. Unlike Irish history, which I had imbibed from the cradle, there seemed to be no logical start to the history of Europe. I had no concept of what feudalism or serfdom meant and it seemed just to start in the Middle Ages. It was all so nebulous and didn't advance in logical terms, as through the centuries our own history did.

This brings to mind a little true story. The sister teacher was concerned that a pupil was not doing well in school and requested that her mother come to the classroom to discuss her progress, or lack thereof. When Sister complained to the mother that "Mary doesn't even know who won the Battle of the Boyne," the mother's immediate response was "What does it matter to our Mary who won the Battle of the Boyne?" Problem solved.

English literature and poetry were way down on my list of favorites. Mother Aloysius, the feared mistress of discipline, was our English teacher in our final year. Unlike other teachers of the subject, she was more interested in getting us to write good prose than in making us memorize long passages from Shakespeare or Milton. The essays she required us to write were conceptual and related to current events rather than being descriptive of landscapes or personal experiences. She would hand back the essays to be rewritten until she was satisfied that they were not only grammatically correct but also precise and to the point. Later, in my professional career, I appreciated that discipline.

Our school offered few science classes. My only encounter with such subjects came as we learned the basics of hygiene and human anatomy during our domestic education classes. I had an aptitude for that learning, but little did I guess the significance it might have in my future.

We had little contact with boys of our age or even adult males. Each morning, we walked in procession two by two to the adjoining parish church for the 7:30 a.m. Mass, where we took our places in the left transept. Across the way in the right transept, with its separate entrance, was a gathering of novices and students preparing to become Patrician Brothers. Even if we'd wanted to, distance prevented us from giving them a glance.

The mores of the time dictated that sexuality was something secret and somewhat sinister. The only time the subject was broached—and tangentially at that—was during our annual three-day retreat when we were in our final two years of secondary school. We were taken aside to the Lady Chapel to listen to the retreat master give us a special talk. It was really a homily on sexual morality, and the language, so veiled that most of it went over our heads, evoked giggles of bashfulness and embarrassment out of us. Looking back on it, I find it amazing that we entered adulthood so ill prepared to deal with our awakening hormones, emotions, and relationships with the opposite sex.

During my first two years in Tullow, World War II continued with ever-increasing destruction and loss of life in Europe. Sometime during that period, three refugee girls arrived at the school; two were French, both named Monique, and the third was English and named Diana. I recall that Diana was especially emotional and expressive about her loneliness at being separated from her parents. She was especially ecstatic the day in May 1945, close to the final days of the war, when it was announced that all three were returning to their native land and to their parents. The whole school joined in the jubilation.

Every week without fail, I received a package of food from the Misses Maher to supplement the rationed foodstuffs of the war. It would contain extra butter, fruit, and sweet cake. We were allowed these extras and kept them in the pantry, to which we had access at mealtimes. I like to think I shared some of these bounties with the girls at my table.

When I recall how much those extras were rationed or in short supply during the war, I recognize how much my godmothers went out of their way for me. Even the nuns recognized how spoiled and special I was.

Outdoor recreation was required every afternoon after classes, and we played different games depending on the season. In the fall, we played camogie, an Irish game with a ball and sticks resembling hurling or field hockey. I never made it to the chosen team that went on to challenge other teams from schools run by the Brigidines.

In the spring term, we played tennis. My playing was mediocre, to say the least.

I was always interested in sports and even followed the national Gaelic hurling and football matches of the day. Whether through lack of coordination or another condition, I was unable to keep my eyes on the ball, as they say, when playing those games.

Even though it was the goal of the school to send us forth as good Christians, we were also expected, to leave as refined and accomplished ladies.

I remember enjoying the ballroom dancing lessons we had on Saturday afternoons. We were also tutored on etiquette. Then there were elocution lessons. We practiced intensely for increasing levels of competency decided by an annual examination. I was once singled out for being animated and able to speak with my eyes. My life experiences have taught me that this skill is a mixed blessing. The expression on my face can often be an open book, even when I do not want to reveal my inner thoughts.

As I was coming to the end of my secondary education, as with the other girls in my class, big decisions regarding what I would do next, loomed large and occupied much of my thoughts and imagination.

## A MISSION EMERGES

There were limited career options in Ireland in the late 1940s, especially for women. Some of my compatriots joined the civil service and took jobs at various government agencies, from the post office to housing and city planning commissions. Women, of course, were likely to end up with clerical positions.

Nurse training was not degree-based, but it was difficult to get into a hospital for the training, which was only offered by large hospitals in the cities. There seemed to be a preference in intake for daughters of the attending physicians. There was also a significant fee to get into nursing school. As for attending medical or dental school, that was mainly the privilege of sons, or occasionally daughters, of parents already in those professions.

Joining the convent to become a nun was an option.

As we matured through our teens, one of the questions often asked of our generation, either by a teacher or a relative, was "Do you think you have a vocation?" That meant "Do you think you are called to live the celibate life as a nun, priest, or monk?" This was held up to us as the most noble and sublime calling, a blessing not only to the one so called but also to the entire family. Getting married and rearing a family was second fiddle and never referred to as a vocation.

The young person so called was immediately put on a

pedestal. With pride, parents would refer to their daughter as "the nun" or their son as "the priest" rather than by their given names. There was even shame attached to any of these young people who decided convent or seminary life was not for them. For seminarians especially, the term *spoiled priest* was applied. It was unheard of for a professed nun or an ordained priest to renege on the commitment and return to secular life.

During our final year at school, a delegation of Brigidine nuns from Australia and New Zealand were attending a meeting in Tullow, the motherhouse. They took the opportunity to talk to the seniors about joining their convents down under. Three girls from my class decided to join them. My best friend, Nora, was one of them. Sadly, her departure put an end to our friendship.

It was like an Irish wake when the three girls boarded a ship. Still aspirants and not yet knowing whether they were suitable for religious life, they set out for lands down under. Because of the distance between Ireland and Australia and New Zealand, neither we nor their families expected to ever see them again.

That was not a unique situation, as many Irish young women of their generation left our shores as aspirants to join various religious congregations in the USA, Canada, or even Britain. Many congregations from those countries saw Ireland as a fertile recruiting ground for new members.

I was not turned on by any of those recruiters.

As I indicated in a previous chapter, since I was a little girl, I had always visualized myself as a teacher. One of the requirements for entry to Carysfort Primary School Training College was that the candidate had to be able to sing and hold a tune.

While I could easily pass the second requirement, which was proficiency in speaking Gaelic, there was no way I could muster through the first, so that choice of a career was not an option for me.

To become a teacher in secondary school, I would need to graduate with a bachelor's degree in either arts or science at a recognized university. While tuition fees to attend university in Ireland were low, a big stumbling block for working-class parents was to come up with living expenses in one of the three cities with national university colleges: Dublin, Cork, and Galway. Another obstacle was Latin, which I had not studied. The requirements for university entrance included having matriculated in Latin either in the leaving certificate examination or by taking a separate matriculation examination set by the university. I seemed to be barred from pursuing that course of action also.

However, with encouragement from my elders, I decided to take a crash course in Latin in the summer while awaiting the results of my leaving certification examination. Mother recruited Mr. Bergin, a retired teacher proficient in Latin, as my tutor.

So began a struggle to learn by rote and absorb the various declensions of nouns and tenses of verbs as rapidly as my brain could assimilate them. Reading and translating works of Cicero and Virgil without having a solid foundation in grammar was even more difficult.

While I didn't consider myself sufficiently proficient, I took a chance and sat for the exam in September. Was I lucky! Staring at me from page two of the exam paper were the only paragraphs from Cicero that I was really familiar with and could translate into decent English. As a result, I matriculated in Latin, which cleared the way for me to enroll in a university degree program.

In mid-August, the anxiously awaited leaving certificate examination results arrived by post from school, and I had done well. I was in the honors category. I was offered a further scholarship from the county to study and attend any college of my choice. Interestingly enough, I had completely forgotten this offer until my sister Bernadette recently reminded me of it. How this slipped my memory is interesting, but I guess by the time the offer was made, I had already set my sights in a different direction.

Amid all of the noise of these possible options, though, a secret that had taken root in my heart many years earlier was starting to break through: I had an ambition to become a missionary in Africa.

In those days, virtually the only way in the Catholic Church to become such a missionary was to join an established religious congregation. Lay organizations, such as the Peace Corps, Trócaire, and Caritas, had not yet been conceived. Although I later realized that the call to be a missionary is not equivalent to the call to live a life as a vowed religious, at the time, there did not seem to be any distinction between the two.

I was at most nine years old—but it is still as clear as the day it happened—when my heart was set on fire by listening to a recently returned missionary sister who visited our school and told us that many babies in Africa were dying from lack of food and health care. From that moment onward, I decided that when I grew up, I was going to spend my life trying to save "the black babies." She probably threw in a bit about saving their souls as well, as that was a prominent feature of our religious beliefs of the time, but that wasn't my propelling motive.

In spite of all the other distractions that had filled my life over the ensuing years, the embers of that calling never stopped smoldering. It kept being rekindled as I encountered and listened to other returned missionaries tell compelling stories of how they were working to feed the bodies and souls of the poor and neglected people in the Far East and Africa. The latter was always referred to as the Dark Continent, and in my childish imagination, I pictured not only a people with dark skin but also a whole continent steeped in darkness, always in the twilight zone.

As I matured, in my reading and research, I was able to fill in the information gaps, and I realized the work, though hard, was adventurous and the travel exotic. I began to imagine leaving a small, often gray-skied island for sun-drenched savannahs, steamy jungles, and breathtaking mountain ranges. It was thrilling to imagine seeing elephants, lions, giraffes, and flamingos in real life.

The young Irish men and women who flocked to missionary congregations in the 1950s did not necessarily have a fervor for converting people to Catholicism. Many of us saw our mission as improving the earthly lives of African, Asian, and South American people through education, medical care, and the tools of economic development, regardless of whether they embraced Christianity.

If I was going to be a nun, I had to decide which congregation to join. There were many choices because several new missionary congregations were formed in Ireland in the early twentieth century, including the Franciscan Missionary Sisters for Africa, the Medical Missionaries of Mary, the Missionary Sisters of the Holy Rosary (MSHR), and the Missionary Sisters of St. Columban.

Fate—or, to put a religious twist on it, the inspiration of the Holy Spirit—seemed to be sending me in the direction of MSHR.

While I was just a teenager, Grandmother, out of the blue, asked me to help answer an appeal for funds from a group of missionary sisters, the MSHRs. Up to that day, I had never heard of that group, neither did my grandmother have any idea of the role her request would play in my future. The appeal consisted of collecting a total of five shillings from contributors paying just a penny to place a pin prick on a printed card, in each bead representing one Hail Mary of the five decades of the rosary. With the help of family members, I duly completed the card and mailed a postal order for the large sum of five shillings to the promotion office of the MSHRs.

Of course, that was only the beginning of future appeals and even of my enrollment in their Missionary Junior Club. That was when I promised to continue to support the missions with prayer and monetary contributions. I even sent a photo of myself, which was published in their mission newsletter.

As I progressed through school with my focus mostly on studies, this involvement was in abeyance.

Then there occurred another sign, this one unambiguous. It occurred during my last few months in Tullow.

One afternoon, a visitor interrupted our homework: Sister Magdalena, a Holy Rosary Sister. She had recently completed her training as a nurse and was on her way to a mission in South Africa. She had come to Tullow to bid farewell to her parents and to Mother Ursulla, her Brigidine biological sister. She gave us an inspirational talk, and I was struck by how elegant she looked in her cream habit, black veil and a headgear much less cumbersome than those of other nuns of my acquaintance.

I was smitten. I wanted to have a private chat with her, but I was too bashful to approach her, and I wasn't yet ready to proclaim my secret ambition.

It is hard to explain it now, but as I was making up my mind to join a missionary congregation that would allow me work in Africa for the rest of my life, I did not discuss these life-altering plans with my parents, siblings, teachers, friends, not even Sarah or Nan Maher.

I am naturally a private person, but I'm not sure why I was so secretive. Were my natural shyness and reticence the only reasons? Or was I afraid someone close to me would disapprove or try to talk me out of it? Or was I afraid of the emotions that might come up if I thought too deeply about the consequences of my choice?

Once you entered the religious life, you were meant to say goodbye to the world, even your closest family members and friends. If I was sent to Africa, it would be years before I saw Ireland again, and I would not be able to spend the night in a private home even with my parents or the Misses Maher. I wouldn't see my siblings grow up, and I probably wouldn't be allowed to attend their weddings.

At the age of seventeen, as I grappled with this momentous decision, the implications of a perpetual vow of celibacy did not loom large in my psyche. Yes, I understood that I would take a vow to never marry, but at the time, that was not a big deal. I had never dated, so I had no practical experience of falling in love or the thrill of the first kiss. I might have been a late bloomer, but I can honestly say that I did not fully understand my emotional or sexual needs, nor had I deeply considered the psychological impact of never marrying or having children.

To my knowledge, there was no such thing as counseling for young adults to sort out if they really were prepared to spend the rest of their lives as obedient, poor celibates. The rules of the congregation and a life of prayer were meant to ward off temptations that reared their heads against the vows and keep you happy forever after.

With the hindsight of more than sixty years, I often think about how naive I was. The bottom line is, I was so intent on becoming a missionary that I was prepared to make any sacrifice to get there.

## A SECRET SLOWLY REVEALED

Eventually, I plucked up my courage and my pen and wrote a letter to the superior general of the Missionary Sisters of the Holy Rosary in Killeshandra, Co. Cavan, telling her of my interest and asking for information as to how to proceed. After some research, I found Killeshandra on the map. It was an out-of-the-way village famed for its creamery, a short distance from and on the south side of the border with Northern Ireland. It was about a hundred miles away, and without a car or direct public transport, there was no possibility of a secret visit to check it out or, for that matter, for the superiors to check me out as to my suitability to join the congregation.

In due course, I received a most welcoming letter from Mother Brigid, the superior general of the congregation, inviting me to join other candidates who were entering on September 8 of that year. A state of panic gripped me. The date was only a few weeks away, and I still hadn't discussed this decision with anybody. Besides, I needed more time to digest the reality of the invitation and come to terms with the humongous step I was taking.

I replied that I wasn't ready. The next date for entrance was set for February 2, 1949, two weeks after my eighteenth birthday. Mother Brigid recommended that I talk over my plans with a priest, probably assuming that my parents and other people in my circle of intimates were already aware of my intention.

All of my dealings with the sisters prior to joining the Holy Rosary were by mail. There was no interview, nor was I asked to provide testimonials as to my suitability. If any inquiries were made as to my background or my suitability for joining the congregation, I am not aware of them. I did not meet another Holy Rosary Sister until the day I entered. It surely was faith in action on both sides.

As recommended, one evening in late August, I rang the doorbell of the parochial house, where all the priests of the parish lived. I asked to speak to my favorite, Father Michael Coughlan. He was a tall, handsome man whom I had already summed up through his sermons and his advice in the confessional, so I felt comfortable discussing my plans with him.

As we were a huge parish and had little individual personal contact with the parochial priests, I was somewhat surprised by how he seemed to recognize me, did not question my motivation, and readily supported my decision. I did not request, nor did he write, a letter of recommendation. The weight of the world was off my shoulders as, with his blessing, I hastily descended those steps and scurried home. My secret had been vocalized. It was going to be easier to talk it over with the other important people in my life.

By that time, I was five months away from the departure date. I was spending my days studying the Latin crash course in preparation to take the examination in Dublin in early September. It was easier to concentrate on my studies than to choose a time to inform my parents of my decision.

Then, one day, I couldn't bear the suspense any longer. Armed with the acceptance letter from Killeshandra, I approached my mother, whom I found alone, performing household tasks. With an embarrassing bashfulness, I told her briefly of my momentous decision. I hastily handed her the letter of acceptance. Then I was gone, back to my safe haven at the Mahers'.

Even today, it is hard to fathom why I could not talk openly about my decision and why I could only inform my mother about the most critical decision of my life in such a cold and detached manner. Was this a sign of my own shyness and awkwardness? Was my family uncomfortable communicating about deeply personal matters? Or was it the long estrangement from the family that made me feel so uncomfortable? No doubt all three played some role.

My recollection of her reaction is that she was not surprised, but we exchanged few words. She didn't say she was happy, and in retrospect, I think I was expecting some affirmation of my decision. Perhaps she didn't know what to say. I still don't know how she felt about my making that big decision without her input and presenting it as I did as a fait accompli.

One day subsequently, I found her in tears as she did the housework, and she told me how much she would miss me. At that stage, I didn't see the bigger picture that she was losing me not only to religious life but also to missionary life far away in Africa.

Here I draw a blank as to when and where I informed my fairy godmothers. I was still enjoying their hospitality. Like Mother, they weren't overly surprised. I think they saw the makings of a nun in me already. I believe their alternative wish was for me to fall in love with and marry one of their nephews. They had, on numerous occasions, suggested I might get interested in the business and indicated they would be happy to pass it on to me if I felt so inclined.

As happens in small communities, the news of my decision spread rapidly. Neighbors and some friends offered congratulations and good wishes. I never found out, nor did I inquire from them, how my siblings reacted to my decision. I know for sure that my sisters disliked, as they progressed through the classes in school, when I was held up as a model for them. They hated hearing, "You are not a patch on your sister Marita." Can anyone blame them if they were not overly sad at the thought of my escaping to the convent? For some time now, I'd been, for all intents and purposes, only a peripheral part of their lives.

I had five months to prepare to leave the world as I knew it. I passed the matric, which was good news. In the intervening months, I just lay low, helped out the Misses Maher wherever I could, and enjoyed serving in the shop. Sometime during that period, Eamon Maher, the older nephew of Sarah and Nan and, by inheritance on the death of his father, the owner of the family farm, asked me on a date. One Saturday evening, while ostensibly visiting his aunts, he took me off guard and asked me if I would like to go to the pictures with him. That was what we called going to the cinema to see a movie. Sheepishly, I refused. To this day, I am not sure if I gave him a reason. I would like to think I did so that I didn't completely hurt his ego. My refusal was a lost opportunity to question the direction I was taking and the possibility that I become a farmer's wife instead.

The Christmas season was tinged with sadness, as I contemplated that it would be my last one with family and friends. I had no earthly possessions, so I did not have to make decisions as to how to dispose of them.

At short notice, the date to enter was changed from February 2 to February 11, 1949. I was ready to take the big step. I made a round of visits to cousins, aunts and uncles, and some friends, all low key. While there was a sense of finality in those goodbyes, I kept my emotions in check. The sense of purpose and the sublimation of the life I was about to embrace seemed to outweigh any apprehension or regrets I was experiencing. It wasn't as if I had to break a close relationship with a girlfriend or, for that matter, a boyfriend.

I guess I could characterize my state of mind as resembling the psychiatric definition of *fugue*, meaning "fleeing from one's own identity." Or I was in the initial stage of grieving for the life I'd known and relished up until then, the stage of denial. In a strange way, it also felt much like going back to boarding school.

I was given a list of items to bring with me. Included was just the generic word *underwear*. I, in my wisdom, had assumed that nuns did not wear brassieres. They always looked so flat-chested under those habits. So neither did I wear one on the day of entrance, nor did I bring any in my trousseau. As with a bride, *trousseau* was the recognized title given to the items in the suitcase that accompanied a lady becoming a bride of Christ. I do not remember in detail the other items on the list; I know it included two pairs of black laced shoes, some black stockings, a work basket, and a mysterious item called a Libra. It indicated that this item could be purchased from Easons, the largest bookstore in Ireland at the time.

To conclude the story of the bra, for the first few months after I donned the postulant's outfit, I was braless and not only quite uncomfortable but also somewhat embarrassed. I add that I am quite well endowed! Then, one day, my appointed angel had the courage to remark on this and indicated that once per month, we were allowed to present in writing a list of essential requisites to be provided from the housekeeping department. I felt more embarrassment as I submitted my request. I never repeated the faux pas.

By that time, I had ascertained that the Libra was not related to the zodiac sign of the same name but was essentially a large hymnal in Latin, which we would hold in two hands as we chanted and sang in the chapel. It arrived in the post about four days before my departure date. On opening the packet, I was horrified to find a manuscript about four inches thick. It had no cover, just pages bound together. It was the last one Easons had in stock.

So where to turn? There was no way I could arrive in Killeshandra with that thing as it was. Sarah Maher came to the rescue. Using her business acumen, she succeeded in persuading the publisher of the *Nationalist Newspaper*, the office of which was a few doors down the street, to bind and make a cover for the raw manuscript.

Recognizing the urgency of the situation, they—gratuitously, I believe—bound the manuscript like a tome of antiquity in heavy black leather. It looked beautiful, and when first produced in chapel sometime later, it became the envy of the other postulants. However, I soon discovered there was a dark side to this beauty. Due to the rich binding, it was heavy to hold, even with two hands, when in chapel.

I was ready. I was reaching. I was on my way.

# CHAPTER 4

# JOINING THE HOLY ROSARY SISTERS

On the morning of the big day, I awoke early and hastily donned my demure outfit, including the black stockings and laced black shoes. I deposited on the dressing table my silver bracelet, which, besides my Child of Mary medal, was the only piece of jewelry I possessed; my Pioneer pin, the emblem of my promise to abstain from alcoholic drinks for life; and my gold faine, the pin I wore signifying that I was a proficient Gaelic speaker.

I had one last look at my visage in the mirror—not with regrets, just to confirm my hair didn't have any strands askew.

There was an awkward silence during breakfast as, amid gulps to keep back the tears, I ingested the eggs and rashers (bacon) so lovingly prepared by Nan Maher. I have completely blocked out any conversation that might have taken place. In the weeks prior, both Sarah and Nan had expressed how much they would miss me but how happy they were that I was becoming a nun. The prospect of my going to Africa didn't seem to loom big in the conversation.

In the cold and still predawn hour, I took my last walk up Staplestown Road, up the back-way path to number 21. I hoped none of the neighbors would see me. I wanted my departure to be as low key as possible.

At home, already assembled were my parents, my five siblings, and my grandmother. A few months prior, Nana had come to live with my parents because she wasn't feeling well. As I held her in my embrace, tears began to flow—tears of sadness and loneliness. I sensed that this goodbye was final and that I would never see her again. She was not aware, nor did I tell her, how the request to complete the prick card so many years previously had played a role leading up to that day. To her thinking, that request would not have been a coincidence as much as the inspiration of the Holy Spirit leading me on.

I remained stoic as I hugged each of my siblings. We were all at that teenage stage where it is awkward to be overly diffusive in showing signs of affection. Mausie, who had just turned seventeen, was an apprentice at Darcy's, a local men's clothing shop. Still schoolgirls, Breed, Bernadette, and Eilish were almost sixteen, fourteen, and twelve, respectively. At eleven, Henry was in primary school, preparing for his Confirmation and already distinguishing himself on the football field.

Although I was the first in our family to plan a move far from home, I would not be the last. Mother and Father would eventually see all but one of their children leave for other countries and continents. Only my sister Breed would remain in Ireland.

In the mid-1950s, on a visit home, forty years after she emigrated, Aunt Annie, one of Father's sisters, persuaded Mausie and Bernadette to immigrate to the United States. There, they would work, find mates, and raise families. Eilish, a nurse midwife, would give up her private practice in Carlow to reach for adventure in Zambia. There, she met an Italian man who would become her husband. After stints in various other countries of Africa, she settled in his hometown in the Italian Alps with their four children. Henry would also join a missionary congregation and spend time in Africa, but he eventually would become laicized from the priesthood. After relocating to the United States, he would marry and raise two sons.

"Uncle" James Pender, whose family lived in Keelogue during the war years and who was beloved by all our family, was recruited to drive me to Killeshandra on the day I entered the Holy Rosary Congregation. Although his chauffer duties required him to come down from Belfast to Carlow the day before we left, he did so generously and graciously. Only he, the driver, and my parents would accompany me on the trip to my future home.

The final stop before leaving the town I loved so well was 92 Tullow Street. The packed suitcase and a listed bedside mat were loaded into the car. Sarah wore her businesslike exterior, but Nan was in tears. Having made my home with them for the better part of seven years, I was aware that like most Irish persons of their generation, they were reserved and not prone to show many external signs of affection. We cursorily embraced and hugged, and I hastily retreated to the car before I would lose my composure.

As I had never seen the Holy Rosary's motherhouse, I vividly remember the last leg of that first journey. After driving through Cavan town, we found the country road that took us through the village of Killeshandra. Beyond it, we skirted a large lake, rolled around a bend, and were suddenly struck by the appearance of a huge, gleaming, fortress-like white complex at the crest of the hill, surrounded by lush, manicured green grounds.

In 1924, the MSHR had established its motherhouse on the site of a gentrified estate to accommodate the women who flocked from all over Ireland—and beyond—to become missionary sisters.

We drove through the open wrought-iron gates, which seemed gigantic, and past the former gatekeeper's lodge. It was now the home of the resident chaplain. We then proceeded up the winding avenue. Anticipation gave way to apprehension as I absorbed the enormity and profundity of the world to which I was committing myself.

But in my mind, there was no turning back.

My family and I received a great welcome from Mother Brigid, the superior general, and her councilors. The four of us were treated to lunch in the front parlor, a sundrenched, spacious, beautifully decorated room. That was my last meal with my family for many a day.

From my perspective, the person I most wanted to meet was the novice mistress. Was she really the monstrous witch of a character that folklore, literature, and movies made her out to be? When she did appear, any reservations I had evaporated.

When it came time for me to cross the threshold into the sisterhood, I noticed Mother shed tears. The sisters were well aware of how difficult this parting could be, so they tried to keep the goodbyes short. They almost immediately whisked me away, removing me not only from my family but also from life as I had always known it.

In the first stage of the process of becoming an avowed sister, a woman is known as a postulant. Two other postulants entered on the same day I did, a newly qualified doctor and another, like me, who had just completed her secondary education.

We were escorted to our cubicles on a third-floor wing of the separate novitiate building. The cubicles were arranged on both sides of a central corridor. Each was at most six feet by ten feet, individually divided by a baseboard partition that rose up to a height of about eight feet. A heavy dark curtain covered the entrance. There was only room for the twin-style iron bed and a small washstand, on which was a white Delph pitcher of water and a washbasin. Hidden in the cupboard of the washstand was the vessel—not for personal use but to convey the soapy water after sponge bathing to the communal bathrooms. It wasn't how empty the unit looked as much as the lack of adequate lighting that bothered me. Each cubicle had a small window that gave light during the day, but after dark, the only light source came from ceiling lights on the central corridor. First impressions aside, we soon learned that our cubicles were purely sleeping quarters and not havens of privacy during the day or reading rooms at night.

Each of us was assigned and introduced to an angel, a second-year novice who helped us clothe ourselves in our new uniform: an unlined, collarless black wool dress reaching almost to the ankles. Over this was a cape that had a removable white cotton collar. While no one ever clarified, I believe this garment was to hide our boobs and any suggestion of femininity. We were encouraged to keep our hands underneath our capes when moving around the precincts or processing in formation. With my hair tightly pulled back off my forehead, I donned the black veil of the postulant.

Once we were dressed in our postulant outfits, the three of us attended a brief initiation ceremony before the entire community in the chapel. Then we processed to the refectory for the evening meal. To process is to walk in measured, contemplative formation two by two; this would quickly become a natural formation for us.

Sometime later that evening, we met the seven other postulants who would comprise the rest of my set. These senior postulants had entered the previous September, and by that time, they were well initiated into the ways of cloister living.

Our angels and the senior postulants were anxious to apprise us of appropriate behavior and decorum for religious life. What they didn't tell us directly, we picked up as we were absorbed into the convent ethos.

One of the first things we had to get used to was responding to the call of the bell. It awakened us in the morning, called us to the preset hours of prayer, and announced the onset of profound silence after the last prayer of the evening. An eerie atmosphere of only whispers prevailed as we retired to our sleeping quarters. We were given twenty minutes to undress and take care of personal matters before lights-out at ten o'clock.

In the morning, as postulants, we were allowed to sleep in for about one half hour after the official rising bell at 5:30 a.m. One of the novices, calling us individually with a knock on the partition adjacent to the closed curtain, would wake us. She waited until we replied to her greeting of *"Bendicamus Domino"* (Let us bless the Lord) with a resounding *"Deo Gratias"* to ensure we really were alert and on the move. Within twenty minutes, we were expected to be in chapel for a period of mental prayer before the community Mass. Breakfast followed Mass. We quickly learned that the refectory (from the Latin verb *reficere*, meaning "to renew" or "to refresh") was a large room with a red terrazzo floor and large windows. It was a sacred place on a par with the chapel. In its precincts, we only spoke in whispers and as briefly as possible. One can get the implication from the Latin terminology: food was only for sustenance and not for enjoyment.

Seating in the refectory was formal and preassigned. A series of tables were arranged in the shape of a U, with two sides that stretched for the full length of the hall to accommodate about sixty women. Each place had its own cubbyhole to hold personal utensils and the large white drinking mug. For those of us used to drinking a cup of tea out of nice bone china, this gave the message that we were renouncing worldly values. Stored under the tables were the backless wooden stools—naturally, one for each sister.

At the base was the table where the superior general and her council members sat. Then, according to rank and longevity in the congregation, sisters took up their places on each side. We followed the white-veiled novices at the other end of the hall. This meant that we newcomers were at the end opposite the superiors.

Silence reigned at all meals, except for the voice of a novice reading from a pedestal in one corner of the hall. At breakfast, a novice read a passage from Thomas à Kempis's classic *The Imitation of Christ*. Still ringing in my ears is the admonition "Vanity of vanities and all is vanity, except to love God and Him alone."

The readings at the midday meal were usually from a recently published book on the life of a saint or holy person, so they were relatively interesting.

The evening meal was preceded by a reading from the Martyrology, essentially a litany of the most obscure first- and second-century martyrs. The poor novice reciting the list invariably stumbled over some of the pronunciations. It was painful to listen to, but more significantly, after the meal, the novice mistress would use the mispronunciations as an opportunity to offer a humiliating reprimand. I can speak from experience because like those before me, I would become a victim in my novice years.

Another firm rule in the refectory and elsewhere in the precincts was custody of the eyes, which meant we were to keep our gaze downward and not look directly at another sister. This was a difficult task, at least when everything was new to us as postulants.

We were not dismissed from the midday and evening meals until, with a knock of her knuckles, the local superior indicated it was time to rise. Grace after meals, recited in unison, preceded another procession. We walked two by two in perfect order as far as the central bell station, where we were free to disperse. This central atrium was sort of a general gathering spot.

I should add here that the usual way to locate a sister or to call her to answer incoming personal phone calls was to ring that same bell and wait for her to answer in person. There were no such things as personal phone extensions or any intercom devices, except in the communal rooms. There was a system of codes. Each professed sister had her own, again allotted by seniority. The code system is too difficult to try to describe on paper. It was complicated and required a listening ear but was even more difficult for the poor bell ringer, who, besides learning how gently to pull on the rope, had also, depending on the complexity of the number, to add a little tinkle between one and nine strokes (e.g., nine solid pulls and then a tinkle would let Sister X know she was wanted on the phone).

As soon as we finished the morning meal, we were allowed to scurry away from the table to perform our assigned duties. We could then speak in whispers but only when it was essential for the performance of chores. Besides performing about two hours of manual work each day—such as helping in the kitchen, doing housekeeping, or working in the promotion office—postulants studied the psalms, the Bible, theology and attended choir practice. Initially, I tried to sing along with the rest of the bunch, but the choir mistress soon politely requested that I vocalize with my lips only. It was another blow to my pride.

We were also assigned to serve the community in the refectory during meals. This entailed pouring the coffee or tea from humongous aluminum teapots. When full, they were extremely heavy, requiring us to hold the handle at the back of the pot with one hand and put the other one on the handle which was in front of the lid. With the excitement of being waitresses, it was not unusual to either overfill a person's mug or otherwise spill from the pot. This was especially embarrassing when, through nervousness, it happened at the mothers' table. Even at an early stage, we appreciated the pecking order and the deference awarded to superiors.

It was taboo to discuss any personal affairs or problems with other sisters in the community. In that respect, we had to learn to keep a firm rein on our emotions. I learned that lesson the hard way in the early months of the postulancy.

My grandmother died about two weeks after I bid her my last farewell. Almost a month passed before Mother got around to writing to inform me of her death and funeral.

The novice mistress read the letter—as all our mail was censored, both coming and going—and called me aside to give me the bad news. She then briefly announced the sad news at a combined meeting of novices and postulants and asked their prayers for me and my family. Other than that, I do not remember any help in dealing with my grief.

The reality of her death hit me hard, but it wasn't until some day in August when the family came for the first visit since I'd entered that I came to terms with it as a reality. When, on entering the parlor, I saw Mother still dressed in her black mourning outfit, I dissolved into tears and released all those pent-up emotions.

There was a strict schedule for family-only visitors, who could come every six months. Our postal communications were limited to one letter home per month. To write to additional people, we had to get permission from the novice mistress or her associate. Because I was too conscientious to ask for any exceptions to the rules, I don't think I ever wrote a letter to Sarah or Nan Maher.

One of my great regrets is that I too easily accepted the rules and essentially abandoned Sarah and Nan. These two ladies who had no blood relationship to me had treated me as their adopted daughter—a treasured and pampered daughter, in fact—for a period of seven or eight years. I realized too late that I never recognized them or thanked them sufficiently after I joined the nunnery.

There was no opportunity to form a close relationship with other members of our set. Conversation, which was only during the two hours of recreation we had daily, one after midday dinner and one the hour before night prayer, was supervised by the assistant novice mistress. Only topics of general interest were discussed, and sometimes those were hard to come up with, especially as we had no recourse to topical events. We learned the codified Latin dictum and established rule of the cloister, *"Numquam duos, semper tres"* (Never two, always three), early on.

We were also advised not to enter another postulant's cubicle at any time, especially after the last bell of the night, when we were to maintain a profound silence until morning.

In my innocence, I never read anything more into these restrictions than the negative effects that particular friendships would create in community living. I don't think the word *lesbian* had yet entered my vocabulary, nor had I any experience of women in such relationships. It was much later that I realized that these rules, mostly passed down through centuries of cloister living, could have had more sinister implications, hence the hypervigilance in preventing any two sisters from becoming too close. As I would later discover, male-female relationships were equally controlled and scrutinized.

In that regard, the MSHRs were no different from any other Catholic religious orders for both women and men of the time. I would spend most of my waking hours as a postulant and novice with the eight other women in my set, the group who entered the same year I did. Because of the rules about silence and the discouragement of personal friendships, I did not really get to know them as individuals. Yet each one did have her own personality.

Norah Quinn was from the Transvaal, South Africa. She had gotten to know the MSHRs in her mid-twenties. Both she and another late vocation in the set before us, Sister Mary Matthew Staunton, deserve the utmost admiration for their courage in going against the apartheid regime of that country, a regime cherished by their families and acquaintances. They were joining a missionary congregation devoted especially to serving the needs of the black population of Africa. Moreover, they left their native land to join, at the time, an almost exclusive Irish group in an insular country with its own peculiar customs and beliefs.

I recall being surprised that when we were each introduced to a visiting Nigerian priest one day, Norah remarked that it was the first time she had ever exchanged a handshake with a black person. After profession, she returned to South Africa and spent many years in the education of young black women. Matthew, already a practicing nurse midwife before she entered was larger than life in personality and compassion. On her return to the Transvaal she practiced for several years at the health clinic in Alexandra, near Soweto, a township that hit the international scene due to its riots during the struggle for independence.

Bernadette Moynihan was the doctor who entered the same day I did. She was always reserved, and I think she found obeying the minute rules of the postulancy and novitiate irritating, to say the least. She appeared to be much more mature than the rest of us and also more deeply spiritual, but at times, she seemed aloof and bored with the silly levity of our conversations.

Then there was Joan Laffan, who was renowned for her hastiness and her ability to beat us all to the chapel each morning. She would be halfway around making the Stations of the Cross before I would appear. The irony of this—and the terrible tragedy for her—was that about nine years later, as a midwifery student in Dublin, she fell off her bicycle under the wheels of a truck and never walked again, as she became a paraplegic. Joan dealt heroically with her disability and actually lived to a ripe old age, evidence of her fighting spirit and the good care she received.

Christine Heslin was from Scotland. In spite of her

fast-flowing, unique Scottish accent, which was unfamiliar to those of us with the Irish brogue, she became the natural leader of the group. She breathed a motherly aura and was the go-to person if there were any issues. She subsequently graduated as a primary school teacher. Strangely enough, our paths crossed again in the wilds of Ortum sometime in the mid-sixties, when, for a brief period, she was the headmistress of the primary school. Besides recognizing that we were of the same set, we did not reestablish any close bonds of friendship. Come to think of it, perhaps I am to blame.

Dymphna McKenna was from Dublin. She was a quiet person with a caring personality who did not make any waves. We were students together for several years while she trained as a nurse in St. Vincent's. I don't think our paths ever crossed again after she went to Nigeria.

Then there was Mary "Mae" McHugh, the little redhead from Ardara (pronounced Arr-dra), County Donegal, the most northwestern of the twenty-six counties of the Republic. She could be quite perky and was sure of her own opinions. Little did I realize in those early years that our lives would be tangentially thrown together at a future date.

Agnes Prendergast entered the same day I did and was six months younger than I. She got quite a teasing for being the junior of the set. Like me, she took everything in stride. The rules and regulations of the postulancy appeared to be just an extension of those of boarding school. After training as a domestic education teacher, Agnes spent most of her active life in Nigeria.

As I said earlier, I became one of nine postulants the day I entered. However, only eight of us made it through the novitiate. I am unable to recall the name of the other young woman, whom I only knew briefly, as she left within a few weeks of my entering. I just remember her as someone pleasant and vibrant, with striking good looks, who did not give the impression of being unhappy.

When a woman left either the postulancy or the novitiate, we were not informed until it was fait accompli, and then we were never to question the reason why or to discuss it among ourselves. I can still recall my bewilderment when the novice mistress informed a joint session of postulants and novices of the above woman's departure. It was like a sudden death, especially as she had joined us for recreation the evening before, and all had seemed well with her. These departures and the callous way they seemed to be handled had an unsettling influence on me, making me wonder if my turn was coming next.

## A BRIEF HISTORY OF THE MSHR

From the early 1900s onward, there arose in Ireland what was generally called the Irish Missionary Movement. It was spurred on by a combination of factors, including our emancipation from British rule and the opening up of previously closed regions of Africa and the Far East not only to international trade but also to the opportunity for Christian evangelization. One of the spearheads of Catholic evangelization in southern Nigeria was Irish-born Bishop Joseph Shanahan. Born in County Tipperary in 1871, he became a priest of the Holy Ghost Congregation, known today as the Spiritans, who, while they had a French origin, were at the time focusing on recruiting young Irish men to become missionaries in anglophone colonial countries, such as Nigeria.

From the first day that Bishop Shanahan set foot in Onitsha, Nigeria, in 1902, he and his volunteer priests were successful in converting thousands of Nigerians to the Catholic faith. This was mainly through the schools they had set up for the young boys of the region. As these men married, there was only a brief catechetical instruction afforded to their as-yet-uneducated brides, which Joseph Shanahan, as bishop, did not see as providing a good foundation for the future of Christian families.

Without going into the details of what is a fascinating story, the Missionary Sisters of the Holy Rosary came into being to answer this need for a cadre of female religious.

By the early 1920s, with the blessing of Pope Pius XI, Bishop Shanahan was openly recruiting young Irish women to join a newly proposed congregation, which Dominican sisters from Cabra in Dublin were willing to sponsor and train in the ways of religious life. Only after this formation would they go forth to serve the educational and medical needs of the people of southern Nigeria or elsewhere in Africa.

The response was dramatic. One can only marvel at the faith and determination of these seven young women who, wanting to dedicate their lives as missionaries, were required through the rules and regulations of the Catholic Church to agree to become nuns. They were also joining an ill-defined entity, a new missionary congregation without any established records or identity.

Among the founding members was Mother Brigid Ryan, who was superior general when I joined. There was Agnes Ryan, who was one of the first female doctors to graduate from the Royal University, Dublin, in 1902. Marie Martin, who had already served as a lay volunteer in Nigeria, was one of them. She became better known later in life as Mother Mary Martin, foundress of the Medical Missionaries of Mary.

There was Sister Mary Joseph Byrnes, whose home was just a few fields away from the convent grounds in Killeshandra. Even after I joined she was still hale and hearty and loved to reminisce about the early days. For whatever reason, I don't think she ever saw the mission fields, but she served for years as bursar at the motherhouse. What struck me as poignant was that even though she could see her home from the front door of the convent, she had never set foot in it from the day she entered. Her nephews used to serve Mass in the convent chapel, and I think that was as close as she got to a relationship with her family.

Sister Mary Peter Shannon was a font of information, often recalling the early days, and enjoyed her time with us greenhorns. Her smile and open-arms approach left an indelible mark on my young mind.

Sister Dominic O'Dwyer, if I recall, was still in Nigeria at the time of my joining. When, in later years, I made her acquaintance, I was struck by her spunk and ability to be a mover and shaker in effecting change in the community, as necessitated by changing times and the needs of the missions.

Sister Philomena Fox, the first American citizen to join the new group, was outstanding in her devotion to Bishop

Shanahan, whose secretary she had been for many years in Nigeria. She played a significant role in my later life, for which I am eternally grateful.

On a cold, snowy day in February 1924, four Dominican nuns set out with Bishop Shanahan to a bleak, derelict house on a large estate in County Cavan. This was Drumallac House, which he had purchased with a bank loan and which was to become the home of the new congregation.

On March 7 of the same year, the seven aspirants joined the group and began the process of their transformation. Having to adopt a distinctive name for the newly formed congregation required some ingenuity, seeing that many names were already taken, such as Mercy Sisters and Holy Spirit Sisters. It ended up with Dominican influence, the rosary having been formulated by their founder, St. Dominick. Although the official name was Missionary Sisters of the Holy Rosary (MSHR), in Ireland, over time and even to the present, we became known as the Killeshandra nuns.

From this humble beginning came an influx of young women from every county in Ireland and a few from Great Britain and even the USA, all eager to join a band of missionaries ready to save the world. We all had good intentions and were ready to leave home and country for the cause of helping our less privileged brothers and sisters. Our set of nine aspirants was actually one of the smallest in several years; just ahead of us was a group of twenty-one, nineteen of whom made it to profession.

From the beginning, essentially against the customs of the day, Bishop Shanahan had the good sense to insist that the newly professed sisters, before they boarded a ship for Africa, be professionally trained, initially with emphasis on education but ultimately with medical credentials sufficient to establish institutes of education and hospitals, which were second to none as far as efficiency and prestige in the countries to which the sisters were sent.

Rome required that members of an established congregation train candidates for any newly formed religious order. That was how the Dominicans came to Killeshandra. Because of that Dominican influence, the Holy Rosary habit was a variation on theirs, with the same cream-colored habit and scapular but a distinguishing headgear. Luckily, this was less cumbersome, as can be seen from early photographs of both groups.

The MSHR history was brought home to me in a personal way when, within days of my entering, celebrations for its landmark twenty-fifth anniversary commenced. These celebrations went on for eleven days and concluded with solemn High Mass of Thanksgiving celebrated by the local bishop. Many of those who played a role in the formation of the Holy Rosary either officiated or were present for the celebratory Mass.

Two of the original Dominican Sisters, Mother Xavier and Sister M. Ursula, spent time with the postulants and novices, recounting the early difficult days in the bleak, damp house by the lake. Hearing stories about the missions as recounted by four of the founding members was especially stimulating. That was the raison d'être we were aspiring to be members. Some parts of the celebrations were more down to earth than devotional, including skits by the novices about the idiosyncrasies of daily living in the convent and performances by the most talented singers among the professed members. There was no effort to disguise the actors by donning costumes. The utmost decorum held sway.

After all these years, I have held on to a printed memento of the occasion, titled "Silver Sheaves." As I thumb through the pages, they help me to document these memories. This paperback booklet has moved with me wherever I have roamed, and it is a treasured possession as a reminder of my deep affection for Holy Rosary.

## THE NOVITIATE YEARS

Novices went through a two-year period of intense preparation before taking the vows of religious life: obedience, poverty, and chastity (now more appropriately called celibacy).

From the first days of joining the postulancy, we were told that we should not enter the adjoining room, the one reserved for the novices. That room, more than one hundred feet in length, with perpetually closed doors opening off the main corridor, was intimidating and sinister, to say the least. I wondered what was going on inside. Was life as a novice as austere as rumors or the tabloids of the day narrated?

Adding to my apprehension, the contemporary novices all seemed so serious. I longed to ask one of them, even my angel, for some enlightenment as to what was going on inside. But the rule of silence forbade us postulants from speaking with novices, except for information regarding our common household duties.

In spite of my observance of custody of the eyes, in my peripheral vision, one day I saw a novice receive a lesson in humility that horrified me after she broke a piece of crockery, most likely by accident. As soon as the community was seated in the refectory, the novice got up from her seat with the broken piece in hand but hidden under her scapular, moved to the middle of the floor in the center of the U, knelt down on a mat, and kissed the floor. She then exposed the broken piece and held it out for all to see. She continued kneeling until the superior gave her a sign. She then kissed the floor again, arose, and took her place to partake of the meal.

I soon learned that this was a typical example of the humiliating penances in vogue in religious life at the time. I had to do it myself a few times, and it cut to the core.

Our induction into the novitiate was marked with a solemn ceremony in the chapel known as the reception of the habit. It was a private ceremony without our families present and was presided over by the local bishop.

A full-dress rehearsal of my set's reception of the habit in August 1949 appeared in an MSHR promotional film titled *Out of the Darkness*, which can still be found on YouTube. We simulated the ceremony for the movie a few weeks before the actual event took place.

Dressed in donated white bridal gowns and veils, as brides of Christ, we processed up the center aisle of the chapel to formally bid goodbye to the material world. After a brief interrogation from the superior general when we expressed our desire to become novices in the congregation, in the adjoining sacristy, we changed our bridal gowns for the cream habits of the sisterhood. After we returned to the chapel, the superior placed the headgear and the white veils of the novice on our heads—a poignant moment symbolizing our renouncing of feminine vanity, as our tresses were supposed to never be seen in public again.

Instead of wedding rings, which we would receive on our final profession day, we were formally given a copy of the Rules and Constitution of the MSHRs. Throughout the two years of the novitiate, we were to study and assimilate them as our guides to observance of the vows and dedication to mission.

Remember that this took place well before the Second Vatican Council (Vatican II), a worldwide assembly of Roman Catholic religious leaders convened by Pope John XXIII between 1962 and 1965. Vatican II heralded profound changes in Catholic practices to make the church more accessible to common people. Over time, this led to the majority of nuns giving up their imposing habits to wear simple veils or to dress more or less similar to contemporary women in the world.

Our reception of the habit also marked the time in which we gave up our birth names and took on religious names, which commemorated saints or some form of the Virgin Mary's attributes. To prevent confusion, there could only be one of us with any given name among the living members of the congregation. With the large number of sisters ahead of us, the options to get an easily recognized name were limited. Many had the Virgin Mary's name in various forms, such as Sister Mary Immaculata, Sister Mary Consolata, and Sister Mary de Lourdes.

Although it was not ultimately up to us to choose our religious names, we were able to offer three suggestions for consideration. Many of us selected masculine saints' names—Kevin, Regis, Fintan, Bruno, and so forth. Killian was one of my choices because it reminded me of St. Killian's Crescent, where I grew up, and as it had not already been taken, I became known as Sister Mary Killian.

Now that we were fully clothed in the religious habit, we had to learn how to take care of it. As the habit and scapular were full length, they were difficult to keep from splattering in the muddy soil of the Irish countryside.

We were allowed two of each, and in order to send the tunic and sleeves to the laundry, we had to detach them from the calico yoke and then reassemble them according to regulations on return from the laundry. In a slow and tedious process, all were sewn by hand with double-layer strong thread. This process occurred about once monthly.

But what demanded more attention was reassembling our headgear each week, usually on Saturday night, when we were given more time before the lights went out. The stiffly starched white forehead band had to be shaped to form three sides of a boxlike structure so that it would sit about three inches above our eyebrows. To this, we attached the cap that covered our head, including our ears, and on top of that the veil, all according to a predetermined uniformity. Getting the process completed before darkness overtook was a source of anxiety, especially for new novices. The results of some bad handiwork could often be seen on a Sunday morning.

Another thing that sticks in my memory from those days in the habit is that in order to not only keep perspiration from staining the linen forehead band but also keep the band from collapsing, we would use folds and folds of white writing paper between the bands and our foreheads in order to absorb the moisture. The frequency of changing this depended on the amount and intensity of the physical work performed. There was a definite need for a change after some hours of scrubbing the red floor tiles of the main thoroughfare, which, as novices, we did once weekly.

In my eyes, the worst of all was the hideous coif we were expected to wear at night—I mean for the whole night! Every time I see lady speed skaters wearing the tight-fitting helmets covering everything except their noses and mouths, my mind recalls those awful night coifs. Not only did they look spooky, but they were also uncomfortable, especially the piece worn under the chin. But nobody complained. After all, we were supposed to be mortifying the body and getting it into subjection.

Becoming a novice brought many changes into our lives.

For one, Mother Gabriel, the novice mistress, became stricter and began to issue the dreaded penances. In the folklore of the time, the novice mistress was meant to be a witchy monstrosity who would challenge the novices with impossible and illogical tasks, such as planting cabbages upside down, but Mother Gabriel, fortunately, was reasonable and not unkind.

The job of the novice mistress, whom we called Mother Mistress, was to focus the novices on humility, obedience, and utter detachment from the goods and possessions of the world. That meant material things were only for our use, not to be regarded as personal possessions. Therefore, any gift an individual received was automatically surrendered to the common stock.

It was not exactly forbidden for a sister to keep an occasional special memento, but she had to ask permission to do so. Invariably, Mother Mistress would ask, "Do you need it, Sister?" with emphasis on the need versus the want. Answering in the affirmative was often tough, especially if it seemed like a little luxury, such as an expensive fountain pen that a relative had given.

During the two years of the novitiate, we studied intensely the rules and constitution and the implications involved in taking the three vows. Even though the life of a missionary would be far different from that of a cloistered religious, the Holy Rosary and other Congregations retained the emphasis on personal perfection, self-denial, detachment from everything worldly, conformity, and uniformity that was more appropriate to the sheltered life of a monastic. I would later understand firsthand how unhelpful and even detrimental these lessons would be when we were dispersed among the various missions.

Obedience was not difficult for me in those early days. I was a strict observer of the rules, partly to keep out of trouble but essentially because I tried to live the ideal that was set before us: that keeping the holy rule was the path to holiness, perfection, and, eventually, heaven.

I was still a novice when I learned that following the rules to the letter was not always practical or realistic.

To assess our leadership abilities each of the second year novices was appointed for a month at a time to be the leader and spokesperson for the entire group. My turn happened to coincide with the time when we were decorating our outdoors in anticipation of the solemn procession and benediction on the

Feast of Corpus Christi. This feast, which occurred in late May or early June, was a solemn one to honor Jesus in the Eucharist. We put weeks of preparation into it, sewing yellow and white bunting and attaching it to stakes that lined both sides of the avenue from the front gate to the altar erected in front of the main entrance. We picked wildflowers, the petals of which we placed in decorated baskets for children in their first communion outfits to strew in front of the priest as he processed along the route while carrying the monstrance. The monstrance is a decorated receptacle for exposing the Eucharistic host during processions or for the service of benediction. This solemn procession was the only celebration the local community from the village of Killeshandra joined us for.

It was regarded as a special privilege for the novitiate to take charge of this solemn preparation, and it fell to me to assign duties and lead the group of twenty novices and ten postulants.

As a stickler for keeping the rules, I was worried that the pressure to finish the decorating would keep us novices from completing all our spiritual exercises, such as study and reading. Left to my own devices, I would have pushed myself and the rest of the group to the breaking point. Fortunately, Sister Mary Matthew, the wise recruit from South Africa, took me aside to remind me that sometimes it was necessary to rob Peter to pay Paul. In other words, it was allowable to put short-term or urgent priorities ahead of the prescribed daily practices of religious life.

That wasn't the last time I used that technique. It came in useful many times henceforth when life-or-death situations fell into my lap in my practice in Africa.

As novices, we were on our honor to take ourselves to the office of the novice mistress whenever we broke a rule or made a mistake. We would knock, listen for her invitation to come in, and get down on our knees as soon as we entered. We would then kiss the ground and say, "I ask pardon and penance for …" Transgressions included ringing the bell for wake-up too early in the morning, breaking a plate in the kitchen, or wasting notepaper, a popular admission. Depending on the offense, the penance could be as easy as saying a Hail Mary or as humiliating as prostrating yourself on the floor of the refectory at mealtime while holding a broken piece of crockery, as I mentioned earlier.

But those everyday humiliations paled in comparison with the chapter of faults, one of the most solemn and intimidating exercises that communities of religious endured in those days. This was a practice not only for novices. Nuns were also expected to engage in it for remainder of their religious lives.

Each religious community, even those as small as three or four, was expected to convene at a set day and time each week for the chapter of faults. The exercise, a carryover from the days of monasticism, was supposed to be penitential and foster the spirit of humility.

At Killeshandra, the session started when the entire community processed from the chapel into the refectory while reciting the De Profundis (Psalm 130), a prayer of penance that begins "From the depths, I have cried out to you, O Lord; Lord, hear my voice. Let your ears be attentive to the voice of my supplication." This is the English translation; we intoned it in Latin, of course.

We then sat in two rows facing each other, with the superior seated at the top of the room. Each sister would take a turn kneeling on the mat placed in the center of the group; kissing the floor; and then asking for "pardon and penance" in a loud voice, proclaiming her errors or offenses. Fortunately, we were limited to a maximum of three faults, none of which should be serious sins or transgressions that would be matter for confession in the sacrament of penance. I found the whole process nerve-racking. Before my turn came, I would find myself racking my brain to recall offenses against rules or regulations. In fact, sometimes I would fabricate them. It was the job of the superior to proclaim a penance, which invariably was to say a short prayer, but it was up to her discretion to mete out a harsher punishment.

One of the most embarrassing parts of the exercise was having to sit through and listen to fellow members of the community recite their litany of peccadilloes. It was always a relief to me—and probably the rest of the community—when the day scheduled for the chapter of faults fell on a feast day or when there was some other good reason to cancel.

On one occasion during my student days, that odious exercise had a comical ending. One of my fellow students, a trainee nurse in the maternity hospital, took to the floor and, after her profound *venia*, proceeded to ask pardon and penance for breaking thirty baby bottles. Evidently, she had dropped a whole tray of them in the neonatal nursery. As soon as the words came out of her mouth, a spurt of nervous laughter shattered the solemnity of the chapter of faults. The sister in charge, who found it so hard to schedule these sessions at the best of times, had no problem calling an immediate halt to proceedings. We all retired with broad smiles on our faces but without even a glance at the culprit. The exercise was so sacred that after we left the room, we could make no reference to what had taken place.

While I never had the experience of being a superior myself, this whole process was so humiliating that I believe those who were in that office found the exercise difficult. Imagine sitting in judgment on your comrades whom you rubbed shoulders with every day, not to speak of realizing that you were just as much a culprit and defaulter as they were. It was more a creator of stress than an exercise in humility. As far as I know, that medieval practice is no longer part of religious life, and I say good riddance.

When it came to the Sacrament of Penance, the official title for going to confession, we were obligated to go at least once each week. The toll of the bell announced that the confessor, usually a local priest, had arrived. Then we would leave whatever we were doing and line up in the Lady Chapel, waiting our turn to enter the confessional. I still found this exercise difficult, as I scrambled to recall the sins I had committed during the intervening week. One of these confessors was overhead to describe this duty as "Now I must go to the convent to dust the lilies." I can only imagine what it was like to listen to up to one hundred of us penitents tell our stories. I am not trying to make light of the sacrament of penance; I just don't think it should have been a compulsory weekly exercise for us.

As the two years of probation were drawing to a close, each of us had to signify that we were ready to move forward and willing to commit our lives to God as vowed religious. It was the responsibility of the novice mistress to recommend each candidate to the general council for approval. Besides her observation of our compliance with the rules, through a series of individual meetings for spiritual direction, she must have known each of us well, including our aspirations and our fitness for this life.

On an assigned day, we were called one by one into the meeting chambers of the superior general and her council, made a deep *venia*, and, on our knees, humbly asked to be allowed to become a professed member of the congregation. The final decision rested with its members. It was a great relief to be told one had passed the litmus test. As an added caution to ensure that we were undertaking this step freely and with no coercion, the local bishop interviewed each of us.

I never hesitated for a moment in my resolution.

## MY MOST SOLEMN DAY

In a solemn ceremony known as first profession, on August 29, 1951, before the bishop, invited clergy, the whole community, and invited guests, I joined the seven remaining members of our set to formally take the vows of obedience, chastity, and poverty according to the constitution of the Missionary Sisters of the Holy Rosary for a temporary period of three years.

Rome, in its wisdom, did not allow religious to take final vows without a further period of probation, usually for a duration of three years. The placing by the superior general of the black veil over the novice's white one concluded the ceremony. We exited the chapel as the choir intoned the missionary hymn. It was on par with the national anthem in terms of the gusto with which the whole congregation sang it. The original was composed by Reverend J. Burke, a Spiritan priest, and the MSHRs were allowed to use it as their signature hymn. Here are some of the stanzas:

> Go, teach all nations, Bear witness unto Me, on earth in every clime, And I with you shall be until the end of time … Lovely appear over the mountains, the feet of them that preach and bring good news of peace … Blessed are they that leave all dearest; In life a hundredfold, shall they rewarded be, With joy, with bliss untold, for all eternity.

It is difficult to describe the emotions of the day. I was in seventh heaven with extreme joy that I had given my whole life to the Lord, and I sincerely but naively believed that fulfilling the vows would be easy. There was a flood of other feelings too, including a certain pride of being at the center of attention, like a bride at her wedding, in spite of the fact that pride was one of the characteristics most frowned upon in a member of a religious congregation. We were human, after all.

We did not interact with our families until the ceremonies were complete and they had enjoyed a festive lunch, called by the French word *déjeuner*, absent our presence. We dined in our separate quarters, even on our "wedding day," because it was not becoming for the female religious to be seen eating in public.

Of course, I was excited to see my parents, but the occasion was even more significant because it was the first time in two and a half years that I saw my two brothers and three sisters as well as Father Coughlin, the priest from my home parish who had encouraged me to pursue my dreams and had followed my progress during the ensuing years. Then there was Sarah Maher. I was shocked to see how much she had aged in the interval. Nan was not there; she was too feeble to undertake the trip.

I was disappointed to find out, however, that they had missed the ceremony due to car trouble along the hundred-mile journey from Carlow to Killeshandra. My disappointment was nothing compared to theirs.

When I see myself in photos of the day, I cringe at how smug I looked. I realize how ill at ease I felt with my family.

I can remember listening for the bell calling us to vespers at four o'clock, an obligatory exercise for us that would signal that it was time to say farewell to our guests. A subtle way to bring the visit to a close was to invite them to listen in on the solemn singing of this prayer from the adjoining Lady Chapel. Our families, mine included, got the message that we belonged to a new tribe that now took precedence over our original familial bonds, and they went on their way.

At the time, I had no consciousness of the sacrifices my family and Sarah Maher had made to come to my profession. The image of a fishbowl comes to mind. I was in my own little world, too caught up to be genuinely interested in the comings and goings of family and friends. In my parents' eyes and with the Misses Maher, I was on a pedestal, and they were immensely proud. As for my siblings, I am not sure of their feelings, and all these years later, I haven't had the courage to ask.

## I PROVE TO BE CHICKEN

With the festivities of Profession Day over, we became known as the junior professed. We left the precincts of the novitiate but were assumed not to be ready to be incorporated into the community at large. We had our own daytime quarters, and Sister Benedicta was appointed as our immediate superior. She was one of the first MSHRs to graduate as a doctor. For health reasons, she was not able to continue to work in the tropics. Instead of Sister Doctor, we now called her Mother.

One of her duties was to assess which profession we were showing aptitude for—the medical field or the educational one. Besides the continued study of spiritual matters, she held sessions in human anatomy and physiology. I showed an interest in this science, which no doubt was not lost on Benny, as we lovingly called her.

She was only about three months in the job when she fell seriously ill, and sooner than expected, we were incorporated into the wider and fully fledged community. We then interacted directly with approximately fifty older members who were living in Killeshandra because, for various reasons, they were not able to serve in the tropics. All of them had unique personalities, of course, and I, for one, soon learned which of the senior members could be grouchy and were best kept at a distance.

I was stunned, I have to admit, when, as newly professed, I was assigned to work on the poultry farm. The sister in charge, Sister Bonaventure, affectionately known as Bonnie, was a woman with a heart as big as herself, God bless her. She had been running the farm for several years and was anxiously hoping to be sent for formal training in preparation for assignment to the missions. She felt her time had come and was optimistically convinced I would be her successor. That didn't sit well with me, but I did not dare to let anyone know how much I feared that would happen.

Regardless of practicality, we wore a full habit to work on the farm, the skirt in front folded and stretched across our waist and then held in place by a large safety pin at the back. The wide outer sleeves were also neatly folded and held in place above our elbows. A long blue cotton apron completed the working outfit.

It was my daily responsibility to feed and bring water to the chickens. On occasion, I was asked to pluck feathers off slaughtered chickens before they were sent to the kitchen, a painstaking task. Taking care of the day-old chicks in their incubators was, comparatively speaking, a pleasant but responsible job.

Because our one paid employee had a day off, it was my duty on Sunday mornings to clean the coops before the solemn High Mass. An odious task at the best of times, I felt sorry for myself to be toiling away while other members of my set were free to pray or read spiritual books. Even more aggravating to me, with my "neat freak" tendencies, was to have to perform this malodorous job in my Sunday's best and just-laundered coif and headgear.

I truly disliked the work on the chicken farm. Was I really

being groomed to take over from Bonnie? How could I ever agree to that assignment which might last for years? As these thoughts kept coming, I felt panicky because I did not trust myself to obey. There I was, only a few months after taking a vow of obedience, and it was already an issue for me.

The situation came to a head when it came time to learn how to kill the chickens destined for the dinner table.

I could not make myself wring the neck of a chicken until it expired, so with trepidation, I presented myself to the superior to accuse myself of refusal to obey the sister in charge in my assigned job. To my surprise, Mother Superior was sympathetic and told me that I was not expected to perform that task if I was not comfortable with it. Rather than the expected reprimand and penance, she gave me a reprieve from that gruesome task, and perhaps more importantly, I did not have to test my vow of obedience.

Early in January, after four months on the dreaded chicken farm, I was called to Mother Superior's office. My heart sank. This is it, I told myself. You are taking charge of the farm. Prepare to bow your head in acceptance.

Instead I was overwhelmed, not to mention overjoyed, to learn of my new assignment. I was taking over the altar bread-making department, where we made hosts to be used during Mass.

Poor Bonnie was devastated, but as we all did, she kept her emotions in check and soldiered on for a few more years before she was sent for domestic education training. Sadly, she died young, before she ever saw the missions.

To be in charge of St. Paschal's department (St. Paschal

was the patron Saint of Eucharistic devotion) was regarded as a sacred and privileged assignment. White flour was mixed with water, made into a thick paste, and then poured onto a bivalve waffle maker that had the impressions of large hosts in the center and smaller ones ringing the periphery. It took some practice and skill to add the right amount of mixture and to assess the timing in the hot irons so as to get the final product just right. Further skill was needed to work the foot pedal of the cutting machines.

When the process was completed, the large and small hosts were packed and sent by mail to parishes in Africa. I often wonder how well the final product stood up to the long trips by sea to reach those destinations. I had two local women employees under my charge, so that assignment was the first test of my administrative skills. The feedback from my superiors was positive, so to paraphrase the words of the lyric from the film The Sound of Music, "I must have done something good."

When we joined the wider community, we were each assigned to our own eight-foot-by-ten-foot room, or cell, located in sequence on both sides of a central corridor. Each cell was equipped with a single iron bed frame and not-too-comfortable mattress; a washbasin; a simple straight chair; and a small cabinet we called a prie-dieu, where we stored our clothing. It got its name because it had a pull-out kneeler as the bottom drawer. The cell was sparsely decorated. We were allowed a crucifix, a statute of Mary, and a framed copy of our declaration of vows.

We used common bathrooms at the end of each corridor. Above the door of each cell was a glass transom window. After lights-out at 10:00 p.m., we would use the glow from the lit corridor that drifted in through the transom to see around our cells.

Even at night, when going to and from the bathroom, we were expected to have our heads covered either with our full headgear or that ugly night coif.

We were encouraged to keep our hair cropped short, which felt more comfortable anyway. Whatever we did with our tresses was done in the privacy of our own cells and self-accomplished. Early in the summer of that first year, I decided to part with mine. In a fit of complete detachment from any semblance of vanity, I snipped and snipped until I reached scalp level. My head felt so cool under the black veil.

Our hanging wardrobe was confined to hooks on the back of the door, where we placed our habit along with our black ceremonial cloak. We wore the latter in chapel on special feast days. Our cloaks used to spread out like wings behind us as we hastened along the corridor to the sacred edifice—amusing, if not practical. A long-sleeved and full-length black coat completed the full regalia, to be worn whenever we were outside the convent precincts—for example, when going to Dublin for a doctor's visit.

As convent life became familiar and relatively comfortable, we were aware that our time in Killeshandra was coming to a close.

In the two and a half years since my arrival as a postulant, I had weathered the difficult and transformative initiation period to become a nun. All the while, I was faithfully anticipating my goal: to set my foot on African soil. I still did not know in what professional capacity I would do so, and I had come to terms with the fact that my assignment would not be of my choosing.

Although it is hard to imagine today, it was my belief that superiors, taking the place of God for me, would decide what I would do for the rest of my working life. One thing I had certitude about was that I would be sent for training in some profession, either educational or medical, before I was assigned to the missions.

We were not informed about this next huge step in any kind of personal way. Rather, we would learn our fates by reading a list posted on our community bulletin board.

When the long-awaited assignments for 1952 were published, I was surprised, to say the least, to see that I was selected to study medicine at University College Dublin. My reaction was one of surprise but also of elation that I was presumed good enough to undertake this extensive training. I have to believe that Sister Doctor Benedicta had some say in deciding my aptitude and that of Sister Mary Fintan McHugh, who would be my companion, to enter this profession. I dare say that all vestiges of humility were flown to the wind as I accepted congratulatory good wishes from members of the community. Notice that I said I was to have a companion on this journey. We were always assigned to study medicine in pairs.

In my wildest dreams as I grew into my teens and contemplated what profession in life I would end up in, becoming a medical doctor was never one of them. For one thing, few women of my generation became doctors. For the young adults who did, it was an expensive training, and due to this factor mostly open to sons of practicing physicians and other professionals. As we knew that our parents would never have been able to afford to send us to medical school it was never a consideration.

CHAPTER 5

# IN TRAINING INCOGNITO

While I was growing up, the Catholic Church's attitude toward pregnancy and childbirth was still stuck in medieval mode. The whole process was considered impure or unholy because of its relationship to that never-spoken word: *sex*.

On one of the first occasions as a child that I was taken to church by my mother, I saw her approach the altar rails after Mass and watched the priest pray over her. I later learned that this was Mother's first time back in church after giving birth to one of my siblings. She was going through the ceremony of churching.

Churching likely had its roots in Old Testament Jewish tradition, in which women were not allowed in the sanctuary for forty days after giving birth to a boy or eighty days after giving birth to a girl. Some have argued that Catholic churching was meant a priori as a thanksgiving prayer after a safe childbirth, but the dominant interpretation in my day was that a ritual purification was required before a new mother could be welcomed back into full membership of the church. Although this was not church doctrine, it was certainly a widely held belief.

Within that environment, the idea of a vowed religious sister studying obstetrics or midwifery bordered on scandalous.

Until 1936, Catholic canon law barred women religious from practicing medicine or midwifery because such practice was seen as threat to their vow of chastity. It took many years for some passionate people—including Anna Dengal, foundress of the Medical Missions Sisters in the United States, and Mary Martin, foundress of the Medical Missionaries of Mary in Ireland—to get the law changed so that women religious could study medicine, including obstetrics, and thus provide much-needed health-care in impoverished countries.

Church leadership in Ireland was slow to allow women religious to study medicine or for nurses to graduate as midwives. For the bishops who agreed, they laid down specific rules for candidates aspiring to enter these professions.

First, we could decline the assignment if we felt uncomfortable studying medicine or obstetrics. Second, those of us undertaking that training were required to wear street clothes instead of our religious habits. For us medical students we underwent an extra three years of temporary vows before being allowed make final profession of vows.

For our part, being a sister doctor was perhaps more of a threat to the vow of obedience than to that of celibacy. We were often in the awkward position of having to balance two opposing roles. I think I speak for a majority of us who completed that training when I say that we soon found ourselves trying to sort out how to be humble and obedient within our small religious communities and be assertive and decisive when our medical training and responsibilities demanded it. At times, I found it disconcerting and personally wrestled with this quandary alot.

As I prepared to leave Killeshandra for our house of studies in Dublin, I had an imminent problem to resolve: my hairstyle. I had chopped off my beautiful locks earlier in the year, never expecting that I would have to expose an unveiled head to the world again. It seemed an act of God would be necessary to get my inexpertly cropped coiffure presentable sufficiently to be shown in public.

Luckily, a Good Samaritan appeared in the person of Miss Kilcoyne, a biological sister of Sister Francis. She had taken care of many of my predecessors in similar circumstances, although my stubble head was one of the biggest challenges she had ever faced. Yet her expertise and the gift of a tight perm were able to make me presentable.

When it came to donning street clothes—or muftis, as we called them—we were allowed to buy the essentials, such as a warm winter coat, skirts, and sweaters. There was also available to us a hamper of clothes worn by aspirants, now professed sisters, on their entry day to the convent. We rummaged through the hamper, picking out the best-fitting and not necessarily the most fashionable items.

I have to give credit to Mother Brigid, the superior general, who was insistent that we were not to stand out from the other female students by looking dowdy. While it was not encouraged, we were also happy to accept gifts of suitable clothes from our families. Mother was especially sensitive to my needs and kept me supplied with quite fashionable outfits. Of course, the idea of wearing jeans or pants was never an issue. But none of the other female students wore them either, at least in class or hospital.

It didn't make sense to me that we were obliged to wear either caps or hats in winter or summer, while traveling to and from college. Luckily, by the time Fintan and I came along, the obligation to wear them in class had been lifted. Our adaptation was to swipe the hat off as soon as we reached the main door of the college, hide it in our bags, and don it again as we exited.

To our fellow students, this rule became a sure giveaway of our identification as the nuns in the class and the men, who were in the majority, quickly recognized we were off limits.

Sister Angela kept us supplied with not-so-fashionable millinery creations, all products of her handiwork. She happened to be the bursar general (treasurer), and in those days of deference to superiors, it was difficult to be honest and tell her that her crocheted hats and caps looked a kind of ridiculous in 1950s Dublin. She continued to gift us with her creations but we found ways to dispose of them without offending her ego.

## PHYSICALLY TOGETHER, EMOTIONALLY DISTANT

In October 1952, Sister Fintan (Mae McHugh) and I started off on a journey that would keep us linked together for the next seven years. We became a threesome when joined in class by a sister from another congregation, Sister Leonie McSweeney, MMM. I find it difficult to answer the oft-repeated question

"How did you two (or three) get along?" The easy answer to this is "We got along fine."

Leonie was an exceptionally caring person and always ready not only to lend a helping hand but to console and encourage if the going was hard. I lost contact with her after our graduation, as she did her internship in a hospital in Drogheda run by her own sisterhood. When we did meet at a reunion of our class forty years later, I don't believe she knew who I was! But that is a story to be told far in the future. In ways, I didn't blame her.

Whether Fintan and I were compatible was never a consideration; we were expected to get along, just as the students studying in the liberal arts faculty were. While we might have had differing personalities, when it came to observing the rules of decorum outside the confines of the cloister, we were of one mind. We were cordial and, for example, never got on each other's nerves by one of us being tardy. But as soon as the front door of the convent closed behind us and we donned the veils and black dresses that covered up our street clothes, we both just melded into the wider community and concentrated on our studies.

Recreation and social interactions took place mostly at mealtimes, when the conversations were of a general nature—a practice meant to have everyone involved with no sidebars—and addressed mainly to the sister in charge, who sat at the top of the table. Talking shop was not encouraged.

We knew a little bit about the comings and goings of our families as they occurred. We shared such details with the other students as deemed fit.

As our studies and training progressed, we had differing

experiences with the clinicians we were assigned to, and while there might have been some petty jealousies between us, they never became a major issue. Actually, Fintan was more popular with the other students, even the guys, than I was, but that didn't overly bother me.

Another rule, which most likely had its origin in safeguards to prevent two sisters from becoming overly friendly with each other, might have been kosher for nuns in habits but was, from the get-go, problematic for Fintan and me.

Rather than sharing experiences, concerns, or any personal information as we walked to and from the college, we were expected to observe the rule of silence. The silence was to be broken only by orally reciting decades of the rosary. While this might have been accepted as normal behavior for nuns in habits, it definitely wasn't for two young ladies in street clothes, walking side by side. We soon came to a mutual understanding that the rule was stupid, and from then onward, we engaged in casual conversation, especially if we realized there was someone close on our heels.

As I will describe further on in this story, our lives went in a different directions upon completion of our studies. I guess to summarize, while our relationship was always cordial, we never became soul mates. Once we parted, neither of us kept up any personal contact. I am sure this sounds odd and disconcerting. It is hard to explain. It was not deliberate on my part. We were both taken up with the intricacies of adapting to a new life. When I did hear news of her a few years later, the different direction our lives had taken, made this connection even more remote.

As it had been more than three years since we had entered the confines of the convent at Killeshandra, it was strange to be walking the streets like laypeople, as if we were in disguise. Fortunately, the house of studies on Lower Leeson Street was just a five-minute walk from Earlsfort Terrace, where all departments of University College Dublin (UCD) were housed at the time. The Holy Rosary House of Studies was actually comprised of two adjoining Georgian-style houses connected at ground level.

Fintan and I shared a lovely, spacious, sun-drenched room on the third floor of the house. Since individual cells were not available in the Dublin townhouses, a dark blue curtain separated our respective spaces in the room. Fintan had the bed nearer to the door, and I was lucky to have the more private area next to the window.

Even in the room we shared, the rule of silence prevailed. The only words I remember exchanging were a quiet "Pardon me" when I had to pass through her allotted space.

We only used the bedroom for sleeping, never for reading or study. Study was done in a room furnished with personal desks in the rear of the house, on the second floor. It faced north and was usually cold, extremely so in the winter. Silence reigned supreme in the study. If anyone wished to speak with a colleague, both had to move to an adjoining room to communicate.

Study hours terminated shortly after nine o'clock at night, when there was a call to evening prayer. Profound silence was in effect until after morning prayers, Mass, and breakfast. This routine was followed without exception, even in the weeks before end-of-term examinations. As burning the midnight oil was an impossibility for us, we had to make sure we studied consistently and absorbed every lecture when it was delivered, hoping all those details would stick in our minds for the duration of the course.

## BACK TO SCHOOL

To get through the premed year, we were required to take four new science subjects at the college level: physics, chemistry, zoology, and botany. I was keeping up well with all of them, as daunting as they were, until it came to the study of electricity in physics. I fell behind in understanding some of the definitions and concepts early on and subsequently found it hard to follow the lectures. Although chemistry required a lot of memorization, I didn't struggle with it.

Botany, I could handle with ease under the tutelage of our senior lecturer, a Jesuit, Father Martin Brennan, SJ. It was unusual having a priest teach in the science department, but the heritage of Jesuit involvement with the university dated back almost a century to its original founding as the Catholic University of Ireland.

As for James Bailey-Butler, our professor of zoology, his reputation was legendary but not in a good way. He talked a lot, regaled us with irrelevant stories, and could not control the class.

In the semidarkness, the guys would respond to his comments with cheers and whistles, even sending flying objects spiraling from the upper levels of the lecture theater. Those of us in the front rows couldn't make head or tail, excuse the pun, of what he was trying to teach.

Our saving grace was his associate professor, Carmel Humphries. She was a good lecturer and had developed a series of notes that covered everything we needed to know to get through the final examination. However, knowing this content alone was not sufficient; we also had to pass a practical that included the dissection of either a frog's circulatory system, a rabbit's brain, or parts of the anatomy of a dogfish. It was a sure F if you cut any of the delicate blood vessels of the frog's circulatory system.

After we passed the premed examination, we moved onward to the real medicine subjects.

The day we were introduced to the anatomy laboratory, we were presented with the human cadavers we were about to dissect muscle by muscle, nerve by nerve, and artery by artery. No matter how well we believed we were prepared for it, it was repulsive and shocking to uncover the naked, emaciated body of a human subject on the dissecting table. As a way of dealing with the sinister reality that the cadaver once had been a walking, living person like ourselves, we irreverently referred to the subject of our dissection as "the stiff."

Enhancing the macabre atmosphere, the shelves on the walls were dotted with clear containers enclosing preserved human organs. Large vats in the center of the lab, filled with formaldehyde, showcased already dissected limbs and body parts.

In sets of two, alphabetically by surname, we were assigned a specific cadaver. For periods of two hours at a time, we would painstakingly dissect and identify every muscle, blood vessel, and nerve in the limbs and torso in the first year and dig into the neck and brain the second year.

For the practical examination, an examiner would pick out a single nerve or blood vessel. Our task was to name it; identify its relationship to adjacent nerves, veins, and arteries; and explain which muscles or organs it related to. If we were presented with a muscle, we would describe its origin, insertion, action, and nerve supply. Suffice it to say that I had become well versed in human anatomy by the end of the two years.

After completing the preclinical courses and passing the second medical examination, each student who had made it so far was required to become affiliated with one of the teaching hospitals in Dublin. For Fintan and me, the natural choice was St. Vincent's Hospital, as it had been for all of our sister predecessors. With a good reputation as a teaching hospital, St. Vincent's had the important advantage of being just five minutes' walk from our house of studies. Let me add that this was years before the hospital moved to its present location in the south Dublin suburbs.

Before we were let loose on the wards, we took tutorials on how to address a patient, take a detailed and appropriate medical history, and perform a thorough physical examination. Included was the ability to give intramuscular and intravenous injections, draw blood samples for laboratory testing, and set up intravenous drips as needed. Nurses were not allowed to perform any of these duties in those days. Neither were there phlebotomists or infusion technicians. We students were called on to perform these functions, all of which, in their newness, were exciting for us.

At the time, the majority, if not all, of the hospitals in Dublin were sponsored either by religious groups or charitable foundations. They were therefore able to determine policy and abide by their beliefs and rules of ethics. At St. Vincent's, each ward—and they were all open wards of about twenty patient beds—was under the firm and watchful control of a Sister of Charity. The physicians who serviced these wards were specialists in their respective interests—medicine, surgery, otolaryngology, and so on. They admitted and treated patients in these public wards pro bono, accepting it as a privilege to be designated as consultants at such prestigious institutions. They earned their income from treating private patients in their consulting rooms and inpatients in private hospitals, which were mostly attached to the public hospital.

There was a pecking order among the consultants: the more senior one was, the greater the retinue, the more deference from the sister in charge of the ward, and the more we were in awe of his presence. Yes, to my recollection all the consultants were male. We quickly learned who the good teachers were and, of course, made sure we attended their rounds. It was also important to attend the rounds of the consultants who would become the clinical examiners in the final examination; it was necessary to learn their techniques, their idiosyncrasies, and their clinical expertise.

On different days of the working week, teaching rounds started at nine o'clock in the morning and were assigned to different consultants. Student attendance was voluntary, but most of us turned up—if not for learning purposes, then at least to be noticed by the chiefs.

This was especially true for the rounds of Professor D. K. O'Donovan, chief of internal medicine at the hospital and the college. He was a force to be reckoned with. He was a good teacher but was prone to humiliating students—or, in the jargon of the day, "wiping the floor with them." As a consequence, when attending his teaching rounds, one preferred to be an observer rather than the student on the mat. This was one area where Fintan and I differed in our assessments of the man: she thought he was the greatest, whereas I couldn't stand his obnoxiousness. However, it was good I continued to attend his rounds and internalized his teachings, as I did meet him at my orals during the final examination.

As you've probably seen on TV, we students would follow a consultant like a flock of baby ducks as he went on his rounds. When we got to certain patients who had agreed beforehand to have their symptoms discussed in public, we would all gather around the bedside. The consultant would then single out one of us to address the patient, take a detailed history, ask appropriate questions, do the indicated physical exam, and discuss a differential diagnosis. The rest of us could be chosen at random to agree or disagree with our colleague and explain why. This ensured we were all actively observing and listening.

It was a rather intimidating way to hone our clinical skills, but it in the days when there were no CAT scans or MRIs, we had to rely almost exclusively on our clinical acumen. This intense practice in diagnosing cases served me well in my professional career, especially in Africa, where we didn't even have the backup of x-rays or anything other than the most basic laboratory tests.

After the morning teaching rounds, Fintan and I would go to the outpatient department, where other consultants were holding clinics. As far as I can recall, patients attending did not have to pay a fee to be seen and treated. Patients were referred either by their general practitioner or the doctor who'd previously treated them in the emergency room.

A favorite clinic was held by Mr. James Maher, a surgeon and a great teacher. Everyone just called him Jamsie.

Let me explain. As in Great Britain, surgeons who had obtained board-qualifying credentials changed their prefix title from doctor to mister. Even though this could be confusing for the public, these surgeons were protective of their title, which they earned only after many years of hard work in postgraduate training.

On our arrival, Jamsie would send us one by one into the examining room to take a complete history of the patient's problems and do an examination. He would then come in and quiz us on our findings and discuss the necessary actions.

Jamsie soon got to know that Fintan and I belonged to a religious congregation and he would refer to us as Sister in the examining room. This could be embarrassing for the patient, but we were so intent on learning that we did not want to miss any opportunity to get more exposure and experience. We were fully aware that once we reached our destination at a mission hospital, we would be on our own to perform major surgical and obstetrical procedures as they presented themselves.

# HOLD ON THERE, SISTER

Part of the training at that time was in the form of hands-on clerkships in internal medicine and surgery. During these rotations, we took complete care, under supervision, of patients admitted to the assigned beds for our consultant. Wanting to get as much exposure to surgical techniques as possible, I requested and was assigned to Mr. Jamsie Maher for my surgical clerkship.

Little did I realize how difficult that rotation would become. Jamsie was slow and careful at operating, and he also took on cases that other surgeons were reluctant to perform. My role was to hold on to a retractor, keeping the abdominal incision open as wide as possible, while he explored and operated on an internal organ. Should he see my strength with the retractor wane, out of the depths of the abdomen, he would mutter, "Hold on there, Sister," and I would give it an extra tug.

Jamsie not only wanted his students by his side while performing surgery in the main hospital but also would take us with him to private hospitals, where he invariably operated on Saturdays and after regular office hours. I found it increasingly difficult to get my studies done, and written finals in pathology were imminent. I became a nervous wreck and began to look sickly and lose weight.

Eventually, I was sent to the infirmary in Killeshandra. What I remember most is the wonderful feeling of being served breakfast in bed. After a few weeks of tender, loving care, I was ready to take up where I'd left off, and I passed the examination.

It is hard to imagine how patients were treated in the days prior to the discovery and regular use of antibiotics. Alexander

Fleming had only discovered penicillin in 1928, and it wasn't available to the general public until after World War II. In the mid-1940s, the discovery of the antibiotic streptomycin would mark the beginning of the end of the scourge of tuberculosis. Penicillin, streptomycin, and the antibiotics that followed revolutionized the way infections were treated and saved countless lives. My generation of medical students had the great distinction of participating in the beginning of that revolution.

In our final year, we studied obstetrics, which included a month's live-in experience in one of the three maternity hospitals in Dublin. Fintan and I chose the National Maternity, colloquially known as, Holles Street Hospital.

We were housed with the other female students in the nurses' hostel. No longer under the tight constraints of convent life, we could study in the library with the other students, where we invariably ended up in deep philosophical discussions—or in plain, mundane interactions, which we had missed for so long. The other students were interested in our lives in the convent, and they especially wondered how we could possibly expect to pass our finals in the coming months if we were not allowed burn midnight oil. We wondered ourselves.

I might add that the two of us, in our last year, had been granted an extension of study hours until ten o'clock on the dot—a big concession!

Within that month of residence, each of us had to personally follow ten women through all the stages of labor and delivery. Otherwise, we would not be allowed to sit for the final examination.

Unlike today, the obstetrician did not supervise every birth, only those with complications. The majority of deliveries were supervised and assisted by nurse-midwives who, through years of practical experience, had developed a sixth sense for when a mother or fetus was in distress. One nurse-midwife, Sister Fahey (not a religious sister), had an uncanny way of recognizing a problem before anyone else, but she also controlled the unit with an iron fist. It was essential to get into her good graces if we were going to be alerted about an upcoming delivery. In our estimation the guys had the advantage!.

To get in on an upcoming opportunity, Fintan and I made nuisances of ourselves and hung around the labor and delivery room more than we planned. We got adept at burning midnight oil, hours that were not popular with our male counterparts. This was not lost on the night staff who knew they could count on us to be available for an imminent delivery. And as is well known babies have an uncanny way of being born during the hours of darkness.

## THE FINAL STRETCH

June 1958 came all too soon in one way and not soon enough in another. That month our class of about a hundred sat for the final medical examinations in internal medicine, obstetrics, and surgery. We had already passed the examination for the so-called small parts in December. Small parts included psychiatry; ear, nose, and throat (ENT); and ophthalmology. For each specialty, external examiners, mostly from university medical schools, some in Britain, were invited to assist our professors and teachers to ensure that we met the gold standard.

The written tests came first. They were all of the essay type. (We had not heard of multiple choice.) For both surgery and medicine, we were also required to take both clinical and oral tests. For obstetrics, we had only an oral test following the written exam.

For the clinical tests, we were each assigned to a hospital different from the one with which we were affiliated. Each of us was assigned to a patient who had agreed to cooperate, and we had to treat the person as if he or she had just walked in off the street. Our task was to take the history of the symptom(s) the patient currently exhibited and to find out previous relevant history. We then examined the patient, came up with a differential diagnosis, discussed the supportive tests that might be needed, and recommended how the patient should be managed.

We did all of this under the supervision of the external examiner and senior consultants from the relevant specialties. As humans, not machines, the examiners and specialists had preferences and ways of evaluating us that differed from one to another, so we all felt prayers and Lady Luck played a role in our fate.

The oral examination was held in the afternoon of the day we took our clinical in that discipline. If one had failed the clinical, his or her name would not be called when we assembled for the oral. It must have been devastating to know you would not pass and humiliating to learn of it while surrounded by your fellow classmates. No matter how well one did in the other disciplines, if one failed one part, he or she had to repeat the whole exam, and the soonest one could retake the exam was six months off.

Those of us who had taken all the written, oral, and clinical tests were not out of the woods. We had to wait a few days in suspense while the results were tallied and the university's board of directors met and decided our fates. The registrar then posted the final results behind a glass case on the wall of the great hall, where most of the class and their friends had gathered. With bated breath, everyone would stand, scanning through the alphabetical list of names, joyful and relieved if one's name was there in black and white and utterly dejected if it was not.

Actually, Fintan and I were not among our classmates anxiously peering at the list. It had been a tradition among our sister predecessors to maintain decorum and not rush to the great hall when the results were posted. We were meant to quietly walk over the next day to search for our names.

I spent the days between the exams and the posting of the results trying to come to terms with the possibility that I might have failed the oral obstetrics exam. One of the examiners had handed me a jar containing preserved organs that I could not identify as part of female anatomy. It wasn't that I didn't recognize them; I just couldn't believe my eyes and didn't have the courage to vocalize what I thought they were. Remarkably, it was a trick question. They were actually male genital organs. So I was left with a question mark. Was I heading for an F or an H, the latter standing for honors? I was convinced it was the former. While the rest of the class was celebrating or mourning,

I was sitting in our house of studies, terribly stressed out and trying not to show it.

Then, as the clock struck nine, the doorbell rang. There, standing on the threshold, were two of our colleagues, Ray Reilly and Billy Waldron, with some good news: we had both made it. Hallelujah!

To this day, I can still feel the sense of relief I felt that night, along with a rush of gratitude for the thoughtfulness of those young gentlemen. Whenever, over the years, I have met Ray or Billy, I always remind them of that kind and unsolicited act and how much we appreciated it.

A few weeks later, there was a ceremony for the conferring of degrees: MB, B.Ch, and BAO. These were the Latin abbreviations for Bachelor of Medicine, Bachelor of Surgery, and Bachelor of the Art of Obstetrics. In deference to humility, we did not attend. We were conferred in absentia, with our diplomas arriving some weeks later in the mail.

There might have been a practical point to the decision not to attend the graduation ceremony: the quandary to decide whether to appear in our muftis or full religious garb. Then there was the question of uniformity, in that sisters graduating in the arts and sciences did not attend graduation ceremonies, so why should we, the medical graduates?

Whatever the reason, the toughest part was being unable to celebrate with our colleagues, many of whom had become our friends during those six years of hard slogging. As we were scattering to various hospitals to start our internships, without classes to bring us together, it was likely we would never again meet—not only our classmates but also our teachers.

## PERMANENT PROMISES

Separate from the medical training that all but consumed my life, in the year before I earned my medical degrees there loomed an important milestone to be addressed in my personal life.

At my profession in August 1951, I had taken the vows of obedience, chastity, and poverty for a preliminary period of three years. In the normal course of events, I was due, as were the other members of our set, to take final vows in August 1954. However, as mentioned earlier, Fintan and I, as students of medicine, were only allowed renew our temporary vows for a further period of three years, on that day.

On August 26, 1957, without even a moment of hesitation, in all sincerity and with full commitment, I took my final, permanent vows and became a full-fledged and avowed member of the Missionary Sisters of the Holy Rosary.

## A STAB AT SEXISM

With the six years of medical school behind us, we had to weather a year-long obligatory internship before we became practicing physicians. Although we could do our internships at any hospital, the majority of us wanted to stay where we had done our clinical clerkship.

Not everyone got his or her first choice. The two of us were accepted at St. Vincent's Hospital (SVH), our first preference. The hospital had a residence for interns, but only men could be live-in occupants at that time, so Fintan and I caused quite a stir with the administration when we requested to stay in the residence and take our turns on night call.

Our logic was simple: the more experience we got at that stage of our careers, the better we would be able to cope when we were on our own in the African bush. Unusual emergencies in a hospital were more likely to appear overnight, and that was when interns could quickly sharpen their skills.

Mother Rectress, the name the Sisters of Charity gave to their superiors, who held the position equivalent to the CEO of the hospital, was scandalized. Even laywomen were not allowed to be live-ins, and two religious sisters were requesting to share living quarters with the men. We persisted, and after she was convinced that we had received clearance from our Holy Rosary superiors, the rectress conceded.

Early in July, we moved in.

The men received us with open arms, as we were now able to share the night-call rotation and, thus, extend the frequency of their answering to emergencies for inpatients and for those showing up in the emergency room. The utmost propriety prevailed in the living quarters, and we were happy to feel we were one with our colleagues. We even shared our meals together. We fulfilled our internship responsibilities without sacrificing our religious vocation, joining the Sisters of Charity for prayers and the celebration of Mass in the hospital chapel. We were determined to give no room for scandal or rumors.

However, our stay was short-lived. Come September, we were told that the rooms we occupied were needed for newly hired male staff. So be it. We had no option but to retire back to our room on the third floor of our house of studies. So ended our stint at taking our turns on the night-call schedule and the experience that would have given us as raw interns.

An intern of today would be aghast at what was the emergency department at one of the largest hospitals in Dublin in the late 1950s. A room of approximately 1000 sq. feet was the extent of the SVH emergency department! There was a bench, or maybe two, as a waiting area. At the reception window, at least during the day, a new arrival would be greeted by Sister Ibar, an elderly, diminutive Sister of Charity and a nurse by profession, who gave the impression that she was a permanent fixture there and a force to be reckoned with. Actually, that was a false impression, as she was most kind not only to patients but also to us greenhorns as we rotated on duty in her department.

I can still see her in my mind's eye as she alerted whichever intern was on call and gave a summary history of the patient's problem. If she saw a raw recruit hesitate, she would be helpful in suggesting a course of action. She knew all the frequent down-and-out characters coming for a checkup or something else. No, not drugs. They usually just needed sobering up.

The emergency room itself contained at most four examining tables. A folding stand-up screen provided a smattering of privacy for the patient. Equipment was at a minimum, consisting mainly of kits for suturing lacerations, retrieval kits to remove foreign objects, and oxygen tanks and masks, not much more. During regular working hours, we could get blood tests done at the main hospital pathology laboratory. Off hours, we had to conduct tests ourselves in a small lab in the basement of an adjoining building.

The hospital was situated just off the verdant oasis of St. Stephen's Green and within walking distance of the fine shops of Grafton Street, in the more respectable part of city center. It was not designated as a trauma center. Victims of auto accidents and other serious injuries were taken to designated emergency centers better equipped to deal with critical patients. On the whole, we interns were able to manage the patients who showed up at St. Vincent's, and we were enthused and excited to be able to practice our newly acquired skills.

Directly across the hallway from the ER was the entrance to the radiology department. The extent of radiology examinations available was not much more than chest and bone x-rays, barium meals, and enemas. Ultrasound, CT scans, and MRIs, to mention just a few, were off in the future. To come up with a diagnosis, we had to rely largely on the history and physical and a lot of intuition. As for myself, learning to rely on what I could discover with my own senses rather than with instruments or sophisticated tests served me well for the rest of my career.

Also worth mentioning is the fact that there were few malpractice cases in those days, so we did not have to practice defensive medicine, the situation often found today, when safeguarding from lawsuits overrides doctors' judgment of what they believe is right for the patient. Back then, we did the best we could to reach a diagnosis and treat accordingly, a decision that most patients and their families never questioned or doubted.

## MEMORABLE INTERNSHIPS

There was a lot of competition and jostling to get assigned to the most senior and prestigious consultants, especially for the internal medicine rotation, but Fintan and I waited to be assigned rather than try to curry favor. I was assigned to Dr. Phil Brennan, a brilliant diagnostician but a junior consultant who was only allotted two patients in each of the female and male wards.

A colleague, Cuimin Doyle, was my comrade serving under Dr. Brennan. A quiet, dignified, and humble guy, Cuimin showed off none of his hidden talents and abilities. He later specialized in pathology and microbiology and became professor of the pathology department in University College Cork. After retirement, he published two books of poems related to the practice of medicine.

Dr. Brennan was not particularly communicative but was an exacting master. We were never sure what time in the morning he would show up for rounds, so Cuimin and I found ourselves hanging out quite a bit, waiting for him. With only four patients to care for, it could become boring at times.

This was quite a contrast to the experiences of interns assigned to some of the hospital's more illustrious consultants. Each morning, the retinue encircling Professor D. K. O'Donovan caught everyone's attention as a wall of white proceeded down the main hallway of the hospital, the entire group lapping up every word that fell from the master's lips. Then the sister in charge of the ward would join the band and answer to his every whim.

Added to my job of being an intern with Dr. Brennan were the responsibilities of admitting patients and assisting in surgeries with Dr. Oliver McCullen, an ENT specialist. He had one operating day per week, when he removed enlarged tonsils and adenoids, mostly from children or teenagers, often as many as six in one sitting.

Taking care of those patients in the first twenty-four hours after the operation could be scary. If a patient developed a significant hemorrhage from the surgical site, it was an emergency of gigantic proportions. Even though a few moments could mean life or death for the patient, the consultant would have to be informed, and nothing could be done until he arrived. I said many prayers of petition during those postoperative hours as I kept vigil on my young patients. Luckily, nothing catastrophic occurred on my watch.

As I attended to actual patients, I learned how difficult it can be to act as a doctor and hold in emotions evoked by some situations. My experience with one patient, a middle-aged man with a lesion in his larynx, still sticks in my memory. After a biopsy indicated he had laryngeal cancer, he was scheduled to undergo a laryngectomy, the total removal of the organ that holds the vocal cords. While assisting Dr. McCullen, I was overcome with emotion as he proceeded to remove the larynx. While rationally I knew the procedure was necessary to save the man's life, it still felt like a mutilation to remove the organ that allows one to speak, to use the unique ability we humans have to communicate.

My emotions were even harder to control when I attended the patient after the operation. He tried to mouth words, but no sound came out. On the bedside tray were a pen and a notebook, vivid reminders of his only means of communication from that point on. My heart melted for him, and I know he could hear it in my emotion-touched voice.

As December came and the first six months ended, I had to decide how I would spend the next rotation, which, in my case, was surgery. Many of my colleagues were not particularly interested in becoming surgeons, so they were looking to work with a surgical team that was not too intense. As I anticipated my future in some remote part of Africa, I was looking for challenge and rigor.

I heard through the grapevine that no one was anxious to join the team of the demanding professor of surgery, Patrick "Paddy" Fitzgerald, so I had the audacity to request that I become his next intern.

Professor Fitzgerald was a pioneer in vascular surgery, a newly emerging subspecialty, and he was performing risky surgeries to repair aortic aneurysms, which involved stopping the patient's heart for part of the procedure. To slow down the patient's metabolism and lower the chance for anoxic brain injury, the anesthetized patient would be plunged in a bathtub of ice to induce hypothermia. There was only one anesthetist in the hospital who would agree to undertake putting these patients under anesthesia. Then, to ensure the best postoperative care for his patients, Mr. Fitzgerald, whom I will henceforth refer to as Prof, insisted that only his intern or resident be involved 24-7, even if they were not on duty.

Because he had not known me as a student, Prof was reluctant to take me on, and he was even more cautious because he knew that I lived outside the confines of the hospital. However, with none of his previous students jumping to sign up for his team, he agreed to take me, on the condition that I get a telephone in my bedroom and be available to answer calls at any time. To comply with this unusual proviso, I was assigned to the only private room in our house of studies, the one usually reserved for VIP visitors. The bedside telephone was installed.

Recalling how important I felt for having a telephone at my bedside seems strange today, but the only access we had to a telephone in the house of studies was in the superior's office, and we had to ask her permission to use it.

I must say that the novelty of being called to the hospital in the dead of night quickly wore off. After I had been called to go out into the dark, ominous streets a few times for minor problems, my immediate boss, Dr. Eddie Guiney, decided that either one of the interns on call would address the issue, or if they were unable, he himself would do it. I appreciated Dr. Guiney's concern for my safety and was happy that Prof agreed to the arrangement.

I started as Professor Fitzgerald's new intern on January 2, 1959. With some fear and trepidation but in true stubborn style, I was determined to prove that I deserved the privilege. I worked hard in admitting patients, answering to any emergencies, and making sure all the laboratory test results were available for morning rounds.

Prof was a man of routine and was well organized and punctual to the minute. He was a man of few words, but when he spoke, his observations could be profound.

One morning, in the presence of the whole retinue, with

his arm around my shoulders, he proclaimed, "But you *are* an angel!" No, Prof was not being sexist. I had already provoked the epithet by claiming that in spite of my busy schedule, one needed to be an angel to deal with a particular patient in the male ward who kept annoying me with calls to his bedside for minor problems. At least by that remark, I knew that I had proven my worth and that Prof appreciated my hard work.

Besides the newly emerging aortic surgeries, Prof performed a lot of ligation and stripping of varicose veins, which seemed to be endemic, mainly in middle-aged women, especially those who had had multiple pregnancies. I was able to scrub, get gowned, and assist him with those cases, which helped to improve my confidence as I contemplated how I would face surgical procedures on my own in the bush. On the operating table, those surgeries caused a bloody mess, but they created little in the way of postoperative complications.

When he performed the precarious surgery on aortic aneurisms, Prof had many senior personnel assist him, so I did not have to scrub. As one such operation could take up most of a day to perform, my role was to attend to any emergencies, admissions, or discharges on the wards.

It is hard to imagine nowadays, but the idea of an intensive care unit (ICU) had not yet materialized. Even in the precarious postop hours, patients were taken back to the same beds and wards they had left before going to the operating room. From that point on, the care of the patient was in the hands of the assigned registrar and the junior house staff. (A registrar is, by definition, a doctor who is receiving advanced training in a specialty field of medicine in order to eventually become a consultant.)

I have vivid memories of sitting for hours at the bedsides of postoperative patients who were barely awake, trying to keep their blood pressure (BP) from falling to dangerous levels. When we noted the BP to be on a downward slope, we would inject epinephrine into their intravenous line.

Unfortunately, most of those patients did not make it, and we could see the disappointment on Prof's face every time. But he was determined to push ahead with this new technology, and many lives have since been saved because of the courage of the early pioneers, such as Professor Paddy Fitzgerald.

Needless to say, it was heartbreaking to have to inform the family of the death of a loved one and worse still to have to ask permission to have an autopsy performed to determine what had gone wrong. Invariably, the postmortem showed the graft to repair the weakness in the aorta had held. Most likely, the cause of death was a chemical and electrolyte imbalance for which we did not have the resources to perform continuous monitoring, as is done today.

One time, I broke with all sisterly decorum and took a ride on the back of a motorcycle to be at Prof's beck and call. On that Saturday afternoon, he requested my assistance as he performed surgery at a private hospital in the suburbs. Although he told me he would pick me up at the main entrance to the hospital, he forgot.

As I stood there wondering what to do, Dr. Billy Waldron, one of the guys who had informed Fintan and me that we had passed our final exam, came by on his motorcycle. He offered to take me to the appointed facility. I hesitated but thought it was more important to show up than to worry about my mode of transport. So off we went, speeding through the streets of Dublin, with me as the pillion passenger. I held on for dear life.

When I eventually appeared in the OR, the surgery was well under way, and Prof was surprised to see me. He apologized for his oversight but never asked how I'd gotten there. I am not sure if I would have had the courage to tell him the truth. I definitely did not mention it back in the cloister, then or ever.

One Friday afternoon near the end of May, I escorted the good professor to his car, as he liked his interns to do. Out of the blue, he said, "I would like to do something special in recognition of your good care of my patients," but he did not know how he could show his appreciation, given my status as a nun.

He suggested that I visit with him and his family on the upcoming Sunday, adding that we could possibly go for a scenic car ride—or anything else I could suggest. He joked that he had a special affection for the Holy Rosary congregation, claiming that he had stolen his wife from our clutches. I gather she planned to join the MSHRs on completion of her medical education, but after she met and fell in love with him, that plan became moot.

Of interest, because of this bond and in recognition of our contribution to the missions, Prof consulted and treated, even surgically, generations of MSHRs, all pro bono.

To get back to my surprise, I told him in an awkward way that I would have to ask permission and get back to him. In that era, sisters did not go visiting, not even to our own family homes. On top of that, the superior of the time was a stickler for the rules, which discouraged asking for extraordinary permissions.

However, this was something unprecedented, so at the first opportunity, I went to the superior's office with my request well practiced. Sister gave me permission to visit with the Fitzgerald family but with the stipulation that I stay on the grounds and not enter the house itself. At least I didn't have to have a companion for the visit.

I still squirm when I think of how I acquiesced without question, but keeping the rules to the letter was ingrained in my philosophy or, more to the point, my religiosity of the time. How I wish I had a second chance to act in a more hospitable and considerate manner to my host and his family. As I see it now, my response and that of the superior to a kindhearted invitation from my professor was discourteous and unchristian.

At precisely two o'clock on a bright Sunday afternoon, Professor Fitzgerald and two of his young sons arrived at our door to pick me up for an afternoon of fun. I was so taken up with the absurdity of the stipulation that I have completely blocked out whether I emerged for the treat as a nun in full regalia or in my best street outfit. I would like to think it was the latter, but knowing my frame of mind in those days—that it was important to wear the habit at all times—it could easily have been the former.

Twenty minutes later, we pulled up at the entrance to his home in the southern suburbs, a beautiful Georgian house on its own grounds. There I met Helen, his wife, and the rest of his family. They had already been apprised that I was not allowed to enter the dwelling, so we all sat on benches on the front lawn and socialized as best as we could. How boring it must have been, especially for the children.

After we had our afternoon tea, Prof suggested we take a ride up the Dublin Mountains. Their six-year-old son was the only one who chose to come with us. For an hour or more, we circled around the narrow mountainous roads, never exiting the car until eventually, we were back in home territory. In my eyes—and, I am sure, in his—the day was a disaster.

My last day being an intern for Professor Fitzgerald came all too soon. I enjoyed working for him and his well-organized team. As we parted, Prof presented me with a thoughtful gift: a leather-encased sphygmomanometer, the well known instrument for measuring blood pressure. He asked what name I would like inscribed on it. In all humility, I answered, "Sister M. Killian," with no prefixes or post-nominal letters.

Prof actually came to Killeshandra with members of his family to personally deliver the gift after it had been inscribed and to wish me well in my future work. The resident sisters were impressed.

I brought that memento to Africa and held on to it for several years as I relocated from place to place. It reminded me of that demure, erudite man with the professorial countenance, ruddy cheeks, Einsteinian style mustache, and high forehead leading to a shiny bald hair line, whose exterior image belied an interior spirit of care and compassion. It was my privilege to have worked with him and to have had him as my inspiration and mentor.

## CHAPTER 6

# AFRICA, FINALLY

We completed our internship on June 30, 1959, after which Fintan and I returned to Killeshandra for the summer months. It had been more than ten years since I'd first stepped inside the imposing motherhouse of the MSHR as a postulant. I had survived the novitiate, become a professed sister, and taken my final vows. I had moved to Dublin and devoted myself to six years of education and a year of internship to become a doctor. I was now registered with the General Medical Counsel of Great Britain and of Ireland, which meant I was recognized to practice medicine not only in Ireland but also in Great Britain and its colonies.

Yet my missionary life in Africa was still a dream. I was twenty-seven years old, and I had not stepped foot outside of Ireland.

We would not find out where we would be assigned for our first missionary posts until August. So it seemed a long summer as we reentered cloistered convent life with the community and focused our attention on spiritual renewal. We were both given light jobs to keep us busy. One I particularly enjoyed was repainting the outdoor benches and the wrought-iron gazebo, which took pride of place in the well-landscaped, flower-strewn private garden behind the main building. There I could be at peace with my beautiful surroundings.

I discovered my first missionary assignment the same way I had learned of my selection to study medicine—by reading the notice board in the community room. My name was next to the words "Ortum, Kenya." I was designated to be the sole physician at a remote mission hospital on the floor of the Rift Valley.

This was a surprise not only to me but also to the more experienced sisters who were home from the missions. While my fellow sisters were generally effusive in their congratulations, many voiced their concern that this was a tough assignment for someone who had no previous experience and would be the only doctor in an isolated rural hospital.

The established custom, logically enough, was to assign newly qualified doctors to understudy more experienced ones in an established hospital. Most of those were in Nigeria and Sierra Leone, where the Holy Rosary Sisters had been working for a longer period of time. In spite of the expressed reservations, which weighed on me, I must admit that I was flattered that my superiors considered me capable of functioning on my own in that isolated region of Kenya.

Sister Fintan was assigned to Nigeria. With all the attention I was getting, at one moment, she voiced her disappointment that no one seemed to care that she was *just* going to Nigeria. Yes, she was joining a line of highly qualified sister nurses and doctors working in busy hospitals where she would be well initiated before having to practice on her own. However, it must have been tough to see the fuss over my assignment. For her that was also a watershed moment, one she had worked hard to accomplish.

We two parted amicably, as she sailed off to West Africa. Little did I guess that would be the last time I would see or hear from her. That was sad; even though we weren't soul mates, we had gotten along well as constant companions over a seven-year period. I cannot fathom why we were so detached from each other, but the detachment appeared to be mutual.

## MISSIONARY ORIGINS IN ORTUM

I would be only the second Holy Rosary doctor to serve in Ortum.

In 1952, the St. Patrick's Fathers obtained permission from the British administration to enter that territory. Young and recently ordained, Father Leo Staples was appointed as resident priest. The exact reason Ortum was chosen as a site for a mission campus is lost to time. The theory is that it was selected because of its location midway between Kapenguria, the district government administrative headquarters of the then British colony, and Sigor, a divisional headquarters, on the only road that traversed the district.

At the time, Ortum was a small market center with one general store (called a *duka*) run by an Indian family and a butchery run by a Somali family. There was also a government-sponsored beer hall, which served as a watering hole and meeting place for the local tribesmen. There was neither a school nor any form of medical care available within miles. The elders of the tribe were ambiguous about allowing their young boys to go to school, but in no way would they allow the girls. They would only tolerate a missionary organization coming into their territory if the group was willing and able to open a hospital.

The people living in the area around Ortum were of the Pokot tribe, seminomadic herders of cattle, goats, and sheep. They inhabited a territory extending from southern Uganda to the western highlands of Kenya. Because of their frequent movement and the difficult terrain in which they lived, the Pokot had been isolated from outside influences, and they lived much as they had for a thousand years previously.

Due to their reluctance to come under the influence of foreigners, the elders, in their first encounter with the British administration, gave the tribe's name as Masuk, later abbreviated to Suk, which, in their language, referred to the nearby tree stumps and not their real name of Pokot. Only after independence in 1963 did the district officially become West Pokot, and their authentic name of Pokot became official.

Monsignor Joseph Houlihan, a member of the St. Patrick's Fathers, was in charge of the new diocese. He supervised the construction of the original hospital in Ortum. He did not have any input from medical personnel as to the appropriate layout or necessary facilities for a well- functioning hospital, which was apparent in the final product. The builder had little formal training, and legend has it that the monsignor did not hesitate to add stones and mortar to the construction himself.

A young volunteer doctor from Ireland, Brendan Murphy, was recruited to run the hospital for the first few years, and he did the best he could with little in the way of staff or resources. He was known to ride his motorcycle the forty-odd miles to the nearest town, Kitale, to procure supplies and medications. When Dr. Murphy left, the locals summarized their appreciation of his services by proclaiming, "He worked hard for us without noise"—an astute observation, as he was a man of few words.

The Holy Rosary Sisters came to the mission in 1956, with Teresa Crowley taking over as the resident sister doctor. Sister Regis Woods, who had previously worked in mission hospitals in Nigeria, served as matron, the British title for the nursing sister in charge. She also functioned as an anesthetist when called on. She was assisted by Sister Rosalie Enright and, after her tour of duty was completed, Sister Kevin Osborne. Sisters Rosalie and Kevin had previously worked in a well-equipped government hospital in Johannesburg, South Africa, so coming to this small and poorly equipped one must have been a culture shock, to say the least.

## DESTINATION LONDON

Shortly after the posting of assignments, when I had not yet digested the full implications, I was sent for by the superior general, Mother Gabriel, who had been my novice mistress. She explained that for health reasons, Sister Doctor Teresa needed to be nearer to Kenya's capital of Nairobi. While she, Mother

General, was aware that I did not have the benefit of experience in a better-established mission hospital, she believed I had a pioneering spirit, and she was confident I would do well in West Suk, as it was still called.

As I would be the only doctor in an expansive region, the staff of the hospital in Ortum suggested that before taking up that appointment, I should get experience in treating diseases specific to the tropics, such as those I would see in the Tropical Diseases Hospital in London. Great Britain still had many colonies in the tropics, and that hospital treated returning civil servants and others who had picked up various infectious and parasitic diseases while in the colonial service. So instead of packing my bags for Kenya, I did so for England.

By the first week of September, I had joined two other sister doctors of our group in a hostel in Kensington, an elegant suburb of London. Rosaire was specializing in surgery and Mona in obstetrics and gynecology. Both of them were attached to well-established hospitals of the greater London area.

It is hard to believe it, but on arrival in London, I felt I had arrived on an alien planet. It was so far removed from any experience I'd had in Dublin. The most significant difference was that everyone seemed to be so busy, and nobody spoke to anyone else, at least in the public forum. For me to get to the Tropical Diseases Hospital, I had to take two different lines on the underground (London's subway system). That in itself was a challenge.

At the hospital, the medical director, Dr. Woodruff, graciously took me under his wing and allowed me to shadow him on hospital rounds. Perhaps perceiving my enthusiasm, he suggested I join the class that had just started the five-month postgraduate course to qualify for the diploma in tropical diseases and hygiene. The classes were held at the School of Tropical Diseases and Hygiene on Gower Street, in center city, which was more accessible to my abode. Mother Gabriel was open to the new proposal, even though attendance at the course involved extra expense and meant I would not be able to take the ship voyage to East Africa planned for late October. The other two sisters assigned there were availing of this booking.

I was in completely unfamiliar territory as I entered into the world of medical entomology, the study of insects, and communicable diseases. I commuted daily to attend lectures and field expeditions and engaged in plenty of homework in the evenings. The hostel was managed by Anglican nuns, who were hospitable but thrifty. The only source of heating in our rooms was a gas-fired radiator that needed to be fed by coins. For a student on a strict budget, the shilling it cost for fifteen minutes of heat was very expensive. Being always sensitive to the cold, I had no option but to sit on top of the radiator, wrapped in my winter coat, woolen socks, and anything else I could muster, as I tried to fulfill assignments and readings for school.

By early November, I was struggling to deal with the expense of keeping warm as well as the time I spent commuting to and from the school. It so happened that Sister Doctor Patricia had commenced postgraduate studies at Great Ormond Street Pediatric Hospital. She had found a hostel run by nuns just a five-minute walk from the School of Tropical Medicine and Hygiene. Like an answer to prayer, a vacancy soon opened up, and I was able to join her in a well-heated place where the cost of heat was included in the rent.

Soon I discovered that there was a downside to living in that place. The hostel was set up as accommodation for young working women and had strict discipline. To get into the dining room for the evening meal, we had to line up and wait until the door was opened. We had to help with cleanup afterward, which delayed my getting to my room to study.

The greatest drawback, however, was that lights in the sleeping quarters were extinguished at 10:00 p.m. on the dot. There were no exceptions, and the sister in charge was known to continuously walk the corridors to ensure compliance. Each room had a transom window over the door, so there was no opportunity to cheat.

As the final examination loomed nearer, I needed to study later into the night, so I resorted to reading by flashlight under the cover of the bedclothes. It was a relief when I completed the course and qualified for the diploma in tropical medicine and hygiene (DTM&H) from the prestigious University of London.

During my sojourn in London, I had two unexpected and special treats. In October, I was invited, along with Sister Doctor Rosaire, to chaperone a group of patients to Lourdes, France, a place of pilgrimage for Catholics since the Marian apparitions to St. Bernadette in 1858. Prayerful visits to the grotto where the apparitions occurred have, over the years, been associated with miraculous healing from even terminal illnesses. While it became a stressful trip due to poor planning and lack of personnel to care for seriously ill patients, and while we did not experience any miraculous healing while there, it was a wonderful experience of faith and spiritual healing for them and for me.

To make up for the stresses we experienced on the trip to Lourdes, the same foundation gave the two of us an opportunity to accompany physically challenged residents of the well-known Cheshire Homes on a trip to Rome, which was to occur over the Christmas holidays. We were able to interrupt our studies to avail of this wonderful opportunity. Our whole group not only experienced Christmas Day Mass in St. Peter's Basilica but also, two days prior, had a special privilege that was the highlight of our pilgrimage: a private audience with the pope, John XXIII.

This simple man who'd assumed head of the church upon the death of Pope Pius X11 was such a breath of fresh air, especially when he immediately called for the unprecedented Vatican II Council on January 25 of that year, 1959. It was awesome to be in his presence. He had no airs about him and chatted amicably with Rosaire and me as if we were the most important persons to meet with him that day. He visited with each of the residents, imparted his blessing individually, and asked us to pray for him.

Forever after, he has been my favorite pope, as he has been for millions. He truly lived the gospel: he was born poor, lived poor, and died poor, leaving to members of his family twenty dollars each, the total sum of his estate, when he died on June 3, 1963. While he never lived to see the end of the council that he so courageously summoned, the monumental effects for the world, the church, and me personally cannot be measured by any known yardstick. He truly deserved to be proclaimed a saint, which he was by Pope Francis in 2014.

With my new diploma in tropical diseases and hygiene, I was readying myself for Ortum and the Rift Valley. Then, out of the blue, Mother Gabriel gave me a temporary reassignment to a newly opened health center in Kilima Mboga. Near the town of Thika, approximately thirty-five miles from Nairobi, Kilima Mboga was in the middle of large sisal and coffee estates owned and worked by settlers, as British landowners in Kenya were called. Elspeth Huxley chronicled this area and the lives of white Europeans in Kenya in the early twentieth century in her book *The Flame Trees of Thika*.

This surprising change of plans required a refocusing on my part. Some of the local estate owners had requested the clinic to care for their employees and their families. The bwanas—Kiswahili for "masters"—did not want to have to transport patients with emergencies to Thika General Hospital, which was some ten miles distant. I would be the first doctor there. The long-term plan was to develop the clinic into a hospital. I was temporarily assigned there until October, when, after a general meeting of the MSHRs in Ireland, I would exchange places with Sister Doctor Teresa and finally proceed to my destination: Ortum.

## A VANISHING BREED

It was Palm Sunday, April 10, 1960, when I first set my foot on African soil. It was just after sunrise, and my plane en route to

Nairobi had landed for refueling in Khartoum, Sudan. While the sisters usually traveled by ship to Africa, I was traveling by plane, by myself, because of the extended time I'd spent in London and the apparent immediate need for my services in Kenya.

I cannot vividly recall my emotions as I bade farewell to my parents and my brother Henry at Dublin Airport. I am sure my emotions were mixed, including loneliness and apprehension. Mother and Father were in good health, and I don't believe it ever occurred to me that I might not see them again. Whatever my initial reaction, it was soon replaced by a sense of awe and wonderment as I soaked up the sunshine and verdant vegetation of my surroundings in Khartum. Seeing the waiters in their long white robes and red fezzes made me realize this was not a dream. I was on my way.

Some two hours later, we arrived at Nairobi International Airport. Three sisters from the Kilima Mboga community, which I was now joining, met me there. As we drove down what was then called Princess Elizabeth Highway to the city center, I thought I had entered paradise. I absorbed and relished the cloudless sky, the landscape bathed in bright sunshine, and the explosions of pink, crimson, and purple bougainvillea on the medians. Profusions of the climber — bignonia venusta, better known as golden shower, clung to the roadside fences.

This was Kenya—finally.

As had been the practice since the first Holy Rosary Sisters arrived in Kenya, we went immediately to St. Austin's Cemetery to pay respects at the grave of our congregation's founder, Bishop Joseph Shanahan, who died in Nairobi on Christmas Day in

1943. His remains had been exhumed some years previously and reburied in the cathedral in Onitsha, Nigeria, where he had pioneered the establishment of the Catholic Church. Still, it was an emotional experience to pray at Bishop Shanahan's graveside and ask his blessing on me personally and my future work in Kenya.

The sisters' ranch-style convent at Kilima Mboga surpassed my expectations, having the modern amenities of electricity and running water. The front door faced Kilima Mboga (which means "Hill of the Buffalo" in Kiswahili), providing a spectacular view of the lone sentinel of a mountain that seemed to rise up out of the mirage and pierce the clouds at more than seven thousand feet. At one time, that territory had been in the possession of the Maasai tribe, who had given it a name that was not as well-known but sounded more exotic: Ol Donyo Sabuk (meaning "Big Mountain").

I became the sixth sister in the community. Four of the sisters were on the staff of the adjacent teacher training college, including Sister Declan, the appointed superior, who already had made a name for herself as a pioneer both in Nigeria and Sierra Leone, and Sister Joseph Miriam, who, with Declan, had been on staff at the college since 1958. In October, newcomers had joined them, including Sister Francesca, whom I knew since she had been one year ahead of me in the novitiate, and Sister Eilish, who was some years junior to me. The other, Sister Martin, was a registered nurse and happy to welcome me. Prior to my arrival, she had single-handedly tried to diagnose and treat the patients who flocked to the clinic as soon as it opened its doors.

After my pleasant first impressions, my tour of the health

center was disheartening. How could I function with minimum diagnostic equipment, no laboratory backup, and no ability to get x-rays? The stock in the pharmacy did not reach much beyond aspirin and chloroquine tablets to treat possible malaria. There was one room with four empty hospital beds, which I was meant to fill with inpatients. At the time, the clinic was only providing outpatient services.

European settlers had not only contributed the land for the building but also financially supported its erection. They couldn't wait to meet the doctor and bring patients in for medical care. From day one, I was invited to visit them at their homes on the estates. Mrs. Kell, a lady who had donated five acres for the site of the health center, was first on the list. She arranged for Martin and me to join her for an English-style afternoon tea on the lawn.

Mrs. Kell was born in Scotland and arrived in Kenya with her husband as a newlywed in the early 1900s, soon after the British colonial administration decided to encourage white settlements in East Africa. The Kells' ranch of approximately three thousand acres cultivated and grew sisal, an agave plant that did not require irrigation during the dry season. It was used extensively to make ropes, twine, rugs, and other such commodities. Even though her husband had long since passed, she still managed the estate—by all accounts, with an iron fist—and was as thrifty as her Scottish stereotype suggested.

As Martin and I headed up the driveway carved out of the parallel rows of two-to-three-foot agave plants stretching as far as the eye could see, I realized I was in another world—a world completely different from my perceptions of the savannah country of Kenya as described by Huxley. The road was unpaved *murram*, a reddish-toned claylike material common in East Africa because the warm, humid weather facilitates the leaching of silica from the soil and leaves a porous top layer high in iron oxide, manganese, and aluminum. When dry, these roads were like hard gravel; in the rainy season, they held water and quickly turned into dangerous muddy streams.

In the glorious afternoon sunshine, we saw men and women working, some cutting the lower spiky branches of the sisal plants with machetes and others weeding in between the rows. At the peak of the incline, an opening revealed a stone-walled ranch house with a red roof, its interior sheltered by an eight-foot-wide covered veranda. The emerald-green grass of the manicured lawn contrasted with the silver gray of the sisal. Islands of shrubs and perennial flowers formed a colorful border at the perimeter. In full sight was the most spectacular view of the big mountain. It took my breath away.

Mrs. Kell, awaiting our arrival and wearing her Sunday best, jewels and all, was seated in a sisal rocking chair on the wrap-around veranda. Her slight and erect frame belied her eighty-plus years. Nearby on the lawn, a circular table covered with an embroidered linen cloth was set with her heirloom tea set. This wedding present, she proudly informed us, had come with her as a new bride, all the way from Scotland. By some miracle, it was still intact after sixty years in the African countryside.

After the customary introductions, our hostess summoned the houseboy. The man, named Patrick, was of the Luo tribe, originally from the western area of Kenya, around Lake Victoria. He was dressed in long khaki pants and a jacket of the same material, buttoned to the neck. On his head, he wore the now-familiar red fez. I didn't know at the time but soon learned that these colonial ladies found it easier to teach men from the Luo tribe how to cook European-style meals. They felt safer having Luo men in their homes rather than the local Kikuyu.

That was just the beginning of my education into Kenya's various tribal distinctions. Native peoples were—and largely remain—more fiercely loyal to their ancestral tribes than to the concept of a nation (or, initially, a colony) imported by the Europeans.

Patrick duly emerged from the dwelling carrying finger-sized ham sandwiches and freshly baked scones with the butter melted and slightly absorbed into the dough, topped with homemade strawberry jam. Tea was served out of a silver teapot, another relic from Mrs. Kell's home country.

Our hostess spoke in Kiswahili to Patrick, and the only answers I could interpret were *"Ndiyo, Memsaab"* (Yes, madam). Immediately, the way the African deferred to his European mistress struck a negative chord in me. We were still three years away from Kenyan independence, and many of the privileged settlers were not ready to face the idea of Africans controlling their country. In their favor, I must add that most of the settlers I met were kind, if condescending, to their employees.

Our hostess inquired about my medical training and was appreciative that there was a doctor on board. Her tone was different, though, when she mentioned that the priest in charge of the mission had requested she donate more land on which they could build a primary school for the children of her workers. In her mind, making sure the people were in good health to work and were not spreading infections among themselves and her household was one thing; helping Africans to become literate, knowledgeable, and independent was quite another.

It was interesting to listen to her reminisce about the early days when she and her husband, like other settlers, took on the gigantic task of turning the savannah, the fertile but undeveloped land of the Rift Valley, into a self-sustaining, productive agricultural mecca. As we listened, enthralled by Mrs. Kell's accounts of those days, when the journey in oxen-drawn carts from Nairobi to Thika took more than two days, we could understand how these settlers were reluctant to accept the reality that they were no longer lords and ladies of the manor. It was easy to have sympathy for her, this wan creature, experiencing the world as she knew it collapse all around her.

I wasn't long in residence when I met another settler of English stock, Mr. Delapp. He was a complete contrast to Mrs. Kell: large in height and girth, well-tanned, and muscular, he made his presence known before one ever laid an eye on him.

His estate of some five thousand acres was completely given over to the cultivation of coffee. Not only did he grow the coffee bushes, but he also had all the equipment necessary to prepare the beans for export. As a hobby, he dabbled in cultivating ornamental shrubs, and he proudly proclaimed that he had given his name to a variety of the bougainvillea plant.

Since Mr. Delapp personally delivered patients to our hospital, we got to know him quite well. He was a likeable guy. As I come to think of it, he didn't seem to have a wife or significant other. At least we never met her. He was excited that our new facility would save him the miles and time of transporting his ill or injured workers to Thika General Hospital. He even invited us to come once or twice per month to hold a clinic at his estate, when we could take care of minor injuries and the illnesses of his employees and their families.

During that time, I undertook driving lessons. As strange as it may seem, I was not unique. Most of us arrived at our mission stations without ever having mastered this rite of passage. At the time, it was a necessity and not a luxury. Sister Martin gave me lessons in the only car the community owned, a Volkswagen Beetle. As I hesitated and expressed fears or reluctance, especially when navigating the muddy mess in or after a rainstorm, she would encourage me with, "If I have learned to drive a car, you can also." On the back roads and the byways leading to Delapp's estate, I honed my skills, and I eventually presented myself at the local police station for the test. I don't recall the details, but I ended up with a valid Kenyan driver's license.

## TRAVELING THROUGH TIME

Two weeks after my arrival in Thika, the three new arrivals, Francesca, Eilish, and I, were encouraged to take a trip up-country to visit West Pokot, still known as West Suk. I was delighted, as this was the district where Ortum—my ultimate destination—was located.

Indian entrepreneurs ran a form of a minibus service from Nairobi to many of the principal towns throughout the country. These *matatus* were mostly Peugeot station wagons that had been modified to fit the greatest number of passengers, the seating capacity allotted to each individual being minimal. To be able to ride in the bucket seat beside the driver, the passenger paid extra. Behind the driver were two rows of seats; the rear one was jerry-rigged into the space traditionally reserved for cargo.

Mother Declan drove us to Nairobi that morning, and around eight o'clock, we boarded a matatu and headed north. I landed in a seat in the last row, which was a little hard on the derriere, to put it nicely. We would be traveling about 240 miles into the Rift Valley to our destination of Kitale through the commercial towns of Nakuru and Eldoret.

The first leg of the journey was on a smooth paved road, but it was replaced by a dusty red murram one with many potholes and ruts after the stop in Nakuru. As we moved north, the expanses of wheat and maize, planted on large European-owned farms, gave way to forests of stately evergreen conifers, and the air became sharper and cooler as we climbed to higher and higher altitudes. A crude billboard on the side of the road marked the spot where the equator crossed the land at an altitude of almost ten thousand feet. I must admit I was disappointed by the inelegance of the sign signifying the place where the Northern and Southern Hemispheres touched.

The taxi had made bathroom stops in both Nakuru and Eldoret, although I believe we greenhorns were too bashful to avail of the opportunity to answer the call of nature. By the time we reached Kitale around two o'clock in the afternoon, we not only had an appetite but also were anxious to reach a comfort station. This we would do, but we first had to make the acquaintance of our driver. We had been forewarned that we would be met by the driver of the Ortum Hospital ambulance. While we were a little apprehensive that we might not recognize him, Zachariah, the driver, had no difficulty in recognizing us, three lost souls covered from head to toe in white.

To our surprise, the ambulance happened to be a Bedford truck. Our first question was how the three of us could fit in the already overloaded vehicle. Our question fell on deaf ears, as Zachariah answered in Kiswahili, of which we had the most limited vocabulary. But as we heard the word *Ortum* now and again in Zachariah's thick accent, we were reassured that we were with the right man.

Our first request was for Zachariah to take us to the Catholic mission in the town. Father Christy Hannon of the St. Patrick Fathers, an Irishman, graciously received us at the priest's house near the church. After having tea and freshly baked scones, we were refreshed and ready for the next step of the journey.

As I'll explain later, the mission in Ortum had a unique relationship with the local government health services in that the ambulance and its driver were seconded to the hospital for very specific purposes, mainly to bring medical personnel and services to outstations. At the time, Bedford S-model trucks, in the seven-ton range, with four-wheel drive and high ground clearance, were the vehicles of choice used by the Kenyan government to navigate the difficult terrain of the remote regions. The trucks were modeled on those used as fire trucks by auxiliary firefighters in Britain during that period and later. British made, they were preferentially imported to its colonies.

There was no way any of us were going to climb into the

open, tarpless back of that vehicle. So the only alternative was for the three of us to squeeze into the cab beside Zachariah. Luckily, none of the resident sisters from Ortum had come to meet us, as there would have been an accommodation problem.

After some gesticulating and plenty of smiles, with some interpreting done by Father Hannon, we climbed aboard. I found myself sandwiched between the other two sisters. A newly repaired radio and a large carton of eggs was sandwiched on the floor between our feet. Zachariah had already taken care of the regular errands around Kitale, including the important task of collecting the mail bag. We were on our way.

As we left behind the rich highlands around Kitale, we came to an obligatory stop at a police-guarded barrier at the small village of Keringet, signifying the entrance to West Pokot District. For the uninitiated, this was an ominous sign that a forbidden valley lay ahead. The askari checked us out and asked a few questions in the local dialect, all of which passed over our heads, and when he was satisfied, he raised the horizontal pole to let us through.

Ortum was situated at the floor of a deep valley in the Cherangani Hills, and the only way to make the three-thousand-foot descent was along a sheer cliff-like escarpment on an unpaved, winding one-lane road with acute hairpin bends. Negotiating the protruding boulders and dry riverbeds demanded full attention and ingenuity on the part of the driver. It was actually safer to navigate in the dark; the hope was that the lights of an oncoming vehicle would warn of its presence before it was too late. We experienced our first such encounter after manipulating a particularly treacherous bend, when we came nearly head-on with a Land Rover belonging to the government administration. Some maneuvering by the drivers ensured that each vehicle could pass the other without touching it.

As we crawled along, the forest gave way to semiarid terrain that seemed uninhabited. In the pitch darkness, there wasn't any sign of humanity, not a single light burning on the hills that engulfed us. The spookiness only increased as the eyes of some wild animal peered at us through the bushes. Did they belong to a lion, a cheetah, or a jackal?

Sister Eilish, with her head halfway out of the passenger window, was in awe of the beautiful landscape and kept exclaiming how much it reminded her of her native Kerry. Francesca, on my right and next to the driver, was a city girl from Dublin. She was scared out of her wits and kept repeating, "Ortum, Ortum," with an implied question mark. We knew by Zachariah's countenance that he was amused, but we were not. As he'd told us that our destination was approximately twenty miles distant from the police barrier, we expected that we would see our journey's end at every turn.

Eventually, we reached what appeared to be level terrain. The dusty landscape was dominated by Moropus, a huge, solitary block of granite around which we twirled and twirled for another half hour of torture. Then, suddenly, the lights of Ortum appeared.

## FIRST SIGHTS OF ORTUM

After passing through a small, bridgeless stream, Zachariah pulled into the driveway of the sisters' convent. Out front was the welcoming committee, which was a little larger than we'd expected. In addition to three of the resident Holy Rosary Sisters—Mother Bernadine, the superior; Sister Regis; and Sister Teresa—gathered on the front lawn, we also saw Father Leo Staples and another priest who was visiting with his two biological sisters, one of them a nun of the congregation of the Medical Missionaries of Mary.

Even the path to the front door was not what I expected. Rather than ascending steps to a front entrance, we descended. The driveway was level with the tin roof of the building. A break in the retaining wall revealed three stone steps leading to the barren front lawn and the entrance door of my future home. It took a little time to get the circulation back in our legs after the cramped conditions of the truck cab, but it was a relief to have arrived.

As I crossed the threshold leading into the living room, I was struck by the ice-cream-pink walls and the apple-green painted doors. Gaudy pink-and-green curtains on the two windows reinforced the color scheme. There were Monet prints in gilded frames on the two end walls, *The Bridge at Argenteuil* and *The Water Lily Pond*. I thought they added a touch of good taste and calm to an otherwise discordant decor.

The floor, polished natural cement, sloped toward the back door, which led onto an open veranda that functioned as the dining room. There was a small spartanly equipped and smoked-filled kitchen directly behind the living room. Cooking was done on a small wood-burning stove in one corner. In the middle of the dining veranda was a kerosene-fueled refrigerator backing up to the wall of the house. Its fumes hit one's nostrils before it appeared in sight.

A dark, narrow corridor emanating midway from the interior wall led to the chapel, which was called the oratory, at the opposite end. Once one entered that corridor, one was within the cloister, which was off limits to everyone except the resident sisters and religious women guests.

On each side of the corridor were three of the same bright green doors. The first two on each side led into eight-by-ten-foot bedrooms. Each was furnished with a single bed that fit so tightly that its end was almost hanging out the door, as well as a wardrobe and, a nice surprise, a sink with running water.

The two bedrooms on the right side had windows opening to the front and outside, so they would have an abundance of sunshine during the twelve hours of daylight, consistently enjoyed in equatorial Africa. Those on the left opened onto the veranda and were depressingly dark and sorely lacking in fresh air.

The third door on the right opened into an indoor common bathroom, an unexpected luxury. One entered it from the interior through the center corridor. It had an exit door to the front of the house. This door had a discreetly covered thirty-inch square window, allowing daylight to enter. The arrangement allowed guests to use the bathroom as requested. They had to be forewarned to make sure they locked the interior door to ensure privacy.

The first thing that caught my eye when I entered the bathroom was the newspaper stuffed into the crevices of the interior batten door. How puzzling was that? It was some time before someone explained the raison d'être: the original planks were unseasoned when made into the doors, and shrinkage had left gaping spaces through which light could penetrate, leading to obvious concerns for privacy.

The pedestal tub, salvaged from a dump in Kitale, was half full of the most off-putting yellow-ochre-colored water imaginable. Fortunately, that water was not for bathing. Rather, it would be used to flush the toilet.

There was a temporary shortage of running water because the people living upstream along the river that supplied the mission had diverted the water to irrigate their shambas (small farms or gardens). I subsequently found out that when that occurred, and not infrequently, we would have to negotiate with the locals, often threatening that the hospital might have to close, to get the supply flowing again.

Tucked away in the right-hand corner of the front yard was the boiler to heat the water for the bathtub. It was an ingenious contraption made of a forty-gallon drum turned upside down and attached to pipes, sitting on some stone bricks so that a fire could be lit underneath. The end result was a supply of piping-hot water, the perquisite for a relaxing body soak. How much I would appreciate that luxury in years to come!

The room I would eventually call my own was still occupied by my predecessor. I took comfort in knowing my abode would be at the front of the house. The doctor's room needed to be accessible to hospital personnel so they could hear the taps on the window and answer calls to take care of an emergency during the night.

However, on that night, the room that had been prepared for me had graciously been offered to one of the unexpected overnight guests. With apologies, I was asked to sleep in temporary quarters: the unoccupied interior bedroom on the left, next to the oratory. It served as pantry and storeroom.

Except for a bed tucked in one corner, it was furnished with wire shelving containing a supply of tinned and other nonperishable foods, along with miscellaneous household objects. I was so ready to hit the pillow that I had no problem with the accommodation. I could have slept on the kitchen floor.

Where the resident sisters bedded down that night was a mystery. There were only four serviceable bedrooms, and there were six of us, plus the two lady visitors. The most likely place was the girls' school dormitory, as the students had already left for a term break. The one place I know it could not have been was in the priests' residence, which was always off-limits. Hospitality was a cherished part of life on the missions, and even unannounced visitors, which most of them happened to be, were treated with the utmost courtesy. No sacrifice was too costly.

The next morning, the sound of the bell at 5:15 a.m. came all too soon, but even after the long trip of the day before, everyone answered the call to Morning Prayer. After the community recitation of the Hours of the Divine Office in Latin and a silent half hour of meditative prayer, we awaited the arrival of Father Leo to celebrate Mass. At that point, I decided to take a moment to peek outside through the door of the sacristy.

## REALITY HITS

There I was, at my first missionary post, the moment I had been looking forward to for as long as I could remember, but my emotional response was not at all what I had expected.

A sense of claustrophobia and isolation caught hold of me as I looked out on a barren landscape hemmed in on all sides by steep, craggy mountain walls. My heart sank to my boots. How could I ever survive in that godforsaken place so thoroughly cut off from the outside world?

The early morning air and temperature weren't a problem. It was pleasant and even cool. The sun had not yet appeared over the mountain peaks, but due to the proximity to the equator, there was adequate daylight to disperse the darkness.

Over the years, I have often been asked questions regarding the climate of the area. In reply, I would say that we had no idea of the grades of temperature; we had no outside thermometers to distract us. The climate, designated as being in the "hot, semiarid" category, ensured that the evenings and nights were cool and pleasant, except for the flying bugs that came out to annoy and feed on us, after sunset.

It wasn't until well after midday that the stifling heat was overwhelming. Then it was time to stretch out in the coolness of the bedroom if duty allowed. Of course, there was no such thing available as a fan, save the leaves of a book if the stagnant air became too oppressive.

With my more recent experience, I would guess the peak of the temperature hit over 100 degrees Fahrenheit most days.

One blessing of being in a semiarid region was that there was little appreciative humidity, so we didn't perspire excessively.

That morning, my prayers at Mass were certainly not ones of thanksgiving as I ruminated over what I had just experienced. I drew some deep breaths and kept my feelings to myself.

If I was caught off guard by the sight of my soon-to-be home, I was even less prepared for what I experienced when taking a tour of the hospital.

The hospital was comprised of just one rectangular building, lengthwise no more than a hundred feet. The exterior walls were made up of large boulders crudely cemented together, and one did not need an experienced eye to note their lack of plumb. The roof of *mabati* (galvanized iron) was partially rusted. Near the entrance was the outdoor kitchen, embedded with the soot of the open wood fire, where simple meals for patients were cooked. The cook, an elderly Pokot man who did not speak English, was standing there watching his newly ground maize being cooked in a blackened pot for the evening meal. The patients and their families were milling all around the entrance and the surrounding grounds.

Many of those waiting were the mothers of sick children. They were wearing their native costumes of animal-skin skirts and concentric collars of blue, red, and yellow beads strung on wires. Their breasts were bare. The rancid-smelling oil they applied around their necks and on their plaited hair was extracted from the native castor oil plant; the earthy odor almost burned my uninitiated nostrils. From their ears hung large circles of brass earrings, the weight of which stretched large open loops into the lobes.

Looking back, I find it amazing that none of my extensive training included language. I could not understand one word of Pokot and wondered how I would ever learn to communicate with the people. The Pokot language, grouped within the Kalenjin language family, is a tonal language, so the meaning of what we Europeans would perceive as a word changes with its inflection. For someone musically challenged like I, this would certainly be difficult to learn.

Despite the gulf between us, I felt I was welcomed as the new "sista daktari."

The main hospital building consisted of two wards off a central corridor, with the men's ward to the right and the women and children's ward to the left. Each room had twelve beds arranged with six on each side of a narrow central passageway just wide enough to walk through in single file. This created some congestion as we wound our way from bed to bed during rounds. The black-iron single beds, no more than twenty inches off the floor, were dressed in faded red linens.

Sister Regis hastened to explain that the sheets had originally been a nice red-and-white gingham, but the red had overtaken the white with laundering to result in this drab, fiery appearance. The reason for colored sheets in the first place was that the charcoal-infused oil in the hair of the female patients left permanent stains on the bed linens. It was therefore necessary to abandon the goal of maintaining the customary clinical setting of snow-white linens.

Sister Doctor Teresa escorted me on rounds in both wards, advising me of the presenting diagnoses on each patient and how he or she was responding. There was much to absorb.

Then, in the matter-of-fact manner for which she was well known, with a touch of a smirk on her countenance, she said, "Now let us go see the laboratory, your office and examining room." I held my breath.

To reach these facilities, we needed to exit the main building and walk around a well-worn footpath to the rear, where, on a narrow veranda, a waist-high cement slab fitted with a faucet and drain resided. That was the totality of the laboratory. The only tests the doctor could do, all by herself, were urine analysis and staining of blood slides for detection of the malaria parasite through one high-powered but out-of-focus microscope.

To the right was a locked door. It opened into complete darkness that was illuminated only when Teresa opened the shuttered, glassless window, which kept out the sunshine and the air. Exposed was a tiny cubicle with an examining couch on the left, a small two-drawered oak desk on the right, a simple folding chair for a seat, and a four-foot-high metal cabinet in the corner. The sight of my future office-cum-examining-room left me speechless.

Regardless of the expression she saw on my face, Teresa was not one to seek or give sympathy. She did, however, try to lessen the shock of the moment by assuring me that plans were under way to build a new inpatient wing and an administration block. We would have not only an outpatient department but also a bona fide theater (operating room), along with a pharmacy and laboratory.

When the plans would be implemented was uncertain and dependent on acquiring the necessary funding. There was already an assurance of a small building grant from the central government, but the rest would have to come from overseas donors. Requests for these funds had already been made to as far away as the Vatican's department for the propagation of the faith.

We must have stayed in Ortum for most of a week. I don't remember much more of the visit except that I breathed a sigh of relief the day we eventually left and climbed the escarpment to gulp in the fresh, cool air of the highlands and interact with civilization once more.

In Kilima Mboga, it was back to work at our small clinic. I began to like the place, the challenges, and the proximity to Thika and Nairobi, especially when compared with my experience of West Pokot. But I dare not express my feelings, not even to my best friends, Sisters Martin and JM, my term of endearment for Joseph Miriam. As always, I must keep my emotions in check and answer to the call of obedience.

## ANOTHER CHANGE OF PLACE

My lack of experience in obstetrics was a concern. The only practical experience I had under my belt was what I had gleaned as a student in the National Maternity Hospital in Dublin. How could I ever intervene or care for obstetrical emergencies when I was the lone practitioner in the bush hospital? It was a sobering thought.

I appreciated that this was the time to hone my skills in this specialty, and after some inquiries, I found a suitable place. It was not difficult to convince the powers that be that this was important for my future practice and that the clinic in Kilima Mboga could carry on without me for awhile longer.

Soon after my trip up north, I found my way to Pumwani Maternity Hospital, in an inner-city environment east of Nairobi city center. It was not only the busiest but also the only one of its kind, serving the fetal and maternal needs of the entire city and surrounding areas.

So I could live on the hospital campus, the nursing sister in charge, an English lady whose name is lost to memory but whose kindness I still recall, offered to have me live with her in her home for the duration of my month-long stay.

In Kenya at the time, not unlike in Ireland, most babies were delivered with the help of midwives, not medical doctors—that was, if the mothers got any trained help at all. Frequently, they didn't; the process of birthing was supervised at home by traditional midwives. Often, people sought services at a hospital only when labor and delivery were not progressing.

Pumwani Maternity Hospital, at that time, had a total of seventy-five beds. With the ever-expanding African population of the capital city, it was extremely busy, frequently with not too highly qualified staff caring for pregnant women at high risk of complications during the birthing process. The only resident obstetrician on staff, Dr. Goosen, originally from South Africa, was a truly dedicated doctor. He lived up to the expectation that he be available 24-7 to deal with any needed interventions.

In that central region of Kenya, cephalopelvic disproportion (CPD) was the greatest problem encountered during labor and delivery. In simple terms, it means the baby's head or body is larger in diameter than the woman's bony pelvis and therefore cannot progress normally through the birth canal. It often meant obstructed labor and required an intervention by the obstetrician to ensure the safe birth of the baby and prevent an untoward event, even death of both.

The reason this condition was so prevalent among the women of childbearing age in that region of Kenya was in dispute. It had never been determined whether it was genetic or due to malnutrition during childhood. Whatever the reason, it meant that many at-term pregnant women needed either emergency or planned cesarean sections (CS).

Dr. Goosen welcomed me and included me in all his deliberations and interventions. Assisting him in performing at least two cesarean sections in a day helped build my confidence to the extent that I was feeling comfortable I could cope with a similar situation on my own in the wilds of West Pokot. However, it wasn't long before that budding confidence came crashing down.

One afternoon, Dr. Goosen left the hospital vicinity for a brief period. At the time of his departure, there was no emergency brewing, but he wasn't long gone before a woman exhausted from an obstructed labor at home was brought into the hospital. She needed an urgent intervention, probably a CS. We got her to the operating table and tried in vain to make contact with the doctor. Unfortunately, he had forgotten to leave a contact telephone number, and in those days, there was no such thing as a cell phone or beeper.

To our horror, we watched as the patient's condition deteriorated. Moments counted. I was beside myself, but even if I were brave enough to perform an emergency CS, I was not authorized to do so. After what seemed like an eternity, Dr. Goosen called in. He was on his way immediately. However, by the time he arrived, it was too late. We lost not only the baby but also the young mother. I was distraught, as was the dedicated doctor. But that was the way it was; he had no coverage if he ever left the hospital precincts, which was cruel and unethical. The ultimate responsibility lay with the local municipal authority, which did not provide sufficient physician coverage.

As I recall the memories I have of those early days, it is hard to visualize how this hospital has grown and thrived. It is listed today as being the largest maternity hospital in East Africa, truly the cradle of the nation. It is a specialized teaching hospital with 354 maternity beds, 144 baby cots, and two operating rooms. There are up to one hundred deliveries each day, of which ten to fifteen are by cesarean section.

Except for that terrible incident, the overall experience boosted my confidence in my ability to cope when I would be alone and challenged with similar situations. I am forever grateful to Dr. Goosen and to the nursing sister who housed and fed me during that eventful month.

When I returned to base, I was able to spend the summer months getting more involved in the expansion of the services at the clinic. I was really settling in. While we were not admitting inpatients, our outpatient load was increasing, and the medical conditions we were handling were getting more complex. I had developed a good rapport with the local community, the settlers, and other medical personnel in the area. At the back of my mind, however, I kept telling myself, *"Don't get too attached. This feeling of bliss might not last."*

## CHAPTER 7

# FIRST TOUR OF DUTY

One afternoon in the middle of November, Mother Declan, the recently appointed regional superior for Kenya, summoned me to her office. She was brief and to the point: I would be traveling north with her in a few days, and the switchover between Sister Doctor Teresa and myself would take place. We would have some time together in Ortum, when Teresa would fill me in on my duties as her replacement. She would then proceed south to take my place in Kilima Mboga.

This timing was chosen because Declan, as regional superior, would represent the Holy Rosary Sisters at the ceremony for consecration and installation of Monsignor Joseph Houlihan as the bishop of Eldoret on November 20, 1960. He had only recently been nominated bishop, with the whole area under his jurisdiction recognized as a free-standing diocese and not an apostolic prefecture, as it had been when it was first broken off from the now larger diocese of Kisumu. While this distinction might not be of interest to the reader, what was of interest to me was that he would now become my bishop. Ortum was one of the outlying areas under his jurisdiction.

Even though I had known about my appointment to Ortum for more than a year and had studied and worked in London and Nairobi to fortify myself for the rigors of being the lone doctor in that remote Rift Valley outpost, I was overwhelmed by the realities I had experienced during my visit there about six months earlier. I had been secretly hoping some circumstance would come about to spare me from the actuality of going there.

Yet obedience called. Hiding my emotions, I packed my meager belongings and bid farewell not only to my fellow sisters of the Kilima Mboga community but also to some of the settlers who, in a way, had become friends.

Eldoret was a provincial town with an unusual history for British colonial Kenya. The settlement was developed by more than a hundred Afrikaner families who had lost their farms and properties in the bloody Anglo-Boer War at the turn of the twentieth century. This had solidified British control of South Africa. Descended from the Dutch, the Afrikaners had traveled by caravan from South Africa to Kenya and hewed farmland from the untamed bush.

The ceremony for consecration and installation of Monsignor Houlihan as bishop was a grand affair by any standard but especially in the Eldoret of the day. It was an outdoor event on the beautiful grounds of Loretto Convent, attended by missionaries, both men and women; dignitaries from municipal and local government agencies; and African chiefs and *wazee* (elders of tribes), all of them decked out in their full ceremonial attire and coming from the four corners of the area to celebrate. Among the dignitaries present was Bishop Fulton Sheen from New York, well known as a television personality. Sheen had known and befriended Houlihan years prior, when the latter was fund-raising for the missions in the United States.

After the day's celebrations, it was time to transfer my belongings to the Jeep of Father Leo Staples. With two of the sisters from Ortum, we set out on the journey of a hundred or so miles to our destination. As the road narrowed, twisted, and became bumpier and dustier, evening turned into the darkest night. The three-thousand-foot drop in elevation mirrored my spirits as I sank deeper into apprehension and turmoil. How would I ever settle into this isolated, desolate place?

I got a fortunate reprieve from my doldrums the day after my arrival. We had visitors, which would be a rare and welcome occurrence throughout my stay in Ortum. As so often happened, our little isolated mission had become somewhat of a showpiece—the legend aloft was that if one wanted to see life in the raw, he or she should come visit Ortum.

Our newly installed bishop arrived along with other VIPs, including Bishop Sheen and the papal delegate to Kenya, creating a buzz of excitement. They did a superficial tour of our facilities, including the hospital, but if I remember correctly, their focus was on getting refreshed after the harrowing road trip. They signed our visitors' book and gave us their blessing, and they were gone. Hopefully the bishop and the diocese benefitted from their largesse, as we did not see any monetary reward.

Financing the hospital was a constant concern. We lived from month to month and worried about being able to meet the payroll. It was necessary for us to contact friends and overseas organizations to request financial help. Help from the latter was slow to materialize; nonprofit agencies were prepared to give funds for the more glamorous capital projects but not often willing to support recurring maintenance expenses that would not be exciting to donors.

While it was a matter of principle that the patients contribute something to the care they received, we never expected their contributions to impact the maintenance costs. So we found ourselves in a bind. For one thing, the Pokot did not have money because their economy was mainly one of barter but we also wanted to encourage usage of the hospital. The Pokot still relied on their traditional medicines and healers, visiting our hospital only as a last resort—and often too late.

The Ortum Mission Hospital, even though it was sponsored by the Catholic Church, depended on government support to keep it functioning and to entitle us to such perks as obtaining drugs and medical supplies at a cheaper rate from central government stores.

In the colonial government of the time, X amount of Kenyan shillings was allotted yearly to each of the church denominations to be distributed as the church authorities deemed fit. There was always some squabbling as to who got which piece of the cake, and it did not necessarily go to the one that deserved it most. Ortum's slice amounted to the large sum of two thousand shillings—supposedly to help with the doctor's salary, but it could be used for other maintenance costs. It was only a drop in the ocean in terms of covering the overall expenses of the hospital. We sisters did not take salaries, only a small monthly stipend for living expenses. In order for us to live frugally, this money had to be supplemented from the general funds in Killeshandra.

The medical officer of health (MOH) for the whole district of West Pokot was located in Kapenguria. In addition to his responsibility for public health, he was the only doctor serving the district hospital of eighty general and twenty maternity beds, which meant he, like myself, had to be always available for emergencies. His supervisory and outreach efforts were therefore restricted. Twenty miles farther into the valley beyond Ortum was a government-sponsored health center in Sigor, staffed by auxiliary medical assistants, who after completing high school, had undergone a three-year training program in diagnosing and treating patients at the primary care level. Other than that, there were no medical facilities in the entire district of approximately 3,500 square miles.

The government welcomed any contribution the missionaries could make while at the same time allowing them independence. To prevent competition between different churches for Kenyan souls, the administration instituted a policy of zoning—that is, only one denomination was allowed to function in a given subdivision of the district, regardless of the breadth of services offered. So if a missionary group from one denomination operated a church and school in a division, a different denomination could not start a mission in the same location, irrespective of the appeals of the local people.

## EARLY HURDLES

Sister Doctor Teresa was to leave just one week after I arrived in Ortum, so it was imperative that I get to work immediately. That was a good thing for me emotionally, because I did not have time to experience loneliness or fearful anticipation of the future.

There was much to compress into the week of transition: take on the care of the twenty or so inpatients, their diagnoses, and their treatments; learn how to compound medications in the pharmacy; visit one of the outlying stations with the mobile unit; and get introduced to the district commissioner and the district medical officer in Kapenguria. How to deal with the cultural realities of the situation was left to osmosis. Unfortunately, neither Teresa nor I had been given the opportunity to study these or the intricacies of the Pokot language.

I had to learn from Teresa an unfamiliar surgical procedure: how to reverse the inverted eyelids of patients presenting with a condition called trichiasis. The upper eyelids of these patients, mostly middle-aged women, turned inside out due to scarring from chronic eye infections caused by the chlamydia bacterium. The inverted lashes coupled with the chronic irritations of the sandy and smoke-filled environment led to corneal scarring and, if not treated, blindness.

Already news had spread among the locals that the sista daktari, who had specialized in ophthalmology, was able to give relief from this painful condition. Tentatively at first, increasing numbers of patients presented for surgery. This helped convince the local inhabitants that our Western-style medicine was good and could be trusted.

Besides my being responsible for the medical care of patients, the administration of the hospital was on my shoulders. Included in this was supervision of the new building under construction, which meant dealing with the contractors, paying the bills—you name it.

When the day of departure arrived, I wasn't sure I had absorbed all the information, but I was determined to undertake the challenge. In retrospect, if I have any regrets, it is that the emphasis was on the doctor being the one in charge and not on a team approach to decision making, a philosophy that I believe would have created a more cordial working relationship but that I learned only much later in life.

So anxious was I to catch up with administrative affairs that I took the makeshift files to bed with me. After the generator had closed down, I would read by candlelight all the previous correspondence between the national and local church and civil authorities. This confirmed that we had been maintaining the hospital on a shoestring and reinforced my concerns that finances, or the lack thereof, would be a major worry and constant headache.

As the only doctor for miles and miles around, I had to do much more than perform surgery. It took time for me to gain confidence in my ability to diagnose and treat the presenting illnesses without the help of a laboratory or x-ray facilities. Having no knowledge of the language was a major obstacle.

One of the first puzzles I encountered was a young woman with a markedly swollen face and an open ulcer over the most prominent part of her cheek. Our English-speaking interpreter and aide was Raymond, one of the first educated Pokot men. He had learned some medical skills during his service in the British army.

On the morning rounds, Raymond noticed my hesitancy in determining what the problem was. He tactfully suggested it could be an infection caused by the anthrax bacillus. Observing the stained bacilli under the microscope confirmed the diagnosis. I learned that anthrax was quite common because the spores could contaminate the cattle skins people used on their beds. The patient responded well to treatment with penicillin.

Another disease that was prevalent, especially among the young herdsmen, was an insect-transmitted protozoal infection called *kala-azar* (leishmaniasis). It is spread by a sand fly found close to the large termite hills common in the area. Parents would appear with a young teenager, most likely a male, who cared for the family's livestock. The boy would appear gaunt, with a distended abdomen, and his black hair turned a copper color.

Invariably, before I had the opportunity to ask any relevant questions, the family spokesperson would give us the diagnosis: *termes*, or "spleen" in their language. They were exactly right. The youngsters so infected would have spleens so enlarged they filled the abdominal cavity.

I did not have a problem getting parents to agree to have their child admitted to the hospital after we had a few successes in treating this condition. They were prescribed daily antimony injections for a period of thirty days. That treatment in combination with a protein-rich hospital diet resulted in the teenagers blossoming before our eyes.

There is one story in relation to this that sticks in my memory. It is sad, but it also portrays the wisdom of some of the cultural dos and don'ts the people had learned over the centuries.

We had almost completed the treatment of one young man; his spleen had shrunken to normal, he had put on weight, and he was looking handsome and nearly ready for discharge. Then, one morning, as I was on my way to an outstation, I was told he had taken ill with diarrhea. I prescribed the routine treatment for that condition. I thought no more about it until, on my return, I was shocked to learn that he had died. A stool sample examined under the microscope confirmed he had been infected with a massive dose of the anthrax bacillus.

By that time, the mother, who had stayed on the hospital compound for the duration of the child's hospitalization, had already absconded. We learned she had been giving him extra titbits of food in the evenings—food that she prepared. Contrary to all custom and completely taboo, on the evening before that incident, she had cooked an already dead rodent and fed it to him. Whether she ate any of it herself, we could not ascertain as she had already disappeared, and we could not treat her prophylactically.

In the hospital, we also cared for patients diagnosed with pulmonary tuberculosis, a disease too common throughout Kenya, not only in our area. Patients infected with tuberculosis needed to be isolated from others. In the early days, the only space we had available was an open veranda where we placed hospital beds. The new building, on its completion, allowed us to treat these patients in separate male and female isolation wards, a necessity.

These patients were particularly challenging to treat because taking medications for at least one year was necessary for cure. Patients and their families liked the initial treatments, which included streptomycin given as an injection. They loved injections. Once we moved to the prescribed oral treatments, then I think they lost faith in the medication and in us.

Besides, staying in the hospital when they weren't feeling sick made no sense to them. It was frustrating—and it happened often—to find out on morning rounds that a patient who was responding well to treatment had absconded without a supply of the medication he or she needed to continue to take, in order to effect cure. Neither were we able to arrange follow-up as required. We had none of today's—or yesterday's, for that matter—methods of communication, such as telephones or the Internet, to track down the escapees or their families.

We did try to contact missing patients by alerting the chief in their home area, but rarely did that result in a patient returning to the hospital. We would have been happy to continue dispensing the necessary medication at one of our mobile outstations, but runaway patients rarely showed up there either.

Unfortunately, the patients who did return usually did so after many months, when their symptoms had returned, and they were in extremis. Sadly, the bugs were now resistant to the first line of medications. As this was a public health issue, the medications were supplied from the district health headquarters. The secondary and tertiary levels of medications needed to be effect cure at that stage were so expensive they were mostly unavailable.

An example of the heartbreaking predicament we were in is the story of Chepta, a young woman who was, at the most, sixteen years old. We had her as an inpatient for about three months. She was doing great, with her fever and respiratory symptoms cleared. She had put on several pounds and looked attractive. She kept pestering us to allow her to go home, but we were doing our best to convince her to stay for another few weeks, at least until we could make arrangements for outpatient follow-up.

Then, one morning, Chepta was gone. Our efforts to locate her failed. About three months later, an emaciated and severely ill young woman was brought in on a makeshift stretcher. It was Chepta. I can still see those sunken eyes gazing up at me and beseeching me to save her life. I tried but in vain; she was too far advanced with the disease. She died within a few days.

We were able to function without an x-ray machine—barely. We could get x-rays free of charge at the government hospitals in either Eldoret or Kitale—a long distance away. Getting patients to agree to go out of their familiar environment was often difficult. We insisted that patients newly diagnosed with tuberculosis had to have a chest x-ray (CXR) before commencing treatment. It was the only way to estimate their response to treatment. They therefore needed follow-up CXRs at determined intervals.

The medical officer of health had told us that in order to avail of these free x-rays, patients needed to be transported to Eldoret, a distance of more than a hundred miles. Today this seems inhumane and unbelievable, but that was the reality of the situation.

A majority of the patients had never been beyond the confines of their village, let alone beyond their district. Witnessing their exclamations of surprise as they saw the streets, buildings, and traffic—all new to them—brought home how isolated and remote this people had been for centuries. It gave me a better understanding of their tardiness and reluctance to accept modern medicine and other practices.

Besides the frustration of not being able to cure individual patients infected with tuberculosis, I had a real concern about the public health repercussions. When patients who had not been cured returned home, they were likely spreading antibiotic-resistant bugs to their families and those in close contact with them. It was a matter of ongoing concern and a topic of frequent communications with the district medical officer of health, who was ultimately responsible for the management of this public health problem.

The temptation was to say we were not going to treat these patients but would refer them to the government hospital. Then a new patient would present, and my heart would melt with compassion and hope that maybe this one would heed our advice and complete the required treatment. It was a constant, heart-wrenching dilemma.

Malaria, the greatest scourge of the tropics, was a seasonal epidemic in West Pokot. We had to deal with the most dangerous form of the disease, malignant, or falciparum, malaria. Red blood cells (erythrocytes) infected with *Plasmodium falciparum*, the causative parasite, adhere to blood vessels and can obstruct the microcirculation of body organs. Potentially fatal cerebral malaria results when these infected erythrocytes block blood flow in the brain.

Malaria infections would break out when the rainy season hit, and children and teenagers were the most likely victims. Often, we did not see these patients until the disease had reached the final stages, and the patients were comatose. We had some dramatic recoveries, but unfortunately, we were unable to save them all.

We expatriates staved off malaria by taking a prophylactic dose of chloroquine every week. For the duration of my time in West Pokot, none of us contracted the disease.

## PERILS OF WOMEN AND CHILDREN

Not long after my arrival in West Pokot, I had the first big test of my ability to perform major surgery. A young woman arrived in obstructed labor. It was her first baby. After many hours of labor, there was evidence of both maternal and fetal distress. I decided there was no alternative but to intervene with a cesarean section (CS).

With the new operating theater (OR) still under construction, the makeshift OR was about five hundred feet away from the main hospital building. After the appropriate preparation, the team wheeled the gurney, patient in labor on board, over the dusty pathway to the hastily prepared OR. I had everyone on alert, including Father Leo, praying for a successful outcome. The patient did not show any anxiety or emotion and seemed to trust me completely, and fortunately, Sister Regis, our competent OR nurse and a skilled anesthetist, was already prepared.

After I scrubbed, gowned, and said a short prayer, which was customary before any surgery, I draped the patient, exposing only the operation site. It was well known that a woman was reluctant to be put to sleep until after the baby was born; she wanted to be aware of the whole labor.

Having infiltrated the skin and muscles of the patient's lower abdomen with an adequate amount of local anesthetic, once numbness was ascertained, I began the procedure. Without going into the gory details, in due course, a healthy baby boy was delivered. Only then did we put the mother to sleep with chloroform, which we delivered drop by drop onto a cloth mask placed over her face—just enough to keep her asleep so that we could complete the surgery.

I had successfully overcome my first big hurdle. The mother and newborn baby were soon being wheeled back to the ward, much to the relief of all concerned.

Several months later, I experienced the same anxiety when I was faced with a woman who was not advancing in labor. With the possibility of having to intervene with a CS, I followed her and her baby's progress throughout the night, adding my prayers that she would deliver on her own. Eventually, it was clear that we needed to get to the OR. With the intervention of a CS, we delivered a healthy baby girl and ensured that the mother was safe and happy.

This time around, I had the advantages of an updated

operating table and the more focused overhead lighting system of the new OR.

I seem to be laboring (excuse the pun) the discussion on performing CSs. There are many issues involved. Knowing that you have two lives in your hands is awesome. Even when one has internalized in one's head the procedure, this intervention is major by any standards, even for specialists in obstetrics. Knowing that your assistants haven't a clue how to hold a surgical instrument or cut a ligature adds to the anxiety of a successful outcome. This is especially hazardous when trying to control the arterial bleeding and suturing of the gaping wound in the uterus after the delivery of the baby.

As in every other activity, practice makes perfect. When I initially started working in Ortum, we did not have enough maternity cases to require frequent intervention and give me the needed confidence.

Many women died in childbirth, which reinforced the practice of polygamy. Delivering babies in the hospital was a new and unfamiliar idea for the local women. Besides, the traditional midwives worked against us, not only by their traditional interventions but also by assuring these women that the customs of centuries were sound and should be maintained.

The other major cause of both maternal and neonatal death was the traditional practice of placing cow dung into the birth passage when a woman was having difficulty delivering her baby. This led to both mother and infant being infected with tetanus. If the infant got to the hospital in time, we were able to save some of them, but once a mother was infected, it was invariably fatal. Watching the typical spasms that these tiny tots suffered was one of the most harrowing experiences we had to witness.

Infants and children formed a major part of our inpatient population. The mother was always admitted with the child. Respiratory infections and diarrheal diseases were rampant. The nursing sisters became adapt at delivering intravenous fluids via small needles into the scalp veins of these severely dehydrated infants. Unfortunately, often, we were able to save children the first time around only for them to succumb later at home or be too moribund to be revived on readmission.

My bedroom window faced the front of the house and was always open to catch whatever breath of fresh air wafted its way in our direction. From that open window I would be summoned to the hospital to take care of an emergency during the night hours. The night nurse would tap, not gently, on the window and, in an audible whisper, proclaim, "Please, Doctor. The child in cot ten has changed the condition."

In the early days of my tenure, I would jump out of bed, dress in full habit, and hasten to the pediatric ward—only to find that the child had already expired, and the mother had absconded. The Pokot had a strict taboo against a mother looking on the face of her dead child. If she did, it would be a bad omen for future pregnancies.

After many of these futile trips, I decided on a different tack. Upon being awakened, after I got the usual spiel, I would inquire, "Has the baby already expired?" Invariably, the answer would be "Yes, Doctor, we found it with no pulse and not breathing."

While it was difficult not to spring into action, the realization that I needed to catch on sleep so as to function the next day, kept me in my room. That did not stop me from worrying at three in the morning as to which child was in cot ten or whether I could have resuscitated him or her had I gone down to the hospital. All were difficult decisions, especially for an overly conscientious personality like me.

## UNKIND CUTTING

For the Pokot women, female genital cutting (FGC), or female genital mutilation (FGM), was part of a traditional rite of passage from girlhood to womanhood. A young woman was not considered marriageable unless she had gone through the process, which involved the removal of the clitoris and the labia minora. The mutilated genitalia were then sewn up, leaving small apertures for the urethra and vagina. Tradition called for this painful procedure to be done without any anesthesia, and the women who did the cutting used unsterilized razor blades, knives, or other sharp objects as they went directly from one girl to the next during the initiation ceremony. If a teenage girl survived the ceremonial cutting, she was married off at the end of the initiation period and soon became pregnant.

Deaths resulted from uncontrolled bleeding or subsequent infections. I took care of quite a few young women with severe infections resulting from the lack of sterile equipment, but it was amazing there were not more.

I never witnessed these ceremonies myself because outsiders were not welcome. What I did witness, however, was how FGM led to the unnecessary complications and deaths of women and babies during the delivery process. Without surgical help, it was difficult for an infant to be delivered vaginally. It was not unusual to meet women who had already had nine pregnancies with only one or two—or no—living children. Of the children who survived the neonatal period, a large majority died before their first birthday from either respiratory or gastrointestinal infections.

Throughout Kenya and many other African countries, young women were maimed with a slip of the knife of the traditionalist performing the ritual circumcision. Countless women were left with lifelong conditions, including recurrent bladder or kidney infections, vaginal infections, infertility, spontaneous abortions, and fistulas. I recall many dark nights when I was awakened to take care of women bleeding profusely from incomplete spontaneous abortions under the dim light of a Tilley lamp.

Frequently, the sister in charge of the girls' school would encounter a young woman walking alone on the road near our compound with her face completely masked in a white chalky substance, her whole body wrapped in a cow skin tied with cord at the waist and two reeds or rods in her hand. Only after hearing "Hello, Sister" would she recognize her absentee pupil. During the initiation period, the young women were not allowed to touch or be touched by another person, so the traditional way of greeting her was to take the sticks and give her a few taps around her buttocks area. If all went well with the cutting, she would appear in class a few weeks later.

As a woman, I reacted negatively when dealing with

complications and deaths resulting from this mutilation. Whenever I expressed my views and frustrations to the nurses, especially the Pokot women, their usual response was "We have to do what our parents want, but we will not subject our daughters to this procedure."

Unfortunately, centuries-old practices are hard to extinguish in one or even several generations. FGC is illegal in Kenya today, but more than one quarter of young Kenyan women undergo the procedure. In West Pokot, the percentage is much higher—estimated at 85 percent as recently as 2009—because FGC is seen as an ancient cultural tradition that should be preserved.

## A LITTLE CONVENT IN THE VALLEY

Even in our remote convent in Kenya with just four sisters, we followed as far as possible the schedule of prayers and community activities we would have observed in the motherhouse in Ireland. The morning call bell would rouse us at 5:15 a.m. Prayers and meditation commenced in the chapel at 5:30 a.m. Mass started promptly at 7:00.

We had a schedule for most of the day, and even those of us working in the hospital tried to arrange our activities around it. One event we rarely missed was the get-together for the ten o'clock morning coffee break, although we, of course, drank tea. Even in that remote valley, we enjoyed a freshly baked, mouthwatering sponge cake. How our African cook was able to produce this delicacy out of that primitive wood-fueled stove was a mystery, but we greatly appreciated the result.

The main meal was in the middle of the day, as it would have been in Ireland. We were encouraged to take a short siesta afterward, but more often than not, we returned to complete unfinished business at the hospital. By five o'clock, all routine work was expected to be completed as we answered the call to recite vespers in the oratory.

Six o'clock in the evening saw the four of us take our stroll, four abreast on the main road as we recited the rosary. This must have been a strange sight to the locals, but we never gave it a thought at the time. As far as the Africans were concerned, we were the four wives of Father Leo and should have been preparing the evening meal at home.

During recreation hour, a scheduled event immediately after supper, we listened to 78-rpm records of classical or Irish music, making sure we also kept busy with needlework. I still have a sample of one of the neat hand towels I embroidered. When I see it, it sends me on a journey down memory lane. Conversation among the four of us was minimal because talking shop, whether about hospital or school affairs, was not encouraged.

Taking care of emergencies at the hospital often required that I miss some of these communal exercises but I was expected afterwards to catch up with missed prayers such as the reading.of the hours of the Divine Office. I had a general permission from the superior that if I were called during the night to take care of an emergency I could lie on in the morning provided I showed up for Mass at 7 a.m.

During some of these make up exercises, I have to acknowledge, my thoughts weren't always on my prayers, as clinical or administrative matters of a more urgent nature dominated.

According to the standards of the time, the Holy Rosary Sisters were considered a modern group. However, we still were obliged to follow the rules and regulations as set out in the constitution and approved by the Vatican. They seemed more appropriate for a larger community living a contemplative, cloistered lifestyle. There was a big disconnect between this ascetic vision and the reality of ministering to the health of people in an outback mission situation.

On a personal level, one of my biggest challenges was dealing with the conflicting roles of individuals in the hospital versus the convent. I was in charge and was the final decision maker in the hospital environment, but as soon as I was back in our convent, I had to ask permission for the most mundane and personal things from the nurse who had the role of superior within the community.

These tense feelings might have been exacerbated by the sense of isolation that often weighed heavily on us. It always seemed an answer to prayer when a car drove up outside our front door, almost invariably unannounced. We were delighted to have contact with the outside world and to share our meager resources with guests. By that time, after the new OR was built, we had converted the previous one into a guesthouse so that overnight guests could be accommodated. On those occasions, we could literally let down our hair and relax, at times under the moon and the stars.

Our only means of communication with the outside world

was via a transistor radio, which often gave a poor reception due to the static incurred by the surrounding mountains. Our news briefings came almost exclusively from the BBC overseas program. At one stage, we tried in vain to get a signal on a borrowed black-and-white television. We would have appreciated anything for diversion and connection to the world at large. We thought perhaps we could get episodes of the *I Love Lucy* sitcom, which we enjoyed when visiting one of our convents in an urban area. Our tastes were far from sophisticated.

## ON THE ROAD

Before I arrived, the hospital had entered into an agreement with the Ministry of Health to carry out a mobile service to the outlying remote areas where there was no access to medical care. We received some financial assistance for this effort. The Bedford truck, which served as ambulance, among other duties, was employed for this purpose, and the driver was on the payroll of the local government health ministry. The maintenance of the vehicle, an allowance for fuel, and one trip per month to Kitale were included in the deal. I doubt we could have survived without this assistance.

These monthly trips in the Bedford were the only means we had to get fresh food and other necessities from Kitale, and most important, they were our lifeline for exchanging personal and business mail. We had no other means of transport, partly due to lack of funds but also because driving on the treacherous roads was deemed too dangerous for women. Several years and many fervent requests later, permission was granted to allow us to take driving lessons and acquire our own car, a black Volkswagen Beetle.

Before that time, visitors who knew our situation would stop in Kitale to pick up our mail bag and fresh groceries, especially milk, before driving down into the valley. We very much appreciated those Good Samaritans. Getting in or out of the compound on other occasions was always a challenge. We were dependent on Father Leo and friendly visitors for a ride, at least as far as Kitale. From there onward, there was public transport, such as the Peugeot taxis, to get us to destinations.

About one year into my stay, the Bedford truck was replaced by a brand-new Land Rover. A new driver replaced Zachariah, who retired. He was an institution in himself, forever loyal to us sisters, so we missed him. Indicative of the esteem we held him in, I do not remember the names of any of his successors.

As we bounced over the rocks and ruts and through dry riverbeds, the ride was much easier on our backs and nerves in an all-terrain vehicle. However, the new Land Rover couldn't change the road conditions. In the dry season, we had to deal with the dust permeating everything. In the wet season, the roads could turn into a sliding, shifting mass of red mud, and control of the steering became tenuous.

To get to Sigor and Lomut, we traveled over the Marich Pass, a one-lane road—barely the width of a car—hewn out of the massive wall of granite. This was a particularly treacherous feat even without the added hazard of wet roads.

When trying to get there on one occasion, we encountered a bus lying on its side across the road, obstructing any passage on solid ground around it. We were faced with the dilemma of returning to base and disappointing the patients waiting for our services or trying to find a passage through the scrub on the downward side of the road. Staring in front of us was a steep slope that would send us crashing hundreds of feet to the rushing waters of the river below, if we made one wrong move. We closed our eyes, clung onto each other, and held our breath as the driver steered onto the soft scrubland for several yards until we could reach terra firma again. We had to go through the same process on the return trip. I get goose bumps even now thinking of the risk we took.

Twice per week, after completing the inpatient rounds and attending to any urgent duties, I would join the other members of the team and set out to one of the designated locations in our mobile unit. We chose locations where we were assured of a welcome from the local people and a good turnout of needy patients.

We adhered as much as possible to a schedule of visits to each outstation, which was either once or twice per month. We had to rely on the chief or the headman of the locale to give advanced notice and remind the local community of our approaching schedule. It did not happen often, but it was most disappointing, not to speak of the waste of time and resources, to get to a location and find nobody waiting because the message had not arrived or the headman had forgotten to inform the people.

Twice monthly, we went to Lomut, an up-and-coming center some five or six miles beyond Sigor on the floor of the valley. We were always assured of large crowds coming for treatment at that center. We would set up the clinic under the shade of an umbrella tree, the common name for acacias native to the area.

By that time, I could speak a little Swahili, the widely accepted language of Kenya, but I never had the time or the capacity to learn kPokot, the language spoken by the Pokot people and not yet available in print. This left me relying on interpreters to ascertain the medical problems or communicate with the patients.

My patience was often tested to the limits. I would have to wait interminably for a simple yes-or-no answer, and I often wondered if the interpreter understood the question in the first place. I depended a lot on intuition, which was difficult with such large crowds, often over a hundred. In essence, the clinic became a triage station.

At a table separate from mine, one of our nurses dispensed medicines, such as eye drops; antimalarial tablets; and gentian violet liquid, an antiseptic dye used to treat fungal infections. Prior to the trip, in the hospital pharmacy, we had already filled the empty penicillin vials with this medication. It was meant to be used topically for thrush, a fungal infection, in the babies' mouths. The Pokot mothers loved this medicine, and they probably found other uses for it once they got it home. On return visits, they relished showing us how well they were using it by getting the children to stick out their tongues.

# SUCCESS SOMEWHAT LACKING

Wherever we traveled, the majority of our patients were babies and children. Depending on the location, they could be malnourished or suffering from eye infections, diarrheal disease, or respiratory problems, often pneumonia. It was our task to convince the mother, and sometimes the father, that the child needed to be treated in the hospital.

We did not always get the parents to agree, often because of fear of the unknown. Others would invoke the excuse that they did not have the money—an excuse that we immediately dismissed. Whatever the reason, it was frustrating and upsetting to have to leave them behind, knowing the youngster was facing certain death. Making the situation more distressing, we knew that the child in question might be the woman's only living child even after six or more pregnancies.

Once a month, we visited Chepkobegh. As the crow flies, Chepkobegh was just a few miles from the hospital, but to get to it by road, we had to drive in the opposite direction toward Kapenguria. About halfway there, we would turn onto a secondary road and travel through arid and stony ground until we reached the small village center.

A boys' primary school was housed in a shack built in the midst of the stones and red dust. Small thorn bushes were the only vegetation, and the goats feasted on them, as nothing else was available. The goats were the only sign of life until the Land Rover came to a halt. Then, out of nowhere, the locals would appear, eager to be treated. It was a recurring question mark for me as to how the inhabitants could survive in such barren conditions. Somehow, they did.

My most memorable story from Chepkobegh is not a happy one, but it brings out the everyday challenges the local people and we ourselves faced. On that visit, Father Leo had come with us to supervise the school while we provided the health services. He was told that one of the pupils, a twelve-year-old boy, had recently become ill. The day before our arrival, people had attempted taking him to the hospital on a makeshift stretcher, but he had died on the way.

The Pokot had a long-established but fairly unusual custom going back centuries regarding the disposal of dead bodies. Due to their relationship and fear of the ancestral spirits, they did not bury a body. It was even taboo for them to look on the features of a dead person. If someone died in the bush, his or her remains were left in the open to be picked apart by birds and other wild animals. Whenever someone died in his or her home, the hut was abandoned with the dead body inside. Only respected old men (wazee) were buried in the ground.

Therefore, this twelve-year-old boy who'd died before making it to the hospital had been abandoned at the spot where he had expired. It was distressing to hear not only that we were just one day too late to intervene and possibly save the boy's life but also that his body had been left out in the scrubland.

I cannot forget the scene we encountered on the way home. Lying among the stones on the side of the road was the bare skull of the young boy. Beside it were a few of his vertebrae but no other parts of his skeleton. With due reverence, we buried the remains in a shallow grave, dug by Father Leo with help from non-Pokot staff members. The whole episode was overwhelmingly morbid and sad.

This Pokot custom created a major and ongoing difficulty for us at the hospital. We dedicated a cemetery in an adjoining piece of ground, where we reverently buried our deceased patients without the recognition or support of their families or villages.

## WILDLIFE ADVENTURES

Whenever I mention my time in Africa, people invariably ask whether I saw any wild animals. The answer is "Yes, many." More significantly, I also treated many patients suffering injuries from their encounters with such animals.

On more than one occasion, we had a cheetah leap over the front hood of the Land Rover. Being the fastest land animals, cheetahs can appear out of nowhere, complete their jump in a flash and disappear without a trace into the bush, leaving us humans wondering if it was for real. After each of these encounters I couldn't wait for the evening meal, to share the awesome experience with the community

Once, when we were approaching the Marich Pass on one of our mobile-unit schedules, a passing local man warned us that up ahead we would encounter a group of people carving up a recently deceased elephant. By the time we arrived on the scene, little was left of the poor animal. Some men were using *pangas* (the Kiswahili word for machetes) to harvest whatever meat was left on the carcass. They threw the bounty to the women who had formed a circle around them to receive it. How this animal came to be killed, we never found out and preferred not to know.

Perhaps morbidly, I had my picture taken beside the meatless pelvic bone held upright on its side. It towered over my five-foot-four frame. The image brings home the enormous size of these beautiful animals. This was a highly unusual scene. My experience with the Pokot in those days was that they did not kill indiscriminately, even though meat was a necessary ingredient of their diet. Actually, until that day on the road, I had no idea that elephants roamed the area, nor have I heard of their presence since then.

Leopards were plentiful in the district, and the people feared their presence. Leopards are night predators, and they were known to not only prey on young herd animals but also, on occasion, attempt to take children out of their beds. Because of that fear, the people kept young calves and goats in their homes with the family.

Regarding the children, it is chilling to imagine the parents' distress as, in the dark of night, they heard the screams of their child being hauled away by one of these animals. We saw a number of severe hand injuries resulting from a father's efforts to rescue his child or an animal from the leopard's jaws. These wounds were difficult to treat due to infection which required a combination of antibiotics to effect healing. The victim was often left with permanent hand deformities.

Snake bites were also common, and many victims did not make it to the hospital for treatment before they succumbed. I remember one patient, a well-educated man working as an agriculture extension officer, who was brought in from the Sigor Health Centre several hours after he was bitten. We were unable to ascertain whether his snake bite had come from a viper or a cobra. The antivenin for each is different, as is the way the poison affects the victim's organs or systems. Even though we gave him the universal antivenin serum and spent the night trying to save him, he died. We did the best we could. It was always painful to deal with tragedies like that. I can still see the desperation on that poor man's face as he implored me to try to save him.

Many times, a patient was brought on a homemade stretcher. The construction was ingenuous in its simplicity. Four posts were assembled from large tree branches, and smaller branches were interwoven to form the floor of the bed. The contraption allowed a patient too weak to walk to be transported from the bush or a mountaintop to the hospital compound. When we saw one of these makeshift ambulances arrive, we knew urgent care was warranted.

On one occasion, the nurse came with haste to the convent to inform me that the man on the stretcher had a hole in his chest and that she could see into his lungs and see his heart beating. It was reported that he had been gored by a rhinoceros, but we could never confirm that. I was suspicious that this had not been a spontaneous encounter with a wild animal. More likely, some behind-the-scenes poaching had been going on.

Regardless of the cause of the goring, it was our task to care for the patient, which entailed closing the gaping wound in his chest and creating a vacuum in the pleural cavity so that his lungs could expand and function once more. To our amazement, the patient survived and was able to be discharged in a matter of weeks.

A short time later, another patient was brought in after being gored by a rhinoceros. He was in even worse shape, with a laceration the full length of his abdomen. Fortunately for him, a traditional doctor had already replaced the eviscerated intestines and sewn up the wound, the full length of his abdomen, with sisal twine or rope. We had the job of replacing this makeshift surgery with more refined sutures and treating the infection with whatever combination of antibiotics we had in stock. Amazingly, that man also survived to tell the tale.

The power of the *sindano kwa dawa* (Kiswahili for "needle of the medicine") was universal. In the minds of the patients, this was the most powerful medicine and cured all ills. There was always disappointment if such treatment was not prescribed. Luckily, most of the infections we treated were sensitive to penicillin, which was delivered by intramuscular injection and therefore greatly appreciated.

I was always surprised by how stoical the patients were and their high tolerance for pain. Even pregnant women would only check in when the baby was about to be born. Invariably, their excuse for not coming sooner was that they did not feel contractions or know that they were in labor. I guess they had been used to suffering pain and discomfort all their lives, and pain was a fact of life.

# UNREASONABLE HUNGER

During those early years, there were often periods of drought that led to widespread scarcity of food and even famine. The young children suffered the most. There are two different types of malnutrition common in Africa: marasmus and kwashiorkor. Marasmus results from a severe or total lack of nutrition in the diet; kwashiorkor is caused by insufficient protein consumption. While children in most other parts of Kenya and tropical Africa suffered from kwashiorkor, our children suffered more from marasmus because the diet on the whole was based on animal products, preventing pure protein malnutrition. The problem was the scarcity of food.

When starving people looked to us for help, we had to turn to other nongovernment organizations (NGOs). One of the funding agencies that helped us greatly was Catholic Relief Services (CRS). Through a special association with the United States Agency for International Development (USAID), we were able to secure bulgur wheat and protein supplements for children under five years of age. The snag was that we could not distribute the aid to the general public because there was never an official proclamation of famine in West Pokot.

When it came to who was entitled to get the food, we had some fundamental differences with the administrators of the CRS program at their headquarters in Nairobi.

The rules were that each child registered in the Under Fives Program (UFP) was to be allowed a monthly ration of one kilo (2.2 pounds) of bulgur wheat. The UFP required parents to keep coming on a regular schedule, and we needed to keep a log of the children's weights and heights and ensure that they had all their immunizations.

In Ortum, we had no such UFP, as the parents had not yet reached the stage where they valued this monitoring program for their children. But we did have parents with hungry young children descending on us from all directions. We were supposed to dispense the food only to those children registered. Were we to turn away all the other hungry, malnourished children imploring us for food? That was the ethical dilemma we faced.

When confronted with our problem, the CRS representatives reported that in order to obtain the food, they had to comply with the restrictions placed by USAID. In our eyes, the system in no way solved the problem of starvation we had on our doorstep. Once, while I was visiting the headquarters and tried to explain the situation, my frustration peeled over into a flood of tears. I realized that the representative, a Kenyan woman and I, were poles apart in understanding of the reality on the ground.

Our solution was to distribute supplies, when we had them, as we saw the need. We suffered no penalties from CRS, but we did experience the heartache of not having enough to serve everyone who came for help. Ultimately, the rains came, the crops grew, and the real emergency abated.

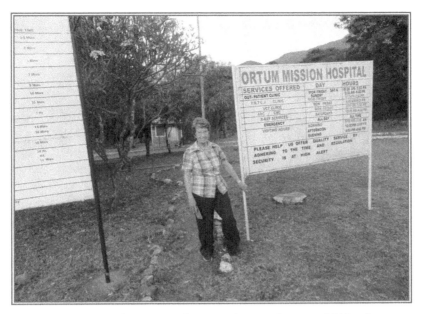

*It is an emotional moment for me when in January 2013, after an absence of 40 years, I revisit Ortum Mission Hospital, Kenya*

*On arrival in Kitale, a joyful meeting with my hosts, (from left) Fathers Fintan Mc Donald and Leo Staples*

*Dr. Miriam Were and I, who had been colleagues in the Department of Community Health, University of Nairobi, are happy to meet again in January 2013*

*This innovative taxi service takes home well-cared for and happy children from Mercy Nursery School in Cheperaria, Kenya, January 2013*

These two Pokot Students from Ortum High School are living witnesses to the progress in education made over the past 40 years

The earliest picture of my parents, John and Mary Malone, taken in their beloved homeland of Killeshin, County Laois, c. 1938

Mother (seated) and Father with the eldest of their six children. From left, Thomas, Breed, Bernadette and me

The studio picture of me on my Confirmation Day, May 1941

The last picture of me taken before I joined the Holy Rosary Sisters. I am proud to display my self-knitted fairisle cardigan

*A family picture taken on the day of my first Profession of Vows on August 29, 1951. With me from left are Henry, Father, Breed, Thomas, Mother, Eilish and Bernadette*

*The gateway to the District of West Pokot, Kenya, as it was in the 1960s and beyond*

*A familiar scene on the roads around Ortum in the 1960s. The truck is similar to the Bedford used as an ambulance and means of transport to the outstations*

*The first convent of the Holy Rosary Sisters in Ortum, built c. 1954*

*In November 1960, I took up residence in the Holy Rosary Convent, Ortum*

*A young Pokot girl, most likely pictured while out minding the family goats, c. 1960*

*A beautiful Pokot woman, one of the many who would become my patients over the years, c. 1960*

*A portrait of a mature Pokot woman. The extended ear lobes torn by the weight of the jewelry often needed suturing.*

*Father Leo Staples is engrossed in conversation with a Pokot elder, c. 1960*

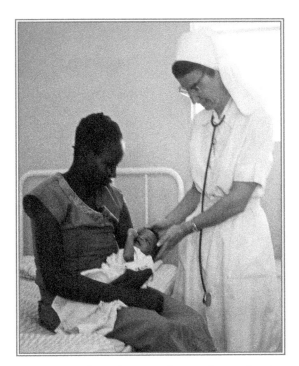

*A concerned mother watches as I examine her sick child in the Pediatric Ward, c. 1970*

*The Mobile Health Unit arrives at an outstation, c. 1966*

*An "Under Fives Clinic" in progress at an outstation, c. 1966*

*A nurse administers immunizations to children at the "Under Fives Clinic", c. 1966*

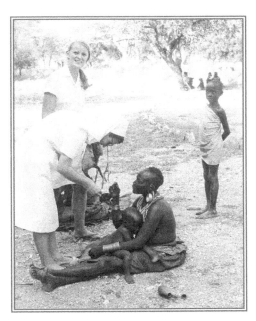

*This mother is anxious to communicate her concerns to Marike (a nurse volunteer from the Netherlands) and me, c.1972*

*It is a proud moment when I graduate with a Master's in Public Health from the Johns Hopkins University, Baltimore, USA in May 1973*

*I am with my sister Bernadette at my graduation wearing the beautiful dress that she made for me for this occasion, May 1973*

*I am listening along with medical students from the University of Nairobi, as the leader expounds on the results of the team's field work project, c. 1978*

*At the close of a busy day it was nice to relax on the patio of the Maisonette, Nairobi, c. 1978*

*Mother and Father at home in Clonmel, County Tipperary, c. 1985*

*Mother and I on the deck of Bernadette's and Gerry's house, Hampton Bays, New York, July 1991. Mother was celebrating her 92nd birthday*

*My siblings and I after Mother's funeral, February 8, 1997. From left, Thomas, me, Breed, Eilish, Bernadette, Henry*

*My friend Sister Áine ni Talbóid and I about to enjoy a sundae during her visit to the USA, July 2009*

*Goofing off with my Mah Jongg friends at an afternoon tea party. From left Marilyn, me, Toby, Laurie and Phyllis, July 2013. Sadly our friend Marilyn passed away shortly thereafter.*

*Enjoying retirement in Florida with my dog, Brooke, January 2017*

# CHAPTER 8

# VOWS PUT TO THE TEST

After three years in Ortum, I had put my early misgivings behind me and settled in well. Although our progress was slow in getting the Pokot people to trust us and our medicine, I was committed to the long haul. I had many plans for how we could develop and improve the health services there. I also realized that improving the health of the people could only progress in relation with developments in other areas, including education, improved farming practices, and the advent of cash crops. At times, it was overwhelming to think of how much it would take to materially change the lives of the people. I knew an abundance of patience was necessary.

Mother Kevin was still the superior of the community and part-time nurse in the hospital. She was our best fund-raiser, writing exhaustively to friends and acquaintances for any help we could get to keep the hospital financially viable. I truly admired this lady, who had come from a wealthy, influential family but was perfectly happy to rough it with the rest of us.

She kept us smiling when things were tough. She was my rock of stability.

In the spring of 1963, the superior general of the Holy Rosary made an official visit to Kenya to fulfill an obligation predicated by rules from the Vatican for all religious communities. Mother Gabriel, who had initially assigned me to that mission, was still in office. My personal interview with her went well, with no problems identified. In fact, she expressed appreciation for the work I was doing in that difficult situation. At the official conclusion of the visitation and after each of us had an opportunity to meet in private with her, Gabriel recognized the financial and other stresses we were under and offered words of encouragement but had no immediate answers to these problems.

A few weeks later, on a business trip to Nairobi, while staying at our house in Thika, Mother Gabriel asked to see me. That seemed a little odd, but I wasn't unduly concerned.

I casually entered the visitors' room and stood in front of the desk where she sat. My feet stuck to the floor after I heard what she had to say to me.

There had been a complaint lodged that I was "too friendly" with Father Leo. She wanted to warn me that I needed to be more careful and reserved in my contacts with him, or something to that effect. In my embarrassment, I only heard the first few words. She qualified her remarks by reassuring me that the report had not been made by a member of my small community in Ortum.

I could feel the blood race through my veins, my cheeks redden as far as my ears, and perspiration roll from under my armpits. I muttered some words in my defense while I wrestled with breathtaking feelings of humiliation, betrayal, and vulnerability.

For those of us who had taken a vow of celibacy, an accusation of any impropriety in our relationships with members of the opposite sex was akin to what a married person would have experienced if accused of adultery. Even the slightest innuendo hinting that there might be anything remiss touched a chord in my being that was sacrosanct and that I'd never envisaged having to discuss, not to mention the implication that I had crossed the line—if not in action, then at least in spirit. I didn't blame Gabriel, as I knew she had a duty to advise me of the report and to warn me.

However, I was angry with the person who'd voiced the complaint. It did not take me long to figure out who most likely was the culprit. I emphasize that even to this day, this is speculation. Anything that happened in the course of the official visitation was secret, so there was no way I could ever challenge anyone or find out.

The person I suspected was someone I had confided in and considered a friend. The most hurtful part was that I'd had no inkling that this was coming. I would have appreciated a prior warning before she made a report to the highest level in the congregation.

Another factor that had worked against me, I suspected, was that I had not taken on the crusade to be independent of the clergy. When the MSHRs first arrived in Nigeria in the 1920s, the congregation's founder, Bishop Shanahan, insisted they not be subservient to the pastors of the parish. This was a new concept at a time when most communities of nuns were dependent on their pastor, not only for funds to do their good works but also for their living expenses. In return, they took care of the priests—down to preparing meals for them and doing their laundry.

When the Holy Rosary Sisters expanded from Nigeria into Kenya, they continued this independence, especially when it came to decisions regarding the administration of the hospital. This did not sit well with Bishop Houlihan or, for that matter, the local clergy. The consequences were not only financial but also mundane, even petty. At one time, the priests were given instructions not to offer rides in their cars to Holy Rosary Sisters, even if they were traveling to the same destination. In Ortum, this hit us hard, as we had no other means of getting out of the place, except once per month in the hospital ambulance. In all fairness, I don't believe any of the priests obeyed that command. Father Leo definitely did not.

## BREAKING WITH TRADITION

In Ortum, we had only one priest, Father Leo, and four sisters. I didn't see the logic of maintaining a hands-off attitude towards him. As he was the overall in charge of the mission, I kept him informed of activities and plans for the medical work. I was cognizant of the fact that he had the respect of the local *watu* (people) and could communicate with them in their own language.

As a small, isolated community, we maintained cordial

relations with Father Leo. We shared meals with him, especially on the occasion of big feast days, such as Christmas and Easter. Whenever he returned from visits up-country, as we called going to Kitale or beyond, he always stopped at our convent to deliver the mail and the latest news. He was always there to support and help whomever of us needed it.

Due to convenience but also his sparse funds to drive in his own Jeep, he took the opportunity to travel to the various outstations in the hospital's vehicle. I had my medical duties, and he had schools to oversee, and it made sense for him to join us. Father Leo and I were never alone on these expeditions. On the front seat of the Land Rover, he was next to the driver, and I sat at the window. My mobile health staff were crowded in the seats behind us.

In our small community, I was more than ten years junior to the next closest in age. Even if friendship had been encouraged among us, I did not have much in common with the other two sisters in the community, both of whom seemed to have a depressive attitude to our situation. They had both worked for many years in Nigeria prior to being assigned to Ortum and found the remoteness and the lack of progress difficult to accept.

I missed any professional collegiality, had huge medical, financial, and administrative responsibilities on my shoulders. Being a nun in the midst of those pressures, I had another set of expectations to fulfill as I tried faithfully to live in two different worlds.

The primitive conditions of the hospital, the heartbreaking loss of patients, the frustrations in trying to convince the Pokot people to use our services, the heat, the exhaustion, the travel to the outstations, the countless difficulties I encountered in trying to get the simplest things done—it all added up emotionally. Although Kevin, the superior, who could easily have been my birth mother, did her best to provide support, I needed much more than she could give, more than any one person could realistically provide.

In Father Leo, I found a good listener who could give me helpful, practical advice, and his sense of humor was a wonderful antidote to the stresses of my life. He was smart and independent-minded, and he had a true passion for missionary work that I admired greatly. He could be serious, witty, brutally honest, and exceptionally kind.

Father Leo had a host of unmet needs too. He lived alone in the priest's house, miles from any of his confreres in the St. Patrick's Society. He had a strong Catholic faith and worked in that remote post because he was dedicated to improving the lives of the people. But it was difficult for him to be constantly giving of himself without receiving understanding and appreciation from someone. Like most of the priests in the diocese, he had many clashes both in person and in writing with the bishop.

I tell no secrets when I state that this Irishman who was our bishop, while he might have had a heart as large as himself, had no idea how to govern his priests or other personnel under his jurisdiction. He caused much turmoil, almost anarchy, and Rome eventually asked him to resign, a highly unusual action in those days.

On return to base after the shocking admonition, I tried to distance myself from Father Leo, but that was difficult. I wasn't about to tell him about the reprimand I had gotten, so I had no reason to curtail our frequent trips to the outstations. When I inevitably encountered him in the mission compound, I was on edge. I felt I was under surveillance, even though I had been told the person who'd lodged the complaint was not one of the sisters I was living with. Having to keep all this in pectore (in my heart) was a burden to my simmering anguish and confusion.

In these days of sexual liberation, it is hard to envisage how embarrassing it was, especially for those of us who had taken a vow of celibacy, to be accused of any impropriety in our relationships with members of the opposite sex. I acknowledge that Father Leo and I had become close friends.

I do not deny that my human emotions played a part in our relationship. It is difficult to explain the situation. I was fully committed to my vow of celibacy, but I also experienced the joy of a close relationship with a person of the opposite sex. It felt good.

At the time of taking the vows, the emphasis was on foregoing marriage and childbearing, but the emotional implications of human sexual love were not emphasized, at least not in my experience. This created a conflict, and I will admit that I was in denial of the presence of these supposedly banished emotions. Now, fifty years later, with the hindsight and wisdom that come with age, I can agree I might not have been as discreet or as tactful about our relationship as religious decorum required. But in the jargon of today, I can vouch that there was no inappropriate behavior.

# FIRST VISIT HOME

In Kenya, the usual tour of duty for each of us Holy Rosary Sisters was five years. After that, we were eligible to return home to Ireland for approximately three months for respite, health and dental care, renewal at the motherhouse and with our families. By this calculation, I was due for home leave in April 1965.

My brother Henry, the youngest in our family, had joined the Holy Ghost Fathers (the Spiritans of today) and was to be ordained to the priesthood in July 1964. An ordination was considered a special blessing for the family. I was encouraged to ask for an earlier home leave so I could be present at the event. Permission was granted.

Because I was a doctor, a replacement, or locum, was needed in order for me to leave my responsibilities in Ortum. It was arranged for Sister Doctor Eileen to come from Sierra Leone as a temporary replacement. That accomplished, I was on my way to home.

One evening shortly after my arrival in Killeshandra, Mother Gabriel asked me to take a walk with her down the Avenue, the proximal half of the driveway leading to the motherhouse, which opened to the most magnificent panoramic vista of the surrounding countryside. I was convinced she wished to inquire about my welfare and my health, seeing that my flight home had been delayed when I developed an FUO (fever of unknown origin).

How wrong I was!

The first shock came when she informed me that Sister

Fintan, my companion of seven years going through medical school, had been dispensed from her vows and was no longer a Holy Rosary Sister. I gasped and muttered something like "Oh no!" Gabriel's response was to ask me to pray for her. I knew better, than to ask for the reason as to why she left. That was a no-no, and even if she felt so inclined, I knew that within the constraints of confidentiality, as superior general, she could not divulge that information.

In the days before the big exodus from religious life post–Vatican II, it was rare for a finally professed sister to ask for or receive a dispensation from her vows. I worried about Fintan and wondered what could have happened. A short while later, the pieces of the puzzle came together when I learned that she was getting married or had been married to a former religious brother she had met while in Nigeria.

The next bombshell was more explosive—and aimed directly at me. I was being reassigned to our congregation's newest mission in Monze, Northern Rhodesia, a British colony that was soon to become independent and renamed Zambia. I would go there at the conclusion of my three-month leave.

My heart sank into my boots. As was expected of an obedient sister, I swallowed all emotion and somehow was able to mutter the formal fiat expected of me. Gabriel went on to voice enthusiasm for the new mission opened under the sponsorship of the Irish Province of the Jesuits, where a new hospital was waiting for the arrival of a resident doctor. She never inquired if I would be disappointed that I was not returning to Kenya. Neither did I voice any of my feelings or the big question I wanted to ask: the real reason why?

Deep down in my innermost being, I was convinced the relocation was related to the previous complaint about my friendship with Father Leo and believed I was being transferred to protect my vocation. Separating sisters from men deemed "too close" was not unprecedented. A few years prior, one of my contemporaries, a good friend, had been transferred from Kenya to Sierra Leone without a good explanation either to her or to us. The move made no sense, except that she was close to one of the priests in the Kenyan mission. I reiterate that this is purely speculation on my part.

Being told of the relocation just before my brother's ordination made the news even harder to bear. I didn't even hint at my transfer to my family during the course of the celebrations, secretly hoping the decision might be reversed.

## ORDINATION AND FAMILY REUNION

I arrived in Ireland about two weeks before the day of Henry's ordination, which was on Saturday, July 4, 1964. He and nineteen classmates were ordained in the chapel of Clonfert Seminary, Dublin, by the archbishop, Dr. John Charles McQuaid. A limited number of tickets were given to each ordinand's family—at the most ten.

I have limited memories of the time surrounding that event, but I do remember being in the crowded chapel, my seat behind one of those mighty decorative columns, and being disappointed not to have full view of the sanctuary. The ritual of ordination to the priesthood is one of the most moving and touching ceremonies in the church and one of the most inspiring to be part of. Seeing these young men prostrate before the altar and proclaim their intention to dedicate their whole lives to God with a vow of celibacy; listening to the prayers of supplication as repeated in the Litany of the Saints; and seeing the presiding bishop lay hands on the head of each ordinand so as to imbue him with the gift of the Holy Spirit and the authority to say Mass and administer the sacraments, are all parts of the ceremony guaranteed to fill with emotion, even the most stoical participant.

As strange as it might seem, I have no recollection of the reunion with my parents. I came to Carlow only the evening before the big event, and I guess we were all so occupied with preparations for the big day, including greeting and meeting some of our out-of-town guests, that it did not stand out. Of course, we were happy to see each other. Mother was more demonstrative than Father, which was typical of Irishmen of his day.

In not-so-happy circumstances, I already met my sister Breed and her husband, Frank, details of which I will later describe. However, it was the first time in four years I was able to greet and embrace Eilish and the first time in ten years I was able to meet Mausie and Bernadette, who had left for America while I was still a medical student.

I was meeting Mausie's wife, Mary, and their two children, Geraldine and Thomas, for the first time. Bernadette, in the later months of her pregnancy with John, had returned to Ireland some time ahead of the big celebration and had delivered him in St. Brigid's Hospital in Carlow at the end of May.

Accompanying her were her two older children, Marie, aged four and Siobhan, aged two years. Her husband, Gerry, due to his duties as an attorney in New York, could not make it for the event, but he came later that week.

By this time Breed and Frank had three children: Marita, Ursula, and Dervla. A few weeks before my arrival back in Ireland, Breed had given birth to another daughter, Jean Marie, who was born with a meningocele and spina bifida. After birth, she was rushed to a pediatric hospital in Dublin. Workup indicated that surgical intervention would not allow her to lead any degree of a normal life. Even though, in my medical experience, I had seen many sad cases in children, I was especially touched to see this little newborn lying there with a huge tumor protruding from her back. I felt bad for my sister and her husband as they kept vigil with their little angel. She was taken to heaven a few days after my visit. About one year later, Breed and Frank were blessed with the birth of another healthy daughter, Niamh. It shows that in life, great joys and sorrows often intermingle.

Meeting the other relatives and friends who were invited was awesome, if a bit intimidating. Many of them I had just known by name and repute, including Uncle Tommy Malone; his wife, Kitty; and their eighteen-year-old son, John. Uncle Tommy had made their first trip back to Ireland since he had left in 1923. Our cousin Rita Clarke also made the trip from the United States. Even distant cousins, including a nun, Sister Bridget Rice, came from Arizona or somewhere out West, all guests invited by our parents to celebrate the momentous occasion.

As was custom, after the ceremony, out on the courtyard of the seminary, in a space allotted to each family, a kneeler was placed. Individually, starting with Mother and Father, family and friends knelt to receive, for the first time, our brother Henry's blessing. It was a touching moment, and of course, the cameras were rolling.

Our rules, while somewhat relaxed, dictated that I stay in one of the convents in town. At least I didn't have to have a companion accompany me, as I had for my cousin's ordination in 1956. I requested and received hospitality at the Presentation Convent, where I had received my early education. It was kind of weird, arriving at the towering front door a few steps away from where I'd lived with the Misses Maher and being welcomed not as a small schoolgirl but as a religious sister.

My memories are blurred, and I have no recollection as to how many of my previous teachers I might have met. As the saying goes, a lot of water had flown under the bridge since I'd first darkened those portals nearly thirty years earlier. I can, however, visualize the sparse cell I was offered in the inner sanctum on the second floor, overlooking familiar Tullow Street. The room spoke to me of the austerity that we always associated with our sister teachers.

These sisters were still restricted in how much they could allow me join them in their community room or refectory. When we were schoolchildren, we were fascinated and felt bad, when we discovered that our teachers were not allowed to leave the convent precincts for any reason, even for a doctor's visit. Only once per year, they were driven as a group in a station-wagon-type car with the curtains drawn to a gentleman's estate in the Wicklow hills, where they enjoyed a two- or three-week secluded vacation. When the school closed for the summer vacation, we kids would watch out for the grand exodus and take delight when we identified the cars speeding away, carrying our sister teachers on their yearly trip outside the walls.

So it wasn't surprising, nor did I take exception, that I had only limited access to them. It suited me fine, as I had come to spend time with my family and only needed somewhere to lay my head at night.

Looking out on Tullow Street brought vivid memories of my sojourn at the Mahers' shop and residence. Unfortunately, both Sarah and Nan had passed to their reward. Sarah had died on Bernadette and Gerry's wedding day in 1958, and Nan had died a few years earlier. The sad thing was that they both ended up in the Sacred Heart Home, originally known as the County Home, as there were no relatives available to care for them in their final days. The shop had been sold and now had a sign over the door replacing the name Maher with Byrne, which I believe remains to this day.

With the wisdom that comes with age and a better appreciation for the gospel message, I truly regret that on entering the convent, in my detachment from the world, I cut these two good ladies out of my life. For their care and kindness to me, they deserved better.

I was not the only Holy Rosary Sister present at the ordination ceremony. Sister Sylvester, with her large family from the west of Ireland, was there celebrating the ordination of her brother. In the reality of the church in the Western world of today, when there might be one or two ordinations in a diocese in a year, it is hard to visualize twenty young men prostrate in a semicircle before the altar, solemnly promising not only to give their lives to clerical ministry but also to serve God in remote areas of Africa or elsewhere in the developing world.

My presence with the family on that occasion was in sharp contrast to what had occurred in 1958, the year I graduated from medical school. Two of my sisters, Breed and Bernadette, had gotten married in that year, both of them in the Cathedral of the Assumption, the church we attended in our youth. Breed's marriage to Francis Browne took place in May, and Bernadette's to Gerald Griffin took place in October.

I was at neither of their weddings. It was not that I was unavailable, but our rules did not allow us to attend marriages or even funerals of family members. On both of those occasions, as the ceremonies and celebrations took place, I went about my duties in St. Vincent's Hospital, Dublin, my mind and heart fifty miles away, regretting that I could not celebrate with family.

Getting back to the events of the ordination day, I was, at best, a little apprehensive as I approached my home in St. Killian's Crescent for the first time in many years. I say "many" because it was not the first time since I'd entered in 1949 that I was crossing the threshold. That previous visit had come out of the blue and been equally as surprising to me as to my family.

In 1953, during one of our breaks from medical school, I was sent to join Sister Patrick, who, at the time, was touring parishes in County Wexford, an adjoining county to Carlow, to show the Holy Rosary Sisters' promotional film *Out of the Darkness*. Patrick, a thoughtful person and never a stickler for rules, aware that I was in close proximity to my hometown of Carlow, had no hesitation in asking permission from the appropriate authorities for me to visit my parents and family at our home.

My parents were ecstatic, as it had been their understanding that once I entered the convent, I would never darken the door again, and there I was, telling them I was coming to visit. The reception Patrick and I received and the sumptuous dinner prepared can only be compared to the parable of the Prodigal Son in the Gospels (see Luke 15:11–32 in the Jerusalem Bible, Popular Edition, 1974)

I have only the vaguest memories of the few days I spent at home after the ceremony. I remember the sense of awe and pride I felt at being present when Henry celebrated his first Mass. My family was welcoming, but I was detached and felt as if I didn't belong. I was made to feel as if I were special, the chosen one, and in spite of my training in humility, I lapped up the attention.

We were at different ends of the totem pole; my siblings were taken up with their lives, their spouses, and their children, and I was still reliving the life I'd experienced in Kenya. There was a big elephant sitting on my chest, the weight of which was more pronounced as, in response to curious questions, I recounted some of my experiences in the remote territory of West Pokot. I did so with a heavy heart but a pretense that nothing was amiss.

There were many young children milling around, the eldest of which was no more than four years old. I have never been googly around infants and toddlers, at least to the extent of wanting to sit and play with them. It is not surprising then that while I would have admired how cute my young nieces and nephews were, I have no recollection of my encounters with them during the visit. I am sure they saw this aloof, statuesque, ghostlike stranger, whom they were told was their aunt, as draconian, if nothing else.

## SOJOURN IN ZAMBIA

As soon as I got back to Killeshandra, the assignation list had been published, and my destiny was sealed. My hurt feelings had not abated in the weeks since I'd first heard about my reassignment to Zambia. I tried to show enthusiasm when the other sisters in the community congratulated me. Two sisters were joining me for the assignment, and one in particular was overflowing with enthusiasm. She couldn't understand my lack thereof. I did my best to avoid her.

In my value system at the time, I had no choice but to follow orders. Obedience was supreme, irrespective of an individual's feelings or desires. Duty required that I start the process of getting visas and medical licensing so I could enter and work in my new African country.

In due course, I received a letter from Sister Eugene, the administrator who had already opened the new hospital in Monze, saying how much she was looking forward to having me come as the hospital's first resident doctor. This was soon followed by a request that the three of us come earlier than planned so as to be present for the celebration of the country's independence from Britain on October 24, 1964.

We duly booked our flights and packed our bags, and we were installed in our new mission before Zambia's Independence Day. In a span of less than one year, I had participated in celebrations in two African countries as they liberated themselves from British rule.

The newly built convent provided by the diocese was a beautiful, well-ventilated two-story building with bedrooms on the second floor. There were now six of us in the Monze community under the leadership of Sister Eugene, an amicable and capable woman. Before that assignment, she had spent more than thirty years in Nigeria in responsible positions not only in our religious community but also as an administrator of successful and busy hospitals. She seemed well suited to the new challenge. She welcomed me and made me aware that she understood the difficulty I was undergoing to adjust to the new and different environment after leaving Kenya.

The other four sisters in the community were more junior than I, all of them on their first mission tour. Sister Therese had opened the new mission with Eugene. I would have close dealings with her, as she was the capable nurse in charge of the inpatient department. I found her bubbliness and enthusiasm for the work in the hospital irritating.

Patricia, a meek, competent teacher, had come from South Africa to teach in the government girls' school. Then there were Teresa and Mary, my companions en route to the new mission, who were full of excitement and wonder as they experienced their first taste of Africa. Teresa was to initiate and develop social service projects, and Mary was given charge of the women's home craft center.

Monze is a town on the Great Northern Highway, 120 miles southwest of Lusaka on the route toward Livingstone, former capital of Northern Rhodesia. Located a few miles from Victoria Falls, which lies on the border between Zambia and Zimbabwe (Southern Rhodesia before 1980), Livingstone is the gateway for tourists to the world-famous falls.

Living in Monze was a considerable change from West Pokot. The township had asphalt roads, and the local people were well dressed in Western garb. Most of them had some level of education, and the majority could speak and understand English. I was often amused by the English words Zambian parents picked as names for their children; they were nontraditional, to say the least. Some I recall are Delicious, Loveliness, Champion, and Magnificent. When I would ask the mothers how they decided on one of these names, which were often English adjectives or adverbs, they proudly answered, "We found it in the dictionary."

Monze was situated midway between two larger government centers, Mazabuka and Choma. Although each of these towns had busy government-sponsored hospitals, the medical care they provided was not considered to be up to standard, hence the political and local push for the Catholic mission to open the hospital in Monze.

The Irish Province of the Jesuits was in charge of the diocese headquartered in Monze. Some years prior, it had been big news in the Irish newspapers when Father James Corboy, SJ, rector of Milltown Seminary in Dublin, had been appointed as the first bishop of the newly formed diocese. The fact that he had never worked in a mission situation made the appointment surprising. At the time, I could never have imagined I would someday be associated with that mission, much less be living next door to the bishop's house and office.

While the hospital building was not yet complete when I arrived, the outpatient department, male and female wards, and maternity suite, including the delivery room, were ready and awaiting my arrival, so as soon as my local license was approved, I set to work seeing and admitting patients—and there was no shortage of patients.

From the start, we were able to get the services of a local laboratory technician who could perform routine blood, urine, and stool examinations, all necessary to establish even a basic diagnosis. As in Kenya, church hospitals were able to avail of the central government medical stores to procure, at a reduced price, necessary medications and supplies. While the issue was not as severe in Monze, we still had to deal with lack of finances, as the fees the patients paid were inadequate to maintain services.

There was a room set up to house an x-ray machine with an attached darkroom for the development of the films. This equipment had not yet been purchased or installed.

## ENCOUNTER WITH HISTORY

The priest who had been appointed as chaplain to us was Father Arthur Cox, an elderly gentleman who was not ordained a priest until two years after his wife passed away. Father Cox said Mass in our convent oratory every morning at seven o'clock and immediately departed back to the priests' house, where he lived with the bishop. We rarely encountered him otherwise. He came across as shy, reserved, and humble.

In spite of his manner, Arthur Cox was renowned in Ireland. The cofounder of a successful law firm on Dublin's prominent St. Stephen's Green, he served one term in the Irish senate (1954–57) and was credited with helping to shape industrial policy for the newly independent country. His widow had previously been married to the Irish patriot Kevin O'Higgins, who was assassinated in 1927. O'Higgins played a major role in setting up the Irish Free State after the signing of the treaty with Britain in 1922 and served as minister of justice in the First Dáil until his tragic death.

Shortly after his wife died in 1961, seventy-year-old Cox began to study for the priesthood at the Milltown Jesuit Seminary, where then Father Corboy was his good friend and mentor. Father Cox was considering but had not yet joined the Jesuit order, when, by taking a vow of poverty, he would renounce all his worldly possessions. In the meantime, he decided to follow Bishop Corboy to serve the church in Zambia. Because Father Cox's considerable wealth was well known, our superiors explicitly warned us not to approach him for monetary help for any of our projects.

One day Father Cox came as a patient to visit me in the hospital. In the course of conversation, he asked if we had a functioning x-ray department. When I informed him that we were still awaiting the installation of the necessary equipment, he immediately offered to finance the cost of the same. I was profusely grateful but had to do a lot of explaining to Eugene to reassure her that this was an unsolicited generous offer.

Shortly after that encounter, we learned Father Cox was involved in a serious motor vehicle accident as he was taking his first trip to a remote mission. He was ejected from the passenger seat of a Jeep and suffered a head injury. He was admitted to the government hospital in Choma, the nearest to the site of the accident, and initially seemed to be doing well. A few days later, one of the Jesuits, after visiting him in the hospital, reported to us in Monze that he was losing the use of his limbs. To my ears, this was an ominous sign.

While we were considering our options, including the possibility of getting Father Cox to a better-equipped hospital, we got the sad news that he had died.

Today a brain hemorrhage similar to the one Father Cox most likely had is surgically treatable if diagnosed and acted on in time. I am a living testament to that, as decades later after a similiar brain injury sustained in Hawaii and with surgical evacuation, I am here to tell the tale.

Diagnosis is by CT scan or MRI of the brain, which, of course, was not available in Choma Hospital—and probably not available in the whole of Zambia at the time. Had this man been immediately airlifted by chartered plane to either South Africa or Ireland, his life might have been saved. Cost would not have been an issue.

I have no doubt that Father Cox would have received a state funeral in his native land. There was no means of refrigeration for corpses in Zambia or elsewhere in tropical Africa, so it was necessary to hold funeral services as soon as possible. His final resting place was the cemetery in Chikuni, where Catholic missionaries who died while on mission were buried. Sisters, priests, and volunteers from far and near came to the Requiem Mass and funeral services, but there were no family members, legal colleagues, or political dignitaries present.

My memory of the funeral procession from the church to the cemetery is still vivid: the unadorned wooden coffin was hoisted onto the back of Brother Dunne's truck. In slow motion and with heavy hearts, we filed to the newly opened grave of red murram soil situated in a remote corner of the cemetery. I could only wonder if that was the way he'd wanted it—just to pass away quietly and without fanfare.

## INNER TURMOIL

I found the whole atmosphere in Zambia different from the camaraderie that had existed among all the various missionaries, both men and women, in Kenya. The Sisters of Charity, the same sisters who owned St. Vincent's Hospital in Dublin, were well established in hospitals and schools, the nearest of which was about ten miles away. On the whole, they kept to themselves and seemed to lead lives of strict observance. We rarely had contact with them, except when we needed hospitality in Lusaka, where, at the time, we did not have a house of our own, and the sisters there were kind and welcoming.

The only other congregation of sisters anywhere near us, the Franciscan Sisters of Mary, was in Livingstone, a distance of a hundred or so miles away, so there was little opportunity to get to know them either.

The Jesuits, while they were a friendly bunch were careful to follow decorum and keep a safe distance from us. Their ministries and ours did not seem to coincide, so we had little opportunity to get to know them individually. There was no such thing as a social hour or sharing of a meal, even at Christmastime. Perhaps we sisters were as much to blame for not issuing an invitation.

I don't believe I or any of the sisters, except perhaps Eugene, ever entered the priests' house, and she only got as far as the bishop's office. Bishop Corboy was cordial and reasonable but reserved. We rarely saw him, and on the whole, he did not interfere in the day-to-day management of the hospital and the other works we were engaged in.

A change from my experience in Kenya was that I was confined exclusively to doctoring, and the administration was fully in the hands of Eugene. While one would think I was relieved that burden was off my shoulders, human nature being as it is, I found it hard to relinquish control. I loved Eugene dearly, but I found the change difficult and resented that she did not include me in policy-making discussions and decisions with the bishop and other public figures.

There wasn't the same challenge as in West Pokot to develop health services. There might have been a need for a hospital in Monze, but it was likely we were forestalling the acquiring of a government-sponsored hospital that would equally serve the local population. Even by that time, quite a few doctors had set up private practices in the area. I could see that the work in the hospital would become more sophisticated and more specialized. We were already receiving patients with severe injuries due to auto accidents, and I questioned my competence in performing major surgery to be able to deal with such trauma and other emergencies. The bottom line was, I didn't see this as my calling, which I believed was to be a missionary serving the least of God's children.

I also kept making comparisons to my previous mission experience in dealing with the European settlers. One or two of the wives made contact with us, but there was nothing like the rapport we'd developed with their counterparts in Kenya. Most of them were considering packing up and returning to either Southern Rhodesia or South Africa, as they assessed there was no future for them in an independent Zambia.

All of this added up to us six sisters being isolated and having to daily put up with each other's foibles, with no good means of escape, not even for a weekend. This was our only house in Zambia. I was also finding it difficult to adjust to a regimented regime of community living predicated by the way life was lived in Nigeria.

While I did my best to settle into my new life, at the back of my mind was a recurring theme I was unable to reverse: *You have to prove that there was nothing inappropriate in your relationship with Father Leo and that you have been unnecessarily victimized.* Adding to the inner turmoil were reactions to changes in the church resulting from the work of Vatican II, especially as we experienced a change in priorities in religious life.

For centuries, the appointed superior, at either the local or general level, was regarded as the interpreter of God's will, and obeying not only made one a good religious but also was the path to eternal salvation. I was a true believer and follower of that philosophy. Even today, I cringe when I remember how I allowed care for the rules to supersede the call of love and compassion in dealings with my own family. These rules kept the communities together, with each one treated the same and outliers regarded as pariahs. There was no reason for petty jealousies; those in authority were held in the highest esteem, and their actions or orders were never questioned.

The emphasis now shifted to a call for the church to be more attuned to the needs of the modern world as defined in the documents of the council. These changes were asking for more fraternal charity in communities, with the discernment of God's will for each, to be determined in group and prayer sessions. Thus, for the first time, the differing personalities of individuals often clashed, as rules and plans were interpreted with hugely divergent opinions.

Some of us, myself included, began to question many of the rules and practices as interpreted not only by our rules and constitutions but also by the very foundation of religious life as we experienced it. The rules had all been drawn up in the days of monasticism and were more suited for the contemplative orders than for active religious sisters, especially in a mission situation like the one where I found myself. I was on duty 24-7 and was still trying to fit in a schedule of prayer and spiritual exercises similar to those with regular working hours. The dictum *"Ora et labora"* (Pray and work) had an emphasis completely opposite the situation I found myself in. The whole idea of having to make up missed spiritual exercises became burdensome, to say the least.

While still in West Pokot, I began to realize and mentally formulate that there was a clear distinction between the call of a missionary vocation and that of a religious celibate life. In fact, the example of a Protestant missionary couple stationed in an even more remote area than we were seemed to be a better witness of Christian marriage and family life that the locals could relate to, than we celibates were. It was a known fact that the people believed we were the four wives of Father Leo. They scoffed at the idea that this was not true. I couldn't blame them, as that was all they knew; polygamy had been practiced for centuries in the tribe.

In this age of liberation, when talk on sexual matters is as common and open as saying, "It is a nice day," I can imagine it is hard to understand what was going on in my head at the time. After all, I was a doctor and had studied not only the anatomy of the genitalia but also the hormonal and emotional responses inherent in the reproductive process. I should not have been in such a state of turmoil and denial. One would have had to live in the time when the Kinsey reports, describing the sexual behavior of the human male and female, were first published, to realize the breathtaking shock they evoked in our puritanical generation. The Masters and Johnson studies, which were even more revolutionary and explicit and essentially established the age of sexual liberalism, had not yet been published. All I can say is that was my reasoning and my emotional state at the time.

From the time I was a teenager, I was so intent on becoming

a missionary that I was prepared to make any sacrifice to get there. In Ireland at that time, we took it for granted that we needed to join a vowed religious congregation to follow the missionary path.

I entered the novitiate just a few weeks after my eighteenth birthday. One of my regrets is that I never dated before I took that significant step, although I did experience a glimpse of romantic love through a distant cousin. During my teens I had a crush on Pat and knew he liked me, but he followed the calling to become a priest with the Passionist Fathers. It was at the same time that I decided to enter the convent, neither of us discussing or knowing of the other's decision.

Our paths crossed again when as a seminarian in Dublin, he came occasionally to visit me in our house of studies. While I so much enjoyed his company- so vibrant, so much fun, a breath of fresh air injected into my stressful lifestyle- we were both ever careful to maintain a healthy distance. Then there was this Sunday afternoon when Pat, now in his final year of study for the priesthood, came to visit. When called to the parlor to meet him, I couldn't believe my eyes There, standing beside him was his immediate superior, the director of seminarians. Conversation that day was awkward, to say the least. Afterward I was left in a quandary and could only surmise that the director was anxious to know who this female 'cousin' really was and perhaps determine his suitability to take a perpetual vow of celibacy. I never did find out the reason for this unusual, supervisory visit, except that Pat was allowed proceed to ordination in May 1956.

When I asked for permission to attend his ordination and

first Mass, it was granted on the condition that another sister accompany me. This rule irked me because I knew my companion, would take the place of a family member, as the number of attendees at such an event was strictly limited.

Cousin Pat subsequently broke my heart in a way I could never have imagined. He volunteered to go as a missionary to Botswana at the same time I left for Kenya. Within months of his arrival, he contracted poliomyelitis with his respiratory system involved. He was emergency airlifted to a hospital in Johannesburg, South Africa, to get the benefit of the iron lung, a precursor of modern-day respirators. Tragically, his frame was too large to fit into the machine, so he died gasping for air. It was Christmas Eve 1960. To add to the poignancy of the moment, his name in religion was Father Emmanuel (God with us), the name so associated with Christmas. He died long before his time, at just thirty-three years.

I did not find out about the tragedy until I received a letter from my mother some time afterward. In remote Ortum, far from the comfort of my family, I was overcome with grief. How could such a vibrant, wonderful human being be taken from the earth in the flicker of an eyelid—and so unnecessarily? I was especially distraught at the thought that he had died alone, far removed not only from family but also from his confreres in religion. However, I later found out that two of his colleagues were with him when he passed. When I received a picture of the simple iron cross marking his grave in Kgale, the remote mission he had just settled into in faraway Botswana, it brought a few more heartbreaking, silent tears.

## A WELCOME CHANGE

About six months into my sojourn in Monze, I was again involved in an official visitation by the superior general, her first visit to Zambia. Yes, it was still Mother Gabriel. I have little recollection of my personal interview with her. I only know that neither of my previous encounters came up for discussion. If she sensed I was unhappy and unsettled, she gave no indication; whether my body language betrayed my inner turmoil, I have no idea. It's possible it played a role in future decision making, but that is only conjecture at best.

During the school break in July or August, which was winter in the Southern Hemisphere, Eugene suggested that I, along with two members of the community, Patricia and Teresa, take a trip to Southern Rhodesia, (Zimbabwe of today). Needless to say, we three embraced the idea enthusiastically. Work in the hospital had not yet reached such a level of busyness that a locum was needed to cover me during my absence for a week or two. We were even offered the community's car, a Volkswagen Beetle, for the duration of the trip, a most generous offer.

Our first stop was the mighty Victoria Falls, where I was invigorated by the awesome power of nature and fascinated by the history of early explorers, such as the legendary Dr. David Livingstone.

We then headed across the border to Southern Rhodesia. Our next planned destination was the capital, Salisbury (now Harare). Unlike Zambia, Southern Rhodesia was still entrenched in British colonialism, and the attitude of the white people toward the native population was startling. For the first time, much to our distress, we witnessed the process of apartheid in action.

We were the guests of the Sisters of the Little Company of Mary, better known as the Blue Sisters, as they wore light blue veils when on duty in their hospitals. I was familiar with the congregation because they staffed a hospital in Carlow town. I had been a patient there when I had my appendix removed as a teenager, and my nephew John had been born there in 1964.

It might seem strange in today's world, but in colonial times in Africa, the hierarchy of the Catholic Church had asked established orders of religious men and women to send members to serve the educational and health needs of the immigrant populations. As such, it was not a surprise that these sisters had established, in Salisbury and in other centers where there was a large European or white population, well-equipped, modern hospitals. This differed from our mind-set in that our mission was to serve the indigenous population especially in areas where they were underserved or neglected.

In our conversations with the sisters, it was obvious we were poles apart in our thinking. It was therefore propitious that a visiting priest offered to take us some miles away to his mission station, where he was working with and answering to the needs of the local indigenous population. That experience was impressive and helped balance our negative impression of the work of the church in the region.

The highlight of our visit was seeing the film *The Sound of Music*, although we had to watch it in a whites-only cinema. For us, just going to the movies was a rare and precious experience, but to see such a beautiful film was beyond our expectations.

Besides enjoying the scenery, heavenly music, lyrics, and love story, I did not equate the movie with any of the personal emotions I was going through. The idea of leaving the convent, falling in love, and marrying a handsome prince never entered my radar at the time.

## TABLES TURN AGAIN

Back in Monze, I still did not feel at home, nor could I put my heart and soul into my work, even after a year in the place.

We had always been taught that when facing any difficulties or temptations, we should take them to God in prayer, and they would go away. Well, I continued to go willy-nilly through the motions of community prayers, but when it came time for private prayer, my whole world was in a state of turmoil and confusion. Only negative thoughts dominated, and I am not sure I even asked God to grant me acceptance or healing.

In spite of my vow of obedience, I was unable to see the present situation as God's will for me. At the core, I was rebelling against the idea that my superiors in the Holy Rosary Sisters represented this will of God. I was no longer the idealist who promised unconditional obedience, yet I was committed to maintain fidelity to the vows I had taken, which I genuinely believed were sacred in the eyes of God.

Then, through the grapevine, I heard news from Kenya that made me feel even more unsettled. The archbishop of Nairobi, answering to the request of the president of Kenya, Mzee Jomo Kenyatta, had asked for the Holy Rosary Sisters, including a doctor, to staff the new hospital he was building in Gatundu, in the heart of Kikuyu country. I was aware that, as there were only nine of us seasoned doctors and two just coming out of internship in the entire congregation, the choice of one of us to answer this request was limited. Was this my opportunity to return to my beloved Kenya?

I could bear the suspense no longer. I plucked up all my courage; knocked on the door of Eugene's office; and, just standing there, blurted out how unhappy I was and told her that in spite of my best efforts, I was not settling into Monze. She did not say much but at least did not lecture me or disagree that I had given it my best effort. I left the office shaking like an aspen leaf—never in a thousand years had I thought I would be so bold.

I don't think it surprised anyone, least of all me, that early in January 1966, a letter came from the superior general apprising me that I was being reassigned to Kenya.

I was to become the doctor in charge at the Gatundu hospital. I was elated that I'd been deemed capable of that post. It would be a privileged but highly scrutinized position because Gatundu, located about eighteen miles west of Thika in the Kiambu District, was the hometown of President Jomo Kenyatta. The hospital was being built as a showpiece and a reward of sorts for the first president's home base and loyal supporters.

As a pet project of the president, this request was an affirmation of the respect given to the Catholic Church in independent Kenya, and it was a huge compliment to the Holy Rosary

Sisters when the archbishop asked them to staff the hospital at the most senior levels.

My emotions at the prospect of returning to Kenya were in conflict. I felt overwhelming joy, but with it came a sense of guilt. Had I manipulated the process by confiding in Sister Eugene, who I suspected had reported my unhappiness to headquarters? I had to acknowledge that I had.

Enhancing the sense of guilt was the fact that the doctor being sent to succeed me, Sister Maureen, was coming straight out of internship and had no previous experience in a mission hospital. It was déjà vu all over again. As I tried to orientate her to her new position, I could see—and she was not slow to voice—how ill prepared she felt for the medical responsibilities she was taking on. It was again a matter of obedience superseding competence.

In their favor, I have to state that the superiors making these decisions that meant life or death for patients and excessive stress for the sister doctors were all professionals in education and could not have fully appreciated the medical perspective. Besides, the limited number of us in the medical profession very much curtailed their choice.

So began an era of turmoil that would define the course of my life for many years to come.

## CHAPTER 9

# FORMATION OF A LARGER VISION

I arrived back in Nairobi toward the end of January 1966 and took up residence in Kilima Mboga, where I had started nearly six years previously. In the interim, in the Thika township, a new maternity hospital had been built and staffed by MSHRs. Sister Doctor Breed was the only doctor serving this hospital and the one in Kilima Mboga, some ten miles away. She had chosen to live in Kilima Mboga, which meant she had to make frequent trips back and forth to Thika, often in the middle of the night to take care of emergencies. She had her own reasons for this arrangement.

Breed had worked for many years in Nigeria and was one of the sisters displaced by the civil war when the eastern province tried to become an independent state known as Biafra. We were already friends since she and I had lived in the same hostel in London, so she was most welcoming, as were the other sisters.

Martin was still there, as gracious and caring as ever. Declan was still the regional superior. I do not remember who the other sisters were. I just remember that I was happy to be back, and nobody questioned motives or reasons for the transfer.

The hospital building in Gatundu was not yet complete, and shortly after my arrival, a harambee was held to raise funds for it. Harkening back to the Kiswahili word for "push or pull together," a harambee is an occasion for people in a community to come together to help themselves. President Kenyatta was a champion of the concept, and the word is emblazoned on the Kenyan coat of arms.

At the event, I was introduced to his Excellency, Mzee Jomo Kenyatta, With him were members of his immediate family, including his wife, Mama Ngina. She had with her a young son of approximately five years, named Uhuru. He presently serves as the fourth president of Kenya. I guess besides reminding me that I am not as young as I used to be, it makes me feel privileged to have met two of the presidents of Kenya. I would like to have met Christine, his oldest daughter with Mama Ngina, as she had been a pupil in Ortum while her father was in detention in Lodwar, Turkana, and when I first landed in Ortum in 1960. I inquired about her and was told that she was in a boarding school, which was plausible, as she was fourteen years old at the time.

Besides the family members present, Mzee was surrounded by chiefs and leaders of the local area, members of Parliament, and other VIPs, all anxious to meet the new doctor.

Mzee, as we generally called him, was cordial and welcoming. His gaze, emphasized by the opaque rings encircling his pupils, medically known as arcus senilis and not atypical for a man of seventy-five, seemed to penetrate to the depths of my soul. After some pleasantries, he remarked, "You appear too young to be a doctor." I wasn't sure whether to take that as a compliment or a reservation on his part. He then added some flattering remarks about my looks, which caused me to blush and feel slightly uncomfortable.

While waiting for the Gatundu hospital to open, I requested and obtained permission to get more experience performing major surgeries. I found a suitable situation in St. Anthony's Hospital near Tororo, just over the border in Uganda. There I attached myself to Sister Doctor Eugene, a Franciscan Missionary Sister for Africa, the only physician serving that large and busy hospital.

There were plenty of maternity emergencies that required intervention in the hospital, but Sister Doctor spent most of her time in the operating room (OR), performing surgery to relieve strangulated inguinal hernias. For reasons not completely understood, groin hernias were endemic in the male population in that area of Uganda. Inguinal hernias are caused when a portion of the intestine or peritoneum protrudes through a weakness in the abdominal wall in the groin area. Strangulation occurs when the herniation becomes nonreversible and the blood flow is cut off, leading to necrosis (death) of the herniated intestine and sepsis.

Even after a busy day in the OR, nearly every night, there was further need to perform these surgeries, which often ended in the early hours of the morning. After assisting Doctor Eugene in all of these operations, I at last felt comfortable enough to offer to hold the fort while she took a week's rest and relaxation.

To everyone's disappointment, especially mine, before Eugene could get away, I had to cancel my offer and return as a matter of urgency to Kenya. I was called back to take over at Thika Maternity Hospital, as Sister Doctor Breed needed, for medical reasons, to return to Ireland, effective immediately.

After a short initiation from Breed, I was on my own to run the busy twenty-bed maternity hospital in the sprawling industrial town of Thika. It had already gained a reputation as a good and safe hospital for labor and delivery.

Many of the presenting women had a difficult time delivering their babies vaginally due to their birth canals being too narrow for the safe delivery of the babies' heads—in medical terms, cephalopelvic disproportion. This demanded intervention by a doctor after a trial of labor had failed. Being the only doctor, I was on call 24-7. Due to the lapse of time, the confidence I had previously developed in that branch of the practice of medicine had faded and needed time and practice to be regained.

Fortunately I had Sister Angelica, an experienced nurse-midwife, in charge of labor and delivery. She had extensive experience in our hospitals in Nigeria. She could smell at a distance that a case was going to go sour, as we used euphemistically to say. But being the genius that she was, she was a little overpowering and slightly difficult to live with in community. I greatly respected her opinion on cases, but the ultimate decision and responsibility for the ensuing course of action was mine. I still got flutters in my abdomen when I had to deliver a baby by cesarean section, but I rose to the occasion and thanked the Lord for good outcomes.

As an example of how emergencies could crop up even at the most unexpected hour, one evening, when everything was quiet in the labor room, I left to drive to the airport in Nairobi to meet Sister Eugene, who was coming from Zambia on a brief visit. One hour after I left, upon my arrival back at the hospital, Angelica met me at the front door. A patient already in the OR required an urgent CS. While I somewhat resented that she had made the decision, which rightfully should have been mine, of course I complied and performed the necessary. This episode brings out that we had no means of emergency contact once we left the precincts of the hospital—no beepers and no access to a land phone.

One case is engraved in my memory. It was a Saturday evening. I had just successfully performed a CS and delivered a healthy baby. In the hospital was a primigravida (a woman giving birth for the first time), whom I had examined that afternoon. She had a history of bronchial asthma, but there were no signs of an asthmatic attack on physical examination, and labor was progressing well.

I had retired to the nearby convent to take forty winks, when the telephone rang. I knew by the urgency of Angelica's voice that something catastrophic was happening. In haste, I got myself back to the labor unit to find that in the half hour or, at the most, three quarters of an hour since I had left, the patient had suffered a series of asthmatic attacks called status asthmaticus and was no longer breathing.

We tried all means of resuscitation but could not bring her

back to life. I listened for the fetal heartbeat, and it was audible, although there were signs of distress. Immediately, I asked for a scalpel, and there in the bed, I performed an emergency CS and delivered a baby boy. He was a little blue from asphyxia but otherwise healthy.

I wasn't sure how to relate the sad outcome to relatives when they came to check on the young woman the next morning. I was especially concerned about how they would react to having a motherless infant to care for. It was a relief and joy to see them welcome the newborn baby while at the same time grieving his mother's loss.

In almost every instance, I found that Kenyan people accepted even the worst tragedies as *Shauri a Mungu* (the will of God). If we doctors were unable to cure a patient or save a life, there was never a suggestion that we were to blame. Filing a malpractice suit would never have entered their minds.

## SURPRISING SWITCH

During the summer of 1966, a general chapter of the congregation was held in Killeshandra. At the meeting were delegates from all the missions of the congregation, about half of them superiors and another half members elected by local or regional communities. Sister Doctor Breed was a delegate from the Kenya region. Even in those years, it was the most democratic process in religious communities. It was held every six years and resulted in the election of the government of congregations, including the mother general and her council. Mother

Gabriel had completed her twelve years as general, and we now had Mother Stanislaus, whom I also had encountered in my young days. She had been my mistress of postulants.

Toward the end of September, the delegates returned to Kenya with a new regional superior, Mother Juliana who, prior to that appointment, had spent most of her career in South Africa. She was a nurse by profession and understood well the intricacies of hospital work.

Soon thereafter, there were reassignments. Instead of me, Breed O'Keeffe would be taking over Gatundu Hospital. Sister Doctor Bruno was moving to Thika Maternity Hospital from her post in Ortum, and I would replace her there. She had been in Ortum for just over one year.

I welcomed this turn of events, not only because I was returning to my beloved Ortum but also because I knew Breed was a better fit than I was for the high-profile Gatundu Hospital. She had considerably more experience than I did—and I suppose she "looked old enough" to be a doctor in the eyes of Mzee Kenyatta. My analysis proved true. Breed served with distinction at that hospital for years and was highly regarded by the president, his family, and the Ministry of Health.

The change over took place almost immediately, I believe in either late October or early November of 1966. Regarding how I physically got back to Ortum, I draw a complete blank. Bruno was anxious to be on her way back to Thika's maternity hospital. We had a brief encounter in Kitale, both of us on our way to our new assignments. Even though we were of the same set, we did not have much in common and had not kept up a relationship over the years.

She had found the transition from the well-developed health-care system in Nigeria, where she had practiced for several years before her sojourn in Kenya, difficult to handle. She had been one of the persona non grata expelled from Nigeria after the Biafran War. Besides, she might have been dealing with personal issues. This became clear a few years later when she left the MSHRs to join a contemplative monastic religious order in Ireland. Henceforth, she would support the missions by prayer and penance. Unfortunately, she died prematurely not many years later.

I returned to West Pokot happy but somewhat nervous. Would the people respond in a positive way to my return?

The enthusiastic welcome I received from the hospital staff and the local people helped dispel any doubts that I was in the right place. Father Leo made no secret that he was happy to have me back, but he was discreet in voicing his opinion on my aptitude to fit into the local situation. I was happy to see him again and determined to prove that there was nothing inappropriate in our friendship. Now back in familiar territory, I was ready and fully aware of the uphill battle I was facing and eager to take up the challenge.

Sister Rosa had by that time been appointed the local superior and was now called Mother Rosa. I cringe when I write these words. It was so archaic to have one of us called Mother. We were only three—she and I in the hospital and a new sister who had come from Nigeria to be headmistress in the girls' school. Again, what a coincidence—she was Sister Alexa, who had been my angel initiating me into the ways of religious life.

We still didn't have our own means of transport, which

meant we were dependent on either the hospital ambulance or Father Leo to get us even as far as Kitale.

I could see signs that progress had been made in our medical efforts in the two years since my departure. The people were making better use of the health services, and quite a few Pokot girls had completed their primary education and were interested in joining the staff of the hospital.

We were delighted in their interest, but we also wanted to address our ongoing problem of maintaining staff after we had trained them. We were in an isolated area, and the lure of the towns was great, even for the local students we had sponsored in the past. With a shortage of trained medical staff throughout the nation, they had no difficulty getting a job elsewhere. Besides, with our precarious finances, we were unable to compete with the salaries and other benefits the government could offer.

The best solution, it seemed, would be to start our own nurse training program. This would give us at least a cadre of local women in training who, under supervision, could perform some of our nursing needs. In today's jargon, they would be called hospital aides. While we would have preferred to try to get a nurse generalists training program, it did not appear feasible to seek such training, not only due to our remoteness but also due to the fact that we did not have the broad spectrum of cases and activities necessary for such training. We therefore decided to focus the training program around our goal of increasing the number of pregnant women who delivered their babies in our hospital.

If we could increase greatly the volume of women delivering

their babies in the hospital, we believed we had a good chance of getting approval to start a midwifery training school. Our goal at a future time would be to advance to a community nurse training program, which was already taking shape generally in Kenya. In fact, I was fully aware that Thika Maternity and Gatundu Hospital were participating in the training of this new cadre of nurse, a multipurpose health worker who could operate as a general nurse, a midwife, and a public health nurse and be better prepared to meet the basic health needs, especially of the rural areas.

At the time, we had only about twenty-five hospital deliveries each year, which was discouraging in light of the high mortality rate among babies from the time of birth through their first year of life due to malnutrition, infection, or both. Many Pokot women had no living child even after multiple pregnancies. The practice of the traditional midwife whereby she inserted cow dung into the mother's birth canal if she was having difficulty delivering her baby, as discussed previously, was still a major factor in the deaths of both mother and child.

Two obvious reasons stood out as to why pregnant women did not give birth at our hospital. First of all, they had no idea of their due dates, or expected date of delivery (EDD) in medical terms. Second, they had no means of transport to the hospital once they went into labor.

After much thought and discussion among ourselves and getting the input of Father Leo, who had the pulse of the local community, we decided on a plan of action.

We would identify pregnant women during our visits to the outstations with the mobile unit. I could estimate their EDDs and know in advance the approximate date they should arrive at the hospital prior to the onset of labor. They still did not have a reliable form of transportation, but that problem could be solved if we could get the women who were nearest to their EDD to be residents on the hospital grounds prior to the onset of labor. That left just one dilemma: Where would the pregnant women stay in the days or weeks before labor started?

We needed a hostel for the ladies in waiting that would include space for them to sleep and an area where they could take care of their own cooking and other day-to-day chores. Short on funds, as we always were, we approached the local elders and asked for their help in rallying the local people in a harambee project to build the hostel on the hospital grounds.

The elders received this suggestion with great enthusiasm. With some moral and monetary assistance from our mission, the hostel was constructed and ready for occupancy within the space of one week. It was a simple structure made of mud-and-wattle walls, as most local homes and buildings were, with a tin roof. Not only was it equipped with cooking facilities, but it even had a bare-bones bathroom. We had a ceremonial official opening when the local women and men, all dressed in their traditional costumes, danced the evening out. The fact that the leaders and elders of the Pokot so enthusiastically entered into the implementation of this project was a real boost to our confidence that we were making inroads into creating better health care for the people.

As soon as the ladies-in-waiting hostel was ready, we introduced rudimentary prenatal clinics at each of the outstations whenever we visited with the mobile unit. In the privacy of a schoolroom, on makeshift benches, I would examine a woman and estimate how far along she was in her pregnancy. When I thought she was near term, I would either take her back to the hospital with us that day or tell her to be ready with her goods and chattels when we next visited.

It was satisfying to return two or four weeks later and find women waiting, ready for the trip to the hospital. Rather than suitcases filled with changes of clothes, they came with gourds filled with sour milk mixed with charcoal and a cooking pot for their diet staple of millet. The combination of this mixture with the moldy, earthy odor of their poorly cured skin skirts, was not pleasant to our nostrils. The joy of having candidates for our maternity services far outweighed the malodorous experience.

Once the women were in the ladies-in-waiting area on hospital grounds, the nursing staff regularly supervised and examined them. As soon as labor contractions started, they were sent to the labor unit to be admitted. Actually, the last sentence needs clarification. It always amazed me, and still does, how tolerant these women were of pain. I cannot tell you how many times it happened that a woman would only present to the labor ward as soon as her baby was ready to be born. When we would say to her, "Why did you not come when you started labor?" invariably, her answer was "I didn't know I was in labor; I didn't feel any pain."

Unlike the situation around Thika and generally in central Kenya, there wasn't the same dominance of cephalopelvic disproportion, so most of the women had normal deliveries. Their main problem was small-for-dates babies. The infants while born at term had weights below average, four to five pounds at most. While many neonates born at home died from tetanus or pneumonia due to infection and exposure in the cold mountain air, most of the infants under one year died due to diarrheal disease superimposed on a degree of malnutrition. It was indeed a happy occasion to see a mother go home with a healthy newborn, and hopefully, through our efforts at basic health education, she was better equipped to care for her infant.

We also saw our share of premature births; some of the infants weighed little more than two pounds. It was amazing how we were able to save those tiny tots without incubators. The ingenuity of the nursing sisters came to the fore as they devised a makeshift neonatal unit, a small room isolated from the rest of the hospital. They developed a regular feeding schedule when the mother's milk was expressed and pipetted into the infant's mouth if he or she was unable to suckle at the breast.

As the temperature of the nights could fall precipitously, we placed on the floor a small charcoal-burning stove on which we had a continuously steaming kettle of water. The combination of heat and steam was as close as we could get to replicate the atmosphere in the mother's womb, which these tots needed to survive and thrive. We made sure to have adequate ventilation due to the danger of carbon monoxide buildup from the burning stove. The mother was allowed to be with the infant as much as she wanted, and there was constant supervision by the nursing staff.

The joy on a mother's face as she was able to go home with a live and thriving infant was worth all the trouble. Often, this was her only living child after numerous pregnancies, sometimes up to ten. We just hoped that while she was in the hospital, she learned the essentials of how to care for her precious child. Of course, we had no way of knowing, as there was rarely follow-up. Need I add that there was no such thing as a register of births, marriages, or deaths, at least in the district of West Pokot.

## SMALL CHANGES BOOST BIRTHS

From the time the hospital opened, we charged a small fee for services for both inpatients and outpatients. It was the rule, however, that no one was refused treatment due to inability to pay. The fees were miniscule by any standards and in line with those of other hospitals in the area. Patients' contributions toward meeting the costs of running the hospital were a mere drop in the ocean, but the practice was based on a principle that generally, people value more what they have to pay for. This was true for our area of West Pokot.

As small as the fees seemed to us, they must have seemed enormous to the locals, who were only just beginning to transition from a barter-based economy to the use of government-issued money. We were familiar with the periodic auction of cattle instituted by the local government to get the families to sell some of their prized herd in order to pay their national and local taxes.

Regardless of our sound logic, I must admit that asking poor people for money was not pleasant. For them, it often involved selling a cow or a goat, their only source of wealth, to get the cash, and the local Somali butcher wasn't overly generous when he purchased the treasured livestock.

Now it was time to do some soul searching and ask ourselves what were the deterrents to more women availing of our maternity services. We had been charging a flat fee of fifty Kenyan shillings for the cost of an admission of a woman for labor and delivery. After consultation with some of the educated elders and Father Leo, who always had the pulse of the community, we determined that besides the two factors mentioned earlier—pregnant women having no idea of their due date and the lack of transportation when at term—was the factor of money. Why spend so much money to deliver a baby, when it was such a natural phenomenon and when help for generations had been provided by the traditional midwives?

We therefore made a big adjustment and reduced our fee to just ten Kenyan shillings, which would include all costs during admission for the care of mother and infant. We publicized the new policy by every means possible, through the church, the chiefs, and the schools. To try to put this fee into perspective, at the time, it was costing each of the sisters about three hundred Kenyan shillings each month to live frugally.

After the implementation of the total program for pregnant women—examinations in outstations, transportation in the mobile unit, accommodations in the ladies-in-waiting hostel, and reduced fees—our deliveries jumped to more than a hundred within a year.

With the increase in the number of inpatients, we had to add another wing to the hospital, and we decided to build a new maternity block. After designing the building ourselves, we were able to get the services of Brother Hugh, a religious brother originally from the United States, to oversee construction. It was heavenly working with him.

In due course, we had beautiful new antenatal and postnatal wards, along with a new labor-and-delivery suite. We were making progress.

Another factor that had a significant impact on the increased numbers not only in the maternity services but also generally was that we had opened a dispensary in Cheperaria, a busy center halfway between Ortum and Kapenguria. This was in response to frequent and compelling invitations from the local elders. During the colonial era, the administration was not in favor of the Catholic mission starting any activities in that center, due to their policy of zoning. That had all changed with independence. At the time, there was no stationary medical facility in the vacinity, nor did a mobile unit visit on a regular basis. For even minor illnesses and trauma, patients were meant to get by any means possible to Kapenguria, a distance of about ten miles on the torturous road of the escarpment.

In spite of our critical finances, we were able to recruit a mature male enrolled nurse to staff the new dispensary. I visited once per week with the mobile unit to supervise, see the most problematic cases, and transport those with serious illnesses back to the hospital for admission. George was well received by the local population, even though he was from the Luo tribe and not a Pokot. From our perspective, seeing a local community anxious to avail of our facilities and responsive to our treatments was a real boost in the arm and kept us motivated.

## STAFFING BY INGENUITY

The number of medical facilities and personnel in the area was inadequate. I was the only doctor in the entire district, an area of more than three thousand square miles, and there had been no resident doctor in the district hospital in Kapenguria for several years. My friend and fellow Irish colleague Dr. Finbarr O'Callaghan was the only doctor in the busy Kitale District Hospital. Plus, he was designated to be the medical officer of health for the district of West Pokot and the adjoining district of Trans Nzoia.

Of course, it was not humanly possible for Dr. O'Callaghan to accomplish all that was needed. As an unconventional remedy, I was asked to visit the district hospital in Kapenguria on a monthly basis to supervise activities there. This came down to signing any documents needing a doctor's signature rather than providing patient care. Occasionally, I was asked for an opinion on a patient's progress or lack thereof.

Any patients requiring surgical treatment at the Kapenguria hospital needed to be transferred to Kitale, a distance of twenty or so miles—an uncomfortable ride in a Land Rover for a seriously ill patient.

In the government medical services in Kenya, as elsewhere throughout East Africa, medical assistants, later called clinical officers, did a good job as primary caregivers. They were the backbone of the health services. The concept of having paramedical personnel trained and functioning as assistants to the few-and-far-between doctors dated back to the beginning of the twentieth century. Initially, the mission hospitals had been prominent in providing this cadre of paramedical staff, but by this time in history, the training of clinical officers was mainly the domain of the Ministry of Health at the medical training center (MTC) in Nairobi.

Without going into details, I'll simply say they were given a mini–medical education so they could diagnose and treat most of the bread-and-butter cases that presented either in the dispensaries and health centers of the rural areas or in the outpatient and inpatient services of the general hospitals. They were meant to have the supervision of a doctor, but that supervision could be as close or as distant as circumstances dictated. Except for suturing of lacerations, they were not allowed to perform major surgeries.

It was a question of economics, but I would also venture to say that it was a question of prestige that we expatriates in mission hospitals did not use this cadre of paramedical personnel. Church hospitals all over the country continued to train nurses at the enrolled level, many of whom ended up working in the government health service. This service was appreciated by all, including the Ministry of Health.

Speaking for myself, I have to acknowledge I had the attitude that only doctors were qualified to diagnose and treat. It took some time to rethink that premise.

In Ortum, I never had more than one nursing sister from the Holy Rosary at any time, and I had to deal with frequent turnover in that role. This meant just like me, the nursing sister was always on duty during day hours. Although she was exempt from night duty in general, she had to be available if she was needed for emergency surgery in the operating room. The administrative duties, which we shared, were an added burden. We desperately needed more staff at the executive level.

Many requests for personnel from the regional headquarters of Holy Rosary got us nowhere, either due to our precarious financial status or the lack of suitable persons to be assigned, in what was still considered a difficult mission. When eventually a sister was appointed to take on some of the administrative duties, it did not work out. Instead, she undertook social and development work in the community. Administrative duties continued to occupy so much of my time and energy, time that I could have better used in patient care and the development of an outreach program.

It was an act of providence that brought two highly trained and motivated nurses to Ortum in 1970. On one of my business trips to Nairobi, by accident or divine intervention, I met an official who was the organizer for the Netherlands' government and was seeking out suitable places where volunteers, somewhat like those in the Peace Corps, could work in developmental projects for the benefit of local communities. I availed of the opportunity to tell him of the needs in our hospital and the local community. After a site visit, he was impressed and offered to recruit two nurses as soon as we could offer suitable accommodation. Their contract would be for two years, and all their expenses would be covered, including a Jeep for their personal use.

The only snag was that we had no suitable accommodation. The offer was too good to let pass, so immediately, I got to work. With no one else available, I became the architect, contractor, and building supervisor for the construction of a simple two-bedroom staff house for the nurses, Elizabeth and Marike. They fit in beautifully. Elizabeth joined the mobile unit, and Marike was willing to be a staff nurse in the hospital.

On another of my infrequent trips to Nairobi, I paid a visit to the headquarters of AMREF (African Medical Service for Research and Education Foundation) Flying Doctor Service to meet with the director and one of the founders, Dr. Michael Woods. I was aware that this service was a great boon to hospitals in the remote areas of East Africa; in fact, they were already extending their services to our neighbors in the desert of Turkana. After I made my case and it was obvious he was amenable, I hastily returned to base to initiate the gigantic task of planning and constructing an airstrip.

This was definitely a job for Father Leo. There were many obstacles to its accomplishment: finding a sufficiently extensive area of level ground in our deep-set valley; getting the local wazee (elders) to agree to the allocation of the land; getting the necessary funds to start construction; and getting the bulldozer and machinery to prepare the proposed strip. I believe the runway had to be a minimum of around five thousand feet. In order to get sufficient length, they had to place a bridge over a stream, and they were still working on the project when Dr. Woods was in the air.

Dr. Woods, an experienced pilot, decided he would make the initial flight, seeing that the approaching terrain was daunting, if not dangerous. At about five o'clock in the afternoon, we heard the drone of the plane as it appeared over the summit of the tallest mountain. Our anticipation and excitement were tempered by breath-stopping anxiety as we observed the rapid descent of the Cessna 402 until it touched down on our newly minted runway.

Once the plane came to a stop and the engine was turned off, the cheers of those on the sidelines—assembled hospital staff and patients; schoolchildren, both boys and girls; and all the locals we could muster, including women in their ceremonial dress and headgear—were deafening and echoed back to us from the surrounding hills. We had achieved a milestone that only dreams were made of.

While the men in the welcoming crowd might have been familiar with airplanes and how they functioned, some of the local women could not believe their eyes that a manmade bird could fly and that a human person could emerge from the open door. In Kiswahili, the word for "airplane" is the same as for "bird," *ndege*, so these women were not the first to see the connection with live birds.

They sought out Father Leo to explain the parts of this amazing bird. They could easily recognize the tail, wings, and body, but then came the question "Where is the head?" It took some explaining to convince them that it didn't have a head, as real birds had, but that there were parts inside the plane that worked like an automobile engine, which was able to make it fly. They were mesmerized. They had never seen a bird like this one.

Dr. Woods stayed overnight in our guesthouse, and the next morning, he performed a few easy surgeries before taking off for Nairobi. Having proved we had a safe place to land and adequate medical facilities, we were approved to be on the regular monthly schedule of visits from the Flying Doctors Service.

The way the routine visits worked was for a team consisting of a surgeon, an operating room nurse, and an anesthetist, with their full complement of instruments and medical apparatuses, to touch down early in the morning, take over the OR, and perform major surgeries on patients we had identified. As soon as they completed the list, they headed for the airstrip, and they were back in Nairobi in a few hours. We were left with the postoperative care of these patients.

This all sounds exotic, but in our remote area and with the mind-set of the locals, it wasn't easy. It was often difficult to convince patients that they needed surgery and more difficult to ensure that they returned for the procedure as scheduled. Even if they were already in house, at the last minute, occasionally they would refuse or abscond.

I recall a lady who had a huge goiter that was causing swallowing and breathing problems who agreed to have a thyroidectomy. The team successfully removed the goiter, but by the next morning, she had absconded, sutures and original dressing in place. We never saw her again.

Another lady, beyond childbearing age, had a uterine fibroid completely filling her abdominal cavity. She agreed to the surgery and was so impressed by the reduced size of her abdomen when she awoke that she got out of bed to dance for joy. One elderly male patient had a large hernia causing his scrotum to reach almost to his knees, and he was most grateful that we made him whole again.

However, most times, developing a list for cold surgery to justify the arrival of the host team was often a scramble and at times embarrassing. The team did not complain; they partially understood.

In between these scheduled surgeries, we had patients requiring urgent intervention beyond my ability to perform. Diagnosing an acute abdomen was particularly challenging. We did not have the necessary laboratory or x-ray facilities to help with the diagnosis.

It takes many hands besides the surgeons to successfully and expeditiously perform surgery beyond the simplest procedure. This assistance I did not have. Besides, the more recently appointed nursing sisters did not have experience to act as anesthetists. I was lucky to have the backup of Finn O'Callaghan in Kitale, who never showed any annoyance if I arrived with a patient requiring urgent surgery, even if he had already spent several hours in the OR.

As a related valuable service, the Flying Doctors Service maintained daily radio contact between isolated stations, such as ours and the main office in Nairobi. We were assigned a time each working day when we could speak with their personnel to request messages to be sent to our sisters' headquarters or order urgent medical supplies or specialist consultations, including a team to come for emergency surgery. If I recall correctly, it was at the hour of midday.

In these days of instant communication, it is nearly impossible to convey the sense of freedom this daily line of communication gave us, even though interference from the high mountains sometimes made transmission difficult. Each time, we transmitted the words "Ortum calling. Over. Can you hear me? Over." Upon hearing the reply of "Roger" from the other end, we knew we were on the air and could talk, listen to any relayed messages, and send our messages. We were no longer isolated—Ortum was on the map.

Only once did I personally land on our airstrip, and it was an unforgettable experience. With help from the United States, the Catholic Church sponsored an air service to serve the personnel and needs of the newly opened mission in the remote Turkana desert. This time, I found myself in Kitale without a means of getting back to Ortum. By some good fortune, Brother Mike, an American who piloted the church plane, was at base and eager to try his skills at landing on the Ortum airstrip. It had developed a reputation as an especially challenging one. I was game to accept his offer to pilot me back to base.

All was well until we neared home territory. Mike seemed to be confused as to his whereabouts. I suddenly recognized the buildings of the mission complex almost directly beneath us and pointed them out to the pilot. Rather than circling around, he made a dive for the airstrip. We dropped from the skies, hit the strip with a mighty bump, and came to a halt just before we reached the end of the runway. Mike got the greatest rush of adrenaline out of the experience, I was petrified.

## ONCE A THIEF ...

Not long after the initiation of the Flying Doctor Service, we needed to contact them for an emergency visit. We encountered the patient when we were halfway to Lomut for a routine clinic visit. A middle-aged man with a green hospital towel tied around his neck was sitting stiffly in the seat next to the driver of a Land Rover coming from the government health center in Sigor. They were on their way to our hospital in an effort to save the patient's life.

It seemed that Njoroke, a Kikuyu living in the upper highlands near Kitale, had been dealing in wild animal skins with the local watu, all hush-hush and illegal. He apparently owed money to some of them for previous purchases. When he wasn't producing the cash, feeling they had been cheated, the locals decided this guy needed to pay in the best or worst way they knew. The end of the encounter was that he had the side of his neck slashed with a machete, and he was left for dead. This all happened way up in the mountains, far removed from the nearest health facility in Sigor.

Because the patient had the resourcefulness to use his shirt as a tourniquet to stop the massive bleeding from the left side of his neck, he survived the cutting. Remarkably, he was able to walk quite a distance down the mountain until he reached the Sigor health center. On arrival, he was not only exhausted but also close to death from blood loss. The clinical officer in Sigor immediately realized this case was beyond his expertise, left the tourniquet in place, covered the whole area with the green surgical towel, and sent him off in the Land Rover to seek my intervention.

A rapid assessment made it clear that this case was also beyond my capability. After a consultation with the Flying Doctor Service, they offered to send a surgical team the next day if we could keep the patient alive overnight. With the help of intravenous fluids and a unit of blood donated by Dominic, our laboratory technician, the patient made it through the night and was ready for the operating room by the time the crew arrived.

It so happened that this was the first rural visit for a newly arrived surgeon from the United States. To add to the oddity of the situation, he arrived on crutches, as he had recently fractured his ankle.

Only after the patient was anesthetized did the surgeon remove the green hospital towel to reveal a gaping wound in the left side of the neck. Luckily, there was no rush of fresh bleeding. The surgeon proceeded to explore and found the laceration was within a hair's breadth of the carotid artery. Although the jugular veins had been severed, the large nerves in that area of the neck were intact. He was one lucky man.

The surgeon complained a lot while performing the surgery, perhaps because of his own anxiety or lack of familiarity with the conditions under which we worked in the bush. At one stage, his assistant nurse responded to his complaints by reminding him that this was the way it was in a rural hospital and that he was not working in a modern OR, as in the United States.

After a few more comments, my patience ran out, and I reacted with "Doctor, I could have taken care of this case myself." He quickly retorted, "Oh no you couldn't, especially if the carotid artery started to spout." Of course, he was right; that was my fear from the beginning. Alone, I could not have dealt with that emergency. In the end, we parted amicably and with a few complimentary comments from him.

We all say things under duress that we regret afterwards. I

can imagine that the two overhead fluorescent bars of an operating light did not award the correct focus; there was no electric cautery to tie off bleeding vessels; and the suction machine, under the power of our low-wattage generator, was temperamental at best. I am sure that standing on his fractured ankle did not help either. Let's hope that with more orientation, this good man settled in and was able to contribute his surgical expertise where it was most needed.

The patient did remarkably well post surgery. Just before we were ready to discharge him, we discovered that he had already gone AMA (against medical advice) without paying anything toward his considerable medical bill. We were aware that he was not a poor man, and we were especially upset that after all we had done to save his life, he had left without a word of appreciation. Because it was well beyond our capability to locate him, we turned to the local chief and requested that he try to find the patient.

About two months later, while I was conducting an outpatient clinic in Chepararia, a local policeman interrupted me. He had the absconded patient in tow. I recognized him immediately. The officer announced that Mr. Njoroke was ready to pay his bill; otherwise, he was going to prison. Before the patient presented the cash, he said he had a complaint.

Pointing to the well-healed scar, he proclaimed, "You did a poor job. You left a rope in my neck." He was referring to the protruding end of a piece of absorbable catgut used as a suture to close his wound. I was incensed and gave him a good piece of my mind. I felt vindicated. Then out of his pocket came the large sum of forty shillings, which nowhere near covered the cost of his care.

I hasten to qualify that this was an unusual case. I have the best memories of patients professing their extreme gratitude for the care we provided. Even if we were unable to save a patient's life, the relatives were always appreciative of our efforts.

In spite of their appreciation the locals did not really understand why they should have to pay for our services. In their minds, we were wealthy people who could more than afford the cost of their care. Even those who had the means to cover their hospital bills commonly absconded in the dark of night, often taking the linens off the bed as a souvenir. It was not unusual for us to meet men out in the bush with kerchiefs around their necks made from our easily recognizable washable baby diapers—the overall teddy bear pattern on the bright green cotton material gave the game away.

As we struggled to keep the hospital going financially, we eventually came up with the idea of charging a patient or his or her family a flat fee of ten shillings before an admission. There were no other charges, regardless of how much an individual's care cost. It wasn't a pleasant task to ask, or sometimes cajole, relatives of a patient or a child to produce the cash.

In order to avoid paying even this modest sum, often, a husband or father would say he had no money to pay for an admission. At the same time, one could easily spy the knot on one corner of his blanket. When this was pointed out to him, with a smile, he would produce the ten-shilling note.

It was not unusual for families to bring a goat in tow with the sick patient. In that case, we would send them over to the local butcher to sell the animal and bring back the proceeds. It was all heart-wrenching, and we longed to be able to dispense with this odious dimension of the admission process.

Another part of the admission process for women was to get them to remove all of their necklaces and give them a shower for probably the first time in their lives. Later, after much discussion, it became the practice to give each woman being admitted a short haircut. This was necessary to solve the problem of the stubborn stains on the bed linens. Amazingly, there were no objections either from the patients or the local elders.

As we made these improvements and established programs, including the busier maternity services, we decided it was time to try to reach our ultimate goal of starting a nurse training school. To initiate this, we had to be approved by the Kenya Nursing Counsel. After my meeting in Nairobi with the chief nursing officer in the Ministry of Health, she was receptive to consider our case but first had to make a site visit.

This good lady had grown up in Central Province, perhaps in a township, so it was an eye-opener for her to leave Kitale, descend the escarpment, and travel another forty miles on our stony, dusty road to the destination. Both she and her retinue of advisers were vocal in their impressions of the trip, and none of their feedback was positive. They were surprised to see our facilities and the uphill work we were doing in providing health care in that deprived area. They were impressed and recognized the dearth of nurse training facilities in the northern part of the country. They also saw that there were Pokot young women sufficiently educated to be the nucleus of this program.

After their return to headquarters, we waited and prayed,

somewhat apprehensive about the staff and monetary implications in starting a training school for nurses. But there was no going back at that stage.

Eventually the letter was in the mail; there was rejoicing all around when we learned that we were approved to start an enrolled midwifery training school

I am a bit vague about dates, but I believe our initial intake was in 1970. It was a two-year program. Each student had to have a certificate of primary education (CPE). From the start, we were able to find the approved number of student midwives from the local school, mostly Pokot women. They each had to supervise ten or more deliveries. Sister Philomena, the nursing sister in charge, took on the added task as the first tutor.

## FROM HUMDRUM TO HEART-WRENCHING

When people discover I spent time as a doctor in Africa, they expect to hear many fascinating and heroic stories. While there were some dramatic moments, life in Ortum was mostly uneventful and often frustrating. As I have mentioned, the sense of being trapped in that isolated place, hemmed in by the hairy mountains, was overwhelming at times. Besides the fatigue of being on call 24-7, there was a sense of futility that we seemed to be making little progress in providing for the medical needs of the people. Because our hospital was seen as a last resort after the traditional healer had failed to cure the patient, it was often beyond our abilities to turn the situation around.

One of the greatest frustrations was how we were losing so many infants and children to diarrheal disease. I can still see these little ones arriving in their mothers' arms, eyes sunken to the back of their heads, ribs showing, and skin wrinkled and prune-like, with barely enough strength to breathe. Intravenous fluids could often save them. Our nursing sisters became true experts in accomplishing this by putting the IV through a scalp vein in the child's head. It was heartbreaking when we were able to save a child on the first episode but were not successful on a repeat admission.

There were many factors contributing to our lack of progress, most of them intertwined. The people were not receptive to a monetary economy. Their wealth came from the number of cattle in their herds, so they were reluctant to sell them for cash. The idea brought back bad memories from colonial days, when the British administration would hold auctions at local centers, such as Ortum, and compel the heads of household to sell their cattle to pay taxes. The status quo was also held together by the lack of formal education, the isolation of the district, and treasured traditions that did not contribute to health or longevity.

We prioritized health and hygiene education in an effort to improve outcomes for the youngest children. The Pokot people had neither traditions nor facilities for washing or dealing with human waste in a sanitary way. I saw many a Pokot mother try to bathe her child in the dry riverbed before she presented at the outstation clinic. First, she would dig in the sand of the dry riverbed to get to some water. Then she would take some in her mouth and spit it toward her offspring like a hose. At least she was responding, even if not convinced, to some of our health education.

On other occasions, if we challenged a mother because her child's face was covered in flies, her answer invariably was that she had no soap. This was true and brought home the reality that health education would be ineffective without improvement in the socioeconomic status of the population.

Recently, through the power of Google, I was made aware of a project carried out some ten years after my sojourn in West Pokot.

The research, part of a philosophy PhD thesis, entitled "The Management of Illness in an East African Society: A Study of Choice and Constraint in Health Care among the Pokot," written by David C. Nyamwaya of Fitzwilliam College, Cambridge, in 1982, gives eye-opening glimpses into the beliefs and practices regarding health and illness of the Pokot. It also makes me acutely aware of how little understanding we had of those beliefs and how lacking we were in addressing them with our Western-style approach.

A few examples may bear this out:

- The birth of a baby is not regarded as an illness but is an important social ceremony in which women play a leading role. Pokot mothers claim that delivery in a hospital deprives them of the company of other women.
- The presence of men during labor is resented.
- A woman should conceive only after the other child has been weaned.

- A woman should stop childbearing when her daughter becomes a mother.
- Infantile diarrhea is caused by the development of so-called false teeth in the gums of the child, usually before the milk teeth appear.
- These false teeth are likened to spirits. They grow in the position where normal canine teeth later grow.
- To prevent false teeth from causing diarrhea, the gums are rubbed with medicines, or alternatively, in a more common practice, they are removed physically by an expert.
- When a child has measles, he or she should not be given an injection.
- The treatment for malaria was to purge and get the patient to vomit.

Yes, we were worlds apart in our actions to address these beliefs and customs. However, I was beginning to see the light and question our status operandi, which will become clear as this saga unfolds.

## FROM BIBLICAL TIMES TO THE MOON

Sometime in the late 1960s, we had a flying visit, literally and figuratively, from high-ranking ecclesiastic representatives of MISEREOR, a nongovernment agency set up by the Catholic bishops of Germany after World War II to financially support needed projects in the developing world. A priori, the agency supported Catholic institutions or missions doing development or medical work in rural areas, such as Ortum.

The delegates expressed a willingness to support an expansion of our facilities. We made them aware of what our priorities were, especially that we needed classrooms for the planned nurse training school and other staff accommodations. The lack of the latter was one of our greatest obstacles to recruiting and keeping qualified staff for the hospital.

While I was taken up with my little world among the Chernagani Hills, my sister Eilish, a nurse midwife, was making her own life-changing decisions. I was still in Zambia, and she had her own private practice of midwifery in Carlow, our hometown, when she started to feel unsettled and wanted to see a bit of the wider world, especially Africa. Knowing that the colonial government gave good packages to expatriates joining the medical services in Zambia, I encouraged her to take a two-year contract. This she did, but by the time she arrived, I had already returned to Kenya.

On the first vacation she had, she made a visit to see me in Kenya and, of course, had to come to West Pokot. She must have accompanied us on one of the mobile clinic visits. There is a photo extinct to record her observing me in action.

When Eilish's second two-year contract was nearing completion, which coincided with my time due for home leave, I received an unexpected letter from her. She made an exciting offer, proposing I travel home with her either sailing around the Cape of South Africa or take a trip to Israel and the Holy Land. She qualified the proposal by stating that we would have a companion on the trip. I held my breath, especially when the next sentence said he wasn't Irish. Orlando was an Italian by birth whom she had met in Zambia, and he was making a proposal of marriage.

To say I was surprised sounds bewildering in these days of mass migration, but for those of us who had grown up in insular Ireland of the forties and fifties, Italy was as far removed as the moon is from the sun. To put it succinctly, there was no such thing as the European Union, and there was no mass intermingling between any of the countries on the mainland of the continent.

As I read Eilish's letter, I could not conceal my surprise and excitement. This was not lost on Mother Juliana, the regional superior, who was visiting and sitting right beside me in the living room. She inquired if I had news to share. After I recounted the contents of the letter, without hesitation, she said, "Of course you cannot turn down a once-in-a-lifetime opportunity to visit the Holy Land; it is actually regarded as a pilgrimage, a spiritual journey that would never otherwise come your way."

*That was easy*, I thought. I didn't have to ruminate on it and pluck up the courage to request one of those outlier permissions not in keeping with the spirit of poverty or available to other members of the community.

Need I add that my choice was to go to the Holy Land? I speedily communicated this to my beloved sister.

In February 1969, Eilish, Orlando, and I met in Nairobi and flew with El Al to Tel Aviv and by coach to Jerusalem, our base, where we were staying in a hostel run by religious sisters. The high security at the airports and elsewhere did not upset us; in fact, it made us feel secure. I was excited to be in that sacred, biblical country.

Even now, it gives me goose bumps—let's call them celestial goose bumps—to recall how awesome it was to have all those places mentioned in the Old and New Testament of the Bible come alive before our eyes. Some of the places, especially in the Old City of Jerusalem, one visited with a degree of skepticism; for example, the Dormition Abbey was supposedly built over the site where Mary fell asleep.

However, for all the places associated with the life and death of Jesus, the positives far outweighed the negatives.

I was completely overcome in the Church of the Nativity in Bethlehem, especially at the Nativity Grotto, the site of the manger where Jesus was born. We approached it on our knees in silence and awe. My silent prayer was broken by the voice of a tour guide. "This is where they laid the baby!" he exclaimed, breaking the spell for me. We had to realize that not only Christians were visiting the historic sites; they were tourist attractions for people of all faiths and even those with none. But for us, in that sacred place, it seemed irreverent.

We felt more comfortable as we traveled north to Nazareth, to the Sea of Galilee, following the footsteps of Jesus into all the places familiar in the Gospels. We even took a trip in a fishing boat, when we experienced an unpredictable storm and were tossed about on the turbulent waters. It was easy to recapture the scene of Jesus rebuking and quieting the stormy waters with His words "Quiet now! Be calm!" and the awe of the disciples as they proclaimed, "Who can this be? Even the wind and sea obey Him" (see Mark 4:35–41 in the Jerusalem Bible).

My visit to the Church of the Holy Sepulcher also had an element of disharmony, like the church itself, divided up as it was by different Christian denominations. To be able to attend Mass at the altar built over the site of the crucifixion was deeply touching.

All in all, the trip was a gift and a spiritual high that I'd never imagined would come my way. I am forever grateful to my sister and brother in law for those unforgettable memories.

From Israel, the plan was for us to fly to Cologne, Germany, where we would part company for a few days. Orlando was taking his fiancée, Eilish, to visit for the first time his home in Villadossola, a suburb of the medieval town of Domodossola, which is beautifully situated in the Italian Alps. It is several miles northwest of Milan, almost on the border with Switzerland.

With the blessing of my superiors, I was traveling to Aachen, the headquarters of MISEREOR, to continue the dialogue on the promise of funding for the necessary expansions in Ortum.

We stayed in a hotel near the famous cathedral, and I was able to attend morning Mass in the gigantic nave. Orlando and Eilish were flying to Milan. I headed to the railway station.

With my third-class ticket in hand as I stood in the station, not only was I concerned that the anticipated train might be going in the wrong direction, but I also was feeling alone and conspicuous in my full black regalia. So when the door of the carriage in front of me opened, I immediately hopped on and sat on the first seat I encountered. There was only one other passenger in the compartment, a middle-aged man. He was dressed in a well-tailored business suit, and while I maintained custody of the eyes, I could see in my peripheral vision that he was somewhat surprised, if disdainful, at my intrusion. When the conductor checked my ticket, he muttered something in German which I did not understand. He then politely asked me in English to vacate the first-class carriage I had unwittingly planked myself in. Sheepishly, I moved to a seat compatible with my ticket. Quite an embarrassment, to say the least.

I made my ten o'clock appointment with the monsignor who was the CEO for MISEREOR. He recalled his visit to Ortum and especially the scary airplane landing with the bishops. Over the time since that first visit, we had been negotiating and relaying our needs by regular mail. Now it was our time to discuss the plans in greater depth.

I had brought with me a dossier of required topographical and other requested data. They were already in the process of drawing up architectural plans. I was excited. I left the meeting with the understanding that not only would they provide the actual money, but also, their organization would take care of everything from nuts to bolts to give us a brand-new, well-equipped hospital using some of the existing buildings. The whole idea was awesome and beyond our hopes and dreams. Mission accomplished!

The meeting must have lasted at least two hours. It was now lunchtime, and as I'd had an early breakfast, I could have done with some food. However, whether Monsignor did not feel it was appropriate to take a fully garbed nun to a restaurant or for whatever reason, no such invitation was forthcoming, so I found my way back alone and hungry to the railway station. On the return ride, I made sure I sat in a third class carriage.

I couldn't for a moment consider assuaging my hunger in a restaurant, and neither was there room service at the hotel. Instead, I snuggled under the down duvet, the continental substitute for blankets, anticipating getting a nap to pass the time until I linked up again with Eilish and Orlando. My attempt to sleep didn't work, so I decided to take the train once more and head to the airport to await their arrival from Milan.

They had only spent one day in Orlando's home territory, but it was enough to get Eilish hooked. She was taken not only by the beauty of the landscape and the sight of Monte Rosa, the highest peak of the Alps on the Italian side, but especially by an almost completed new home that Orlando had built on his vacations from his overseas contracts as an electrical engineer. She was going to make her home there after they were married.

It was well into the evening when their plane arrived, and they were surprised to find me waiting at the gate to greet them. We ate at the airport that night, and food had never tasted so good. I was starving.

The next morning, the three of us traveled to Dublin, where we parted company; Eilish and Orlando were going to Carlow to meet our parents, and I was going to the Holy Rosary base for returned missionaries in Raheny, not far from the airport.

In spite of the awe and inspiration I felt during my Holy Land visit, I do not think I shared my experience with many sisters in the community. Extraordinary trips like that, no matter who paid for them, were not encouraged and best kept quiet.

Eilish and Orlando set the date for their wedding for July of that year. It would take place in a country village near Clonmel, Co Tipperary. I was thrilled that I not only would be able to attend but also could help with the preparations. Among other changes happening in our communities, the congregation was getting more family friendly than we had been in 1958, when my other two sisters got married, as I discussed earlier.

Not long after the wedding, I attended a gathering at the home of my sister Breed in Clonmel to see remarkable images from the moon as Neil Armstrong and Buzz Aldrin took their first historic steps on its surface. Although Americans saw the Apollo 11 mission through the lens of national pride, millions of other people around the world were glued to television sets too and viewed the unprecedented moment as an accomplishment for all humanity.

There on the floor in front of the television screen, I couldn't take my eyes off Ursula, aged eight, and Dervla, aged six, as they continued to play their board game, oblivious of what we were whispering and cheering about. While we were so in awe of that momentous occasion, Marita, aged ten, was able to appreciate that the myth of the man in the moon was about to be defunct.

The situation sticks in my memory not so much for the wonder of it all but for what happened on my return to Kenya and Ortum shortly thereafter.

I was admitting a new patient, asking the usual questions with the help of an interpreter. Suddenly, she looked up at the ceiling, where the electric light bulb was ensconced in a spherical shade. She asked the nurse in kPokot, "Is that the moon?"

The contrast between the two worlds couldn't have been more pronounced.

## MY AHA MOMENT

Later in the autumn of 1969 even though I returned to Ortum refreshed and with renewed vigor, I continued to grapple with the question as to whether our hospital-based approach was the right one to answer to the health needs of the people that we served. I realized I was not alone in my doubts when I discovered a recently published book that formulated a completely new approach to health care in the developing world.

*Medical Care in Developing Countries, a Symposium from Makere* edited by Maurice King and published by Oxford University Press in 1966, gave me food for thought and validated my experiences and my thinking. My approach to medical care would never be the same again.

I never could have guessed it at the time, but this aha moment was to be a life changer in a way I could not have predicted.

Twelve groups of axioms on medical care were set forth, all of them logical but in the climate of the time, revolutionary. It is not within the confines of this treatise to record them all. Some can be summarized as follows:

- Developing nations and colonies of the European powers—which housed the majority of the world's population—required radically different methods of healthcare delivery.

- Those of us engaged in medical work in developing countries needed to devise a model that could provide the greatest health benefits to the largest number of people at the least cost while using the lowest level of staff capable of doing it.
- Rather than having just one hospital, probably with only one doctor, cover vast areas with people clustered in towns and villages far away from that one facility, it proposed "taking services to the people" through freestanding clinics (which he called health centers) that "should be the fundamental units providing both preventative and curative care."
- Because of the shortage of doctors, health centers would be staffed by a trained medical assistant and a small staff. Depending on the patient's condition, he or she could be referred to facilities up the chain that could provide a higher level of medical care. Only if surgery or inpatient hospitalization was required would a fully trained doctor and hospital be needed. To get preventive care information and education in critical areas, such as hygiene, to small villages, this comprehensive system could enlist local midwives or even traditional healers and train them to change their practices and become community advocates for modern medicine.

I read, reread, and digested the treatise. I was smitten and convinced that it made so much sense and answered to the reality of the situation in West Pokot.

I also realized that I was beginning to burn out from the

uphill battle we were waging and was deeply discouraged by the futility of many of our efforts. We were really not getting through to the majority of the people who needed us. I longed to be free to develop a series of maternal and child welfare clinics according to the proposed health center model. However, I felt I was not adequately prepared from an educational standpoint to launch into that new arena of health care.

While I was going through this revolutionary period of my thinking, the priest representative of the bishop asked me to be an adviser for medical affairs for the diocese. There were some issues of policy that needed attention.

Invariably, when a new mission opened in a more remote area of the diocese, one of the first requests from the local communities would be for the church to build and maintain a hospital. The task of the medical secretary was to recommend to the bishop the feasibility of such requests. It was easy to convince Father Joe that building hospitals in all these places neither fit in with the policy of the Ministry of Health nor was within the constraints of diocesan personnel and finances. It was not so easy to convince the priest in charge of such stations, who invariably was under pressure not only from the people but also from the local politicians.

In order to address these concerns, it was decided that we should call a meeting of the involved priests and any others who were interested. I had already shared with Father Joe the results of my new discoveries and how I felt we should attempt to implement a new approach to our medical work based on the twelve axioms as explained above. I had also made him aware that I was hoping to implement some of this new approach from our base in Ortum and was working on a plan to extricate myself from inpatient care to lead a team pioneering this project.

The meeting with the clergy went well. I succinctly put forth a new approach à la King's axioms and was able to use the uphill battle we had in maintaining the hospital in Ortum as an example of, if not the wrong approach, then at least the more difficult one. As the majority of the audience were younger men, some of them on their first mission assignment, they were open to new ideas, and it was not difficult for them to be convinced that this approach made sense. They indicated that they would be on board if we should implement any of these new ideas in their areas.

The contemplated plan was that I would be based in Ortum; another doctor would be recruited who would do most of the inpatient care at the hospital; I would take my share of night calls and stand in on the weekends and whenever the other doctor needed to get away; and we would start the new approach in the more responsive locales on our mobile-unit schedule. In each of these areas, we would initially develop well-run mother-child health clinics with the local community being involved from the get-go.

As they say, the devil is in the details. I was not ready to think any further outside the box—that is, until I got some more training and consultations with experts in that field. I had communicated my dreams and plans as they evolved, not only with my Holy Rosary community both local and regional but also with, the diocesan medical secretary. He understood and seemed enthusiastic about the suggestion that as we implemented a viable program in the underserved areas around

Ortum, we could expand it into other deserving areas in the diocese, all with the approval of the bishop, the local clergy, and the local community.

With the wisdom that comes with age, I can see the worst faux pas I made was not to commit any of this to writing and give copies to everyone concerned. This line of action seems basic to me now, but in my naïveté, it did not appear necessary at the time.

There were other things going on at home and abroad during those turbulent times. In response to directives of Vatican II mandating that religious communities make themselves more relevant to the church in the modern world, we Holy Rosary Sisters were responding to the call for modernization.

We were transitioning from an authoritarian form of government to a more democratic one. It was no longer only the mother superior who defined the will of God for us. That will was meant to be discerned after prayer and dialogue in community, even in the most basic communities of two or three, as was ours in Ortum.

However, the reality did not always live up to the ideal. Speaking for myself, I found some of the new approach irksome, and as we were not used to confrontation in the prescribed community forums, there was a lot of tension, which wasn't pleasant and became magnified in our isolated, small community.

Amidst all the changes of personnel among the Holy Rosaries, Father Leo continued to be a constant presence. His understanding of the Pokot people and their traditions, aspirations, and taboos helped us make decisions that were acceptable to them and would advance their overall welfare. He used every means possible at meetings and during his church sermons to proclaim the benefits to be derived from attendance at the hospital or mobile-unit clinics. He was always there to encourage us but also never slow to point out when we had not acted in the spirit of faith and justice.

While I still had not mastered the Pokot language, I had picked up a few words necessary to make connection with patients in the hospital. On morning rounds, when a mother would say, *"Wete kwaa"* (I want to go home), I knew that she meant action and that she would abscond with her sick child, even if we did not consider him or her well enough for discharge. So reluctantly we would discharge her admonishing her to continue treatment with the prescribed medications. How often I wished I had been blessed with the gift of tongues so that I could communicate better with my patients and their relatives.

When it came to church services, the language was slowly transitioning from the Latin to the vernacular. That meant Father Leo had his work cut out for him to translate the rituals of the Masses, and sacraments into kPokot. The Latin- and English-style hymns were being replaced by ones in the Pokot language incorporating them into their own melodic tunes,

To attend Sunday Mass in the church and hear the congregation pour forth their hearts and souls in song and, at times, even in dance before their *Tororot* (kPokot for "God") was thrilling and worth the moments of patience needed when we had to listen to Father deliver his homily in the vernacular, not a word of which we understood.

It must have been satisfying to Father Leo as the years moved on to see more and more local people request to accept the faith of the Catholic Church, including both men and women, some of whom had never been to school. I still recall with joy the day that five or six middle-aged Pokot women, dressed in their native costumes, were baptized and officially received as members of the church. I never thought that day would come, especially when they did not have to wear the usual Western-style white baptismal dress.

Being attuned to Father Leo's deep spirituality and prayerful desire to spread the gospel message, combined with his pioneering spirit, it was not surprising that in the early seventies he began to set his eyes on underserved areas in which to pitch his tent. Father Michael Dillon, a newly ordained priest was willing to replace him in Ortum and had already started learning the Pokot language.

One day in the spring of 1972, Father Leo announced the decision he had made in consultation and with the blessing of the bishop: he was leaving Ortum to start a new mission some twenty miles away in Sigor, the government sub-headquarters, a fertile valley that could only be reached after going through the Marich Pass. While I knew I would miss his presence, I also knew it was a needed move; there would be more opportunity to serve the people of the lower regions of the valley, including Lomut.

Sometime after he had taken up residence I visited the site to find he was domiciled in a small one-bedroom prefab building with no running water or electricity. Furnishings were at a minimum, a bed, a table and a chair. The tiny windows were curtainless. Inside, the heat and the air was stifling.

I was feeling sorry for him in such spartan surroundings but he would have none of it. He was too engrossed in the details of building a church, schools for girls and boys and earning the goodwill of the local community.

Having experienced the humble beginnings of this mission center it explains how during my visit in 2013, I got so excited to come upon the luxury coach transporting Pokot high school girls to Kitale and emblazoned on the side of the bus in large letters *Fr. Staples Girls Sec.School.* I could never have envisaged such a spectacle.

I am not sure of my dates for this experience. It was probably late 1970. I only know that Sister Rosa was still the nursing sister in charge. It was a Saturday afternoon; the energy had been completely sucked out of us after the busy week and the overwhelming torrid atmosphere. We were on our way up to the convent to get a much-need siesta. We saw a Volkswagen Beetle parked outside our front door. We turned to each other and let out a few sighs.

Mustering our best smiles, we welcomed our guests, a priest whom we knew from near Kisumu on Lake Victoria and a lady whom we did not know. She was introduced as Dr. Nora Moriarty. I couldn't believe my eyes or my ears—she was a classmate of mine from medical school in Dublin.

She was completing a tour of duty at a mission hospital in Kaplong in western Kenya. Her aunt was the superior of a congregation of sisters who'd established that hospital. The latter had prevailed on Nora to give two years of voluntary service to this hospital. Before she went back to the United Kingdom, she wanted to see what life in the real bush was like, and our priest friend had chosen our mission for this experience.

Nora must have recognized that I needed some r and r (rest and recuperation) so she kindly offered to cover for me while I took some time off. So instead of heading off to Mombasa for an oceanic vacation, I was able to arrange to take a crash course in Kiswahili near the town of Moshi in Tanzania. I had the pleasure of a boat cruise on Lake Victoria and then an overnight train ride to my destination: a bare-bones mission set up under the tutelage of a well-seasoned and strict teacher, Father Van der Peet.

For one month, I struggled to learn classic Swahili as only the people of Tanzania speak it and to try to forget the kitchen phrases and poor grammar I had picked up over the years, in Kenya. But my ability to learn languages was limited, and I had many frustrating moments during my stay there. I had undertaken this course in preparation for my entry into the community health arena when it would be so important to be able to communicate with the community in their language. Of course, in retrospect, I realize it would have been more appropriate to learn kPokot; however, except under the tutelage of Father Leo, there was no easy way to learn that language.

Into this whole mix of upheavals came the reality that I was due to take a medical sabbatical, which was recommended for all of us doctors. I began considering my options.

After some research, I applied to and was accepted into a six-month course in maternal and child health at the University of Liverpool Medical School in England. It seemed that all plans were going well, until I received a letter from regional headquarters advising me that there was no replacement available to allow me to proceed. The sister doctor who'd been asked to replace me for the duration of the course was unable or unwilling to come. I was devastated, shed a few tears, and resigned myself to carrying on. There was no other choice. I could not leave the hospital without a resident doctor.

I still had my heart and mind set on moving into the community health field, and my odds of accomplishing that goal seemed dim at best. Then there was hope!

Toward the end of May 1973, I was in Nairobi and shared some of my frustrations with Sister Doctor Breed, who was now medical consultant to the National Conference of Catholic Bishops. In that capacity, she had attended a meeting where she encountered Dr. William Reinke, an associate professor at the Johns Hopkins School of Public Health in Baltimore, Maryland. The two discussed Johns Hopkins' program in international health, which they felt was appropriate for seasoned medical personnel who planned to move into the public health field, as I did. I even think Breed mentioned to him that she knew someone who might be interested.

My first reaction was that the idea of my studying in the United States at the prestigious Johns Hopkins School of Public Health was beyond the realm of possibility. First of all, I thought it was unlikely that someone like me, who had been practicing medicine in the bush for twelve years, would be accepted into the program. Even if I was, I had no source of funding for such an adventure. Besides tuition, I needed accommodation. I could not afford to stay in my own apartment, and there was no convent of the Holy Rosary Sisters in Baltimore. Finally, regional headquarters had already advised me that it was my responsibility to find a doctor willing to replace me for such a long absence. I have to admit that I took umbrage at the suggestion that I find my own replacement and I didn't know how to take it. Could nobody see that I was burning out and needed a break?

## THE IMPOSSIBLE BECOMES POSSIBLE

Despite my ambiguity, I decided to send a letter of application to the Johns Hopkins School of Public Health. It was now June, and I was hoping to be accepted for the master's program starting in early September. The idea was so far-fetched that it would almost require a miracle to become reality, but as sure as God made little green apples, big and little miracles do occur.

Within days of my mailing my application, a young man with a knapsack on his back arrived at the hospital compound. It was not unusual for a solitary young man to arrive unannounced at our mission. Remember, we had no telephone service or Internet, and neither was there public transport in or out of our area. Somehow, word got around among these young adventurers that they could do the rounds and experience life in the raw before they settled to a boring lifestyle in their own country. From Kitale they would descend the escarpment by foot or, if lucky, by thumbing a lift; trek though the valley; and then ascend the escarpment again, witnessing the most fabulous views of the Rift Valley through Marakwet back to Eldoret.

We usually paid little attention to these passerbys but this guy was different. He was a recently graduated medical doctor named Serge Tettamanti from Switzerland. He was the first doctor who had come our way in that manner.

His story was that he had recently completed his training in family medicine, and before he settled down to practice in his hometown and country, he wanted to experience how medicine was practiced in the bush or the rural areas of a country like Kenya. He sounded sincere and interested. I offered him hospitality and was willing to have him shadow me on daily rounds of the inpatients and assist in any procedures I was performing. He was in the process of getting a license to practice medicine in Kenya, but it had not yet come through. His English was perfect. He fit in beautifully.

Serge and I were working well together. From my perspective, it was wonderful to be able to discuss a patient's diagnosis and treatment with a colleague.

In July, my eagerly anticipated letter arrived. I had been accepted for the course leading to a master's in public health at Johns Hopkins, starting the first week in September, barely eight weeks from then.

Not confident of a favorable reply, I decided to ask Dr. Serge if he would consider holding down the fort for me while I went to Baltimore for ten months. Without hesitation, he said he was willing and would be able to get funding from sources in his own country to cover his expenses. He so much agreed with the plans I had to enter the community health field that he was prepared to stay for two years so that the program could get going.

I was ecstatic and started making plans for my departure, even though I had not yet found accommodations near Baltimore. I took a leap of faith that a solution to that problem would come in due course.

The regional council of the Holy Rosary was fully aware of my long-range plans for working in West Pokot after I earned my master's degree. I had their approval and blessing. However, despite my many entreaties to the diocesan medical secretary, Bishop John had not been apprised of my plans to transition into community medicine based in Ortum with plans for expansion if feasible.

On passing through Eldoret on the way to Nairobi International Airport and to home, as was our custom, I called to the bishop's house to pay my respects to His Excellency. Before I was ushered into his presence, I asked Father Joe, who lived with the bishop, if he had already apprised him of my plans. When his reply was negative, I suggested that I be up front and discuss them. Joe was adamant that it was better not to raise the subject and said that when there was an opportune moment, he would speak with the bishop; he was confident it would all work out well. I am a straight shooter, and I must admit that I did not feel completely okay with that arrangement or completely at ease as Bishop John bade me farewell, gave me his blessing and hoped I would return in good health and with renewed energy to Ortum.

I went from Kenya to Killeshandra to spend a few relaxing weeks in the good country air of my native land and to complete the requirement of a yearly retreat, a time of peace and quiet. My discussions with the sister on the council who represented medical work went well. Sister Margaret thought it was a good idea and saw the need to focus more on community and preventive medicine, especially in the territory of West Pokot. There seemed to be no doubt that I would be returning there at the completion of the course. The congregation, although financially stretched, was prepared to cover my tuition costs but was hoping I might be able to supplement the expenses from other sources.

The solution to the last piece of the puzzle—where I would live while studying in Baltimore—came from an unexpected source. One day, while I was driving through County Wicklow with my sister and my parents, we took a detour and visited the home base of the St. Patrick Fathers in Kiltegan. There I met the superior general at the time, the late Father Peter O'Reilly, whom I had previously met when he visited Ortum. On learning of my plans and that I still had not found a place to stay in Baltimore, he graciously informed me that his biological sister was the superior of a Franciscan convent in that city, and he gave me her address to contact her. Time was of the essence, so I did not hesitate to write to her.

Her reply was an answer to a prayer beyond my hopes and dreams. She assured me that I was welcome to stay at the convent for the duration of my course and that I would not be expected to pay for my lodging. The Franciscan Sisters considered their hospitality as their contribution to the aid of the missions in the developing world. I greatly appreciated the magnanimity of the offer.

CHAPTER 10

# GREAT ACCOMPLISHMENT, GREAT HEARTACHE

In August 1972, I arrived at New York's Kennedy Airport. It was my second visit to the New York area after a brief stop some years earlier, so it wasn't too much of a culture shock. I visited with my sister Bernadette; her husband, Gerry; and their three children in Bayside, Queens, officially part of the city of New York but suburban in character.

By that point, we were well beyond Vatican II, with most orders of nuns reviewing the relevance of their religious garb as part of the *aggiornamento* (renewal) mandated by the council. While most of us welcomed the modernization of our habits, with even some of our hair appearing, we were committed to the symbolism of a distinct uniform. Many religious, especially in the United States, were completely abandoning their religious garb in favor of street clothes. A majority of us, myself included, were proud to wear a modified habit to proclaim to the world that we were set apart as vowed religious women. Especially important was to wear the veil as a symbol of our vow of celibacy.

While I had worn secular garb in medical school in the 1950s, as mandated by the archbishop, the clothes were not of my choosing, and fashion was not an issue. I was happy to have left those days behind, but as I was now about to enter the medical field again in a US city, and not familiar with the environment I would be in, I was in quite a quandary over my wardrobe. Bernadette was excited about helping me put together a trousseau of clothes for my new adventure, but she became frustrated as I vacillated between the decision to attend the course in religious garb or don regular street clothes.

In the end, I arrived at my new abode with two separate lines of clothing! At the Franciscan Sisters' convent in northeast Baltimore, I quickly assessed that some members of the community were not as progressive in their thinking as I was, so I needed to tread lightly. My hosts felt strongly that I should wear my habit, including the veil, both as symbolism and for my own safety in the inner-city area, where the school of public health was located.

The convent itself was huge. It had been an orphanage before the idea of warehousing children in such facilities was disbanded in favor of smaller group homes or foster care. It was also the motherhouse and a place of retirement for members of the Franciscan Sisters congregation. My room was among a group of mostly retired sisters. Many of them had come from

Ireland several years previously and had never been home since the day they'd left our shores.

The walls between the rooms were far from soundproof, meaning they were not conducive to late-night study or the tap-tap of my typewriter when I was trying to fulfill written assignments. On the corridor were the shared community bathrooms. It was my first experience with that kind of setup. The lack of privacy was difficult to get used to, but I had to remind myself that I was a nonpaying guest.

The day after Labor Day, Sister Cecelia drove me to the front door of the Johns Hopkins School of Public Health (now the Johns Hopkins Bloomberg School of Public Health), which was across the street from the Johns Hopkins Hospital in the harbor area of Baltimore. I was wearing my full religious outfit. I was joining the department of international health under the leadership of Professor Carl E. Taylor, MD, DrPH.

I soon found out that commuting to and from the campus by public transport would entail a bus ride to the Homewood campus, where I could pick up another bus to the school of public health. It involved quite a bit of walking and was time consuming. With the encouragement of the welcoming committee at the school, I posted a notice to see if a fellow student would be interested in sharing rides.

Shortly thereafter, I met a tall, elegant blonde lady who introduced herself as Lillian, She said she had read my notice. She jovially shared that she thought she had bid farewell to the nuns several years beforehand, but an inner voice told her that she should offer me a ride, especially since she passed by the gate of the convent each day. Thus, I had secured my ride to school. It turned out that our schedules for the day did not coincide. We agreed that she would pick me up at the gate each morning, but I would have to find my own way back after classes ended. Nonetheless, I was thrilled with my good fortune.

It did not take long for Lillian and me to become buddies. She admitted that her hesitation in responding to my posting was because she had been a Maryknoll Missionary Sister before deciding that the lifestyle was not for her. She was now pursuing a Ph.D in maternal and child health after ministering for several years as a nurse in Peru. As we got to know each other, she challenged me on some of the tenets I held. She probed to find out why I found it important to proclaim that I was a religious by wearing the veil and other symbols of my commitment. I didn't have any reasonable answers.

My habit was a simple, none-too-shapely dark blue one-piece dress with white trimmings and a matching veil showing a few inches of hair in front. In spite of its modernity as far as I was concerned, it still made me stick out like a sore thumb in the sea of mostly male students who filled the lecture halls. A majority of the master's candidates in the department of international health were from third-world countries, many sponsored by their government health services. Wrestling with my own innate shyness and hesitating to be anything but an exemplary student, I rarely, if ever, spoke to any of them.

If I had received a call that I was needed in West Pokot during those first few weeks in that strange place—which involved dealing with biostatistics, epidemiology, the use of computers for the first time, and more—I admit that I would have eagerly boarded the first plane back.

The first weekend in October, I needed a break and decided to take a bus to Philadelphia to join the members of the Holy Rosary celebrating a special feast. As I entered the full-to-capacity Greyhound bus, I noticed only one unoccupied seat: the last one at the back. I could feel all eyes upon me as I made my way toward it.

The empty seat was on the aisle, and I asked the male occupant at the window to please remove the books he had placed on the seat so that I could sit down. To my embarrassment, he responded that he did not want a nun sitting beside him—although his exact words were not so nice and were peppered with choice expletives. The eyes of all occupants were now fixed on the commotion in the back of the bus. Reluctantly, the man moved his books. I opened one of my textbooks as soon as I sat down and pretended to read. If anyone had glanced over, he or she would have seen that I had the book upside down! As we sped along the turnpike, my neighbor called out medical jargon from the textbook he was reading to his friends seated in front of him. He was probably trying to impress me.

On arrival in Philadelphia, I was met at the bus terminal by a Holy Rosary Sister, another Sister Cecelia. She already knew me because she had been in charge in our house of studies in Dublin while I was a medical student. I told her of the episode on the bus and how uncomfortable I felt wearing my habit at school.

In contrast to my Franciscan hosts in Baltimore, Sister Cecilia and the other sisters in my own community couldn't understand, especially considering my previous experience as a medical student, why I was so reluctant to don street clothes.

In fact, most of them were already wearing secular clothing. When I returned to Baltimore, my mind was made up: I was going for wardrobe number two. The only question was how to do it diplomatically. I guessed some of the sisters at the Franciscan convent would not understand.

The next day, I went to school in full religious uniform, as usual. That evening, I asked Sister Cecelia to come visit me in my room. With stubborn determination, I made her aware of my decision. I added that it would be effective immediately. Obviously disappointed, she accepted it.

I appeared in chapel the next morning minus the veil but still wearing the drab blue dress. Lillian was impressed that I had the gumption to take action. The following day, I stepped out in what would have been considered ordinary street clothes, although they were on the conservative side so as not to make the transition too obvious.

On the school elevator that day, one of the male students, who, like the others, had never before spoken to me, said, "Hi! I notice that you have taken that thing off your head." Although his words were a bit rude, I felt from that moment onward that the class welcomed me, and I was able to participate freely in the conversations and camaraderie. This lasted to the end of the course.

The program was grueling. Besides the required copious reading material, there were numerous papers to write. I was never a fast typist, so I would have to bang away at those keys far into the night and frequently interrupt the process to deftly use the "write-out" not only to correct the originals but the carbon copies as well. I had no access to a copying machine.

Although I was worried that my late-night use of the Olivetti was disturbing the slumber of my fellow sisters, I really had no option.

Lillian, who lived in the neighborhood, graciously invited me for dinner on the occasional Friday evening, knowing I needed a chance to relax. The hour of my return was invariably around ten o'clock at night. The first few times, the superior general (the highest superior in the order) waited up to open the main door for me when I got back. She wanted to ensure that I had come home safely and that the convent was properly secured for the night. I found this to be an awkward and embarrassing situation.

Eventually, I was able to convince Sister Cecilia, that I would let myself in via the front door and make sure it was securely locked if I were given a key. As soon as I closed the door, I would remove my shoes and climb the creaky steps as quietly as I could. I would then tiptoe along the corridor until I reached my room. I always left my door open prior to going out so that I would not enter another sister's cell by mistake. Unfortunately, the more unobtrusive I tried to be, the more it seemed that something went wrong, like the time a shoe slipped out of my hand and somersaulted down several steps of the oak stairway.

A horrible event occurred in 1993. While it happened twenty years after I domiciled there, it still brings shivers up my spine. That same superior general, Sister MaryAnn Glink, OSF, who stayed up late to ensure I arrived home safely was found murdered, bound, and sexually assaulted inside the convent door one morning after she had gone to investigate why the alarm had sounded in the middle of the night. I read about the tragedy in *Time* magazine and could visualize the whole scenario. So there may have been good reasons for her concern, even during the time of my stay there.

My living situation was obviously compounding the stresses of my school life, but I dared not complain. Adding to the sense of isolation was the fact that I did not have access to a telephone except for the use of the community telephone on Sunday evenings, when the rates were cheaper, and Sister Cecelia would invite me to call my sister Bernadette in New York. I had little communication with the rest of my family other than letters from Mother. Neither do I remember hearing from members of my own community, either in Ireland or Kenya. Luckily, I was too busy to brood over that or to be lonely.

As the term progressed, I needed to study later and later into the evening. Then I learned that one sister had moved to a room in a previously closed wing of the building because her frequent night coughing had disturbed sisters in adjoining rooms. I sheepishly asked Cecelia for another favor—to be moved into the same wing as that sister. After some hesitation, she gave me the okay. My new neighbor, who was much younger and actively teaching, confirmed that I could bang away at the typewriter to my heart's content and that my late working hours were not a problem for her. She and I became fast friends. An added bonus was that I had a large multi-person bathroom to myself.

## UNWELCOME SURPRISE

The master's program proceeded at a fast pace, and it was not easy to keep up. Although I was more comfortable socializing with my classmates, I found it difficult to express my opinions in small group discussions. Some members of the class who had no field experience tended to dominate the conversations. My reality of conditions on the ground in third-world countries often conflicted with the views expressed. My personal adviser tried to get me to overcome this reluctance, assuring me that my contribution would be valuable. Over time, with some effort, I was able to hold my own.

When it came to written tests, even the unfamiliar multiple-choice ones, I did well. After one test, I received a letter from the head of the division of health-care administration congratulating me for being the only one in the class to receive an A. He commented that if I did not agree with that grade, I should call his office!

A critical element of the master's program for all of us in the department of international health was to develop a plan for some area of health services in our respective countries. For many, this was purely an academic exercise. In my case, I fully expected my project would be implemented upon my return to Kenya. This made my work more interesting to the professors, especially Dr. Carl Taylor, than the purely theoretical proposals. He himself was the leader of a maternal child health project in Narangwal, India, and was well aware of the need for such services and the difficulties involved in carrying them out.

My project was titled "Maternal and Child Health Services

for the Kerio-Weiwei Valley." This was to be a community-based primary preventive and curative program specifically focused on maternal and young children's health issues. The Kerio-Weiwei Valley was situated in West Pokot and neighboring Maraquet District, the fertile area past the Marich Pass and before ascending the Elgeyo Escarpment, which formed the eastern boundary of the Rift Valley. It included the market centers of Sigor, Lomut in West Pokot, and Chesegon and Tot in the neighboring Marakwet District. The two rivers, the Weiwei and the Kerio, which flowed north into Lake Turkana, made it a fertile valley and supported a large population of the two tribes, Pokot and Marakwet. Both were Kalenjin in origin, although at times, they were enemies due to cattle thefts between them.

I had chosen that area as our pilot project based mainly on the good response we had with the mobile unit to Lomut, the high density of the local population, and the potential not only for a positive response to our health efforts but also for general social and economic development.

While the details are rusty to my memory at this time, it was based on the development of a series of basic centers where the mobile unit would visit once each week. The community would decide the centers, and there would a harambee effort to construct a small mud-and-wattle clinic where we could examine the patients and especially allow privacy for the examination of pregnant women.

The successful protocol Dr. Taylor and his team had spearheaded with the Narangwal Rural Health Research Project in India would be modified to suit the needs of the local population. As I explained earlier, I would still be based in Ortum;

would use the mobile unit's transport and the staff seconded to the clinic, including nursing students as they got experience in practical field work; and would be able to transport any patients needing inpatient care back to the hospital.

As the project formed a major part of the master's program, I had to approach it scientifically, applying the newly learned tools of biostatics, epidemiology, and sociology, with an extensive literature review, goals and objectives, measurements of success and financial budget, and projections. I spent hours and hours teasing it out in my brain, consulting with teachers, and typing in duplicate on that old Olivetti typewriter. The final write-up made it for the deadline of the middle of April, was well received by the faculty, and earned me an A+.

Getting funding for my project was a worry. I knew I could not rely on local sources to financially support the program, at least in the early stages. In due course I acquired an answer to this concern.

On arrival in Baltimore, I had the chance to become reacquainted with on old friend from my early days in Kenya, Father Patrick Cullen. Like Father Leo, Paddy was one of the St. Patrick's Fathers and he had always been a good friend to us in Ortum. He was now appointed to promotion work for the society, essentially fund-raising for the missions, and was stationed in Camden, New Jersey, just outside of Philadelphia, about two hours' drive away from Baltimore.

I was only a few weeks in Baltimore, still adrift and missing my former familiar territory, when he showed up at the convent, where he was already well known. It lifted my spirits to be able to chat with someone who knew where I had come from and understood the difficult time I had adjusting to my new environment. From then on, Father Paddy took me under his wing, and on more than one occasion, he was kind enough to drive me to New York City to meet my family.

He was just as enthusiastic as I was with my new project for West Pokot, as he'd been one of the first priests to tour the area in 1952. He was aware of the needs of the beneficiaries of the program from his extensive familiarity with the territory, both as diocesan education supervisor and as the vicar in charge of the diocese in the absence of the bishop during Vatican II.

Not only was he available to give me advice, but he also assured me that he most likely could get seed funds for the proposed project. He had been a founding member of an NGO (non-government organization), a consortium of various Christian denominations that were coordinating efforts to request funds from foundations willing to finance projects in the developing world, instead of each group going separately to these agencies. Its name was CODEL (Coordination in Development). I felt positive this would come through.

However, there still were some aspects of the plan that were not confirmed and that had me feeling uneasy, to put it mildly.

This uneasiness was confirmed when, in the final stages of writing up my project, I got disturbing news in a letter. The letter was from Sister Margaret, a member of the Holy Rosary General Council in Ireland, who was deputed to monitor and advise on all medical works of the congregation. She had just completed one such official visit in Kenya. Before she set out on tour, she would have been advised by the regional superior as to future plans for medical personnel such as me. On her rounds, she duly paid a courtesy call on Bishop John in Eldoret, the outcome of which was the content of the letter she wrote to me on her return to Ireland.

She evidently raised the issue with the bishop that on my return after the course in the United States, my plan was to develop community maternal and child health clinics in the surrounding areas of Ortum. With their success and his blessing, I would then oversee the development of these services throughout the diocese.

To her surprise, Margaret found the bishop was unaware of my plan. In her letter, she advised me to clarify the situation, not only with the bishop but also with my own regional council, which was responsible for our local assignments. I'd never anticipated such a situation. I knew I was in trouble.

From the moment I had left Kenya, I'd been worried that the proposed plan for my return had not been clarified with the bishop, and I had written several letters, even in the midst of my studies, to Father Joe, the medical secretary, to clarify the situation. His replies were always to the effect of "Continue on, and I will inform the bishop in due course."

I should clarify here that there was no question that I was planning on being an employee or on the pay roll of the diocese. I would be part of the Holy Rosary community in Ortum. Dr. Tettamanti was doing well in taking care of patients and would be in place for at least another year. All his expenses were paid from his home country of Switzerland.

In retrospect, I often wonder if Father Joe was afraid to tell the bishop, as he may have understood that I was expecting to be an employee and therefore a burden on the diocese. Maybe, but to this day, I do not understand his lack of action. Why could he not have been more open with me? That I will never know. In the meantime, there were consequences.

While I was mulling over what Sister Margaret had told me, I received a letter written personally by the bishop. The gist of it was this: Who did I think I was to make all these arrangements without consulting him? He said I was welcome to come back to work in the hospital in Ortum, but other than that, he had nothing to offer at the diocesan level. It was clear to me that there was a misunderstanding: he thought I was coming back to take care of medical work for the diocese and would probably be a financial burden. In a way, I could empathize with his reaction if he thought I had made all these arrangements behind his back, usurping his authority. Unfortunately, I had no means of an explanation except by a letter, which I sent posthaste.

I was devastated. I needed someone to talk to, as they say in Swahili, *mara moja* (immediately), but there was no one who would understand.

The next day, I turned to Dr. Taylor. He was one of those special people who would put you at ease the minute you entered his office. He saw immediately that I was stressed out, looked me straight in the eyes, and gave me his full attention. He read the bishop's letter. He shared my disappointment but encouraged me to keep up hope that the misunderstanding could be resolved.

I realized there was no point in contacting Father Joe again; neither did I ever hear from him. I felt betrayed.

As I still had papers to write and further classes to attend, I did my best to be optimistic. I had confidence that when I got back to Ireland and especially back to Kenya, all would be well, and I could implement the plan under the umbrella of the hospital in Ortum. We would take it *pole pole* (slowly, slowly), just as we had done with all other decisions regarding the expansion of our services, and keep the bishop informed as needed.

Whether by coincidence or as a foreboding of things to come, one of the associate professors approached me, asking if I would be interested in taking a job with USAID (United States Agency for International Development). While flattered by the offer, I had no hesitation in turning it down. My commitment was 100 percent to my life as a missionary doctor in West Pokot.

By mid-May, after I'd conceived, typed, and submitted my last paper, I had reached the pinnacle of my intellectual and physical endurance. It had been a long time—and eighty credits—since that first Tuesday in September when this greenhorn from the African bush had graced the steps of that august institution. I was ready for graduation, which occurred on May 25, 1973.

It was a bittersweet moment. I was proud to graduate from the Johns Hopkins School of Public Health, a branch of a prestigious US university. My joy was tempered by the chance that the project I had poured myself into during the whole school year would never be implemented. However, positive feelings won the day, as in the presence of my sister Bernadette, my brother Henry, my thirteen-year-old niece Marie, and Father Paddy Cullen, I accepted my degree—master's in public health (MPH) from Dr. Steve Mueller, president of the Johns Hopkins University.

For the occasion, Bernadette, an excellent seamstress, had

fashioned out of a *Vogue* pattern a beautiful, elegant off-white dress that made me feel like a princess. How would I ever go back to the drab dark blue modified habit and veil? That remained to be seen, as my attitude toward religious dress had shifted 180 degrees from the first day I'd set foot in Baltimore.

As Dr. Taylor had suggested, I decided to be optimistic about the future of my MCH project for the Kerio-Weiwei Valley.

One of my happy memories is my appreciation of the late Dr. Carl E. Taylor, MD, DrPH. He had become my mentor and inspiration. He was born into a missionary family in the Indian Himalayas, graduated from Harvard Medical School, worked as a missionary doctor in India, and saw the need to move into the public health and preventive medicine field. He started the department of international health at the Johns Hopkins School of Public Health, the first of its kind in the medical world.

It is a tribute to his goodness and character that this gentle giant kept on working up to one week before his death in February 2010 at the age of ninety-three, having delivered his last lecture, "Case Studies in Primary Health Care," to MPH students at the school of public health.

He will be forever remembered as the primary World Health Organization consultant who prepared the documents in 1978 for the Alma Alta World Conference on Primary Health Care, and he was a key contributor to the Alma Alta Declaration. These ten axioms trace a map as to how the nations of the world should address the basic human right of good health, and they are still cogent today, if not yet universally implemented.

He looked me up some years after I had graduated as he passed through Nairobi, and he treated me to dinner at the hotel where he was staying. It was my introduction to sushi. Our conversation that evening was about what I was up to and not much about his agenda or his achievements. He was a truly great guy.

Let's get back to my itinerary. After the commencement ceremony, the family treated me to dinner at a nice restaurant recommended by Lillian, who also came to celebrate with us. Believe it or not, that was my first time seeing the lights and skyscrapers of downtown Baltimore. I had kept my nose to the grindstone throughout the year, going from convent to school and school to convent, except of course, for my occasional evening escapades to Lillian's apartment.

One special treat I thank Lillian for is a visit to Washington, DC, on a Saturday in May, not only to see the spectacle of the cherry blossoms in bloom but to catch a glimpse of the White House, the Capitol, the Mall, and the Lincoln Memorial. As she said, I couldn't say I had spent a year in that area of the United States without taking in a visit to these monuments to democracy. That was a day to remember and enjoy.

I was sad to say goodbye to Lillian. She had been my lifeline, yet in no way did she try to divert me from my chosen path. Neither of us had any notion of how our lives would enfold. It was several years later before we linked up again under different circumstances, when both of us had some catching up to do and a tale to tell.

The next day, I bade farewell to my hosts. The sisters kindly allowed my family to stay the night in the block of the building where I had set up my abode. I greatly appreciated the gesture. On the way to New York with my family, we stopped off to greet the Holy Rosary Sisters in Villanova. I was happy to spend time with old and some new friends. They were proud of me for surviving the grueling academic year.

In the next few weeks, I was able to spend time with Bernadette's family and also visit my brother Thomas and his family in New Jersey.

It must have been into July before I headed back to Ireland. While I still had hope that my project had a chance of survival, I was anxious. Little could I have guessed how events would unfold.

## WRESTLING WITH DEVASTATION

One sunny afternoon in August 1973, I had an appointment with my regional superior, Sister Felice, in a retreat center on the north side of Dublin to talk about my next assignment and future work in Kenya. The superiors of all the regions had gathered in that spot for their biannual meeting with the MSHR general council, the ultimate decision makers for the congregation.

Having had time to think and pray about the meeting, I came prepared that I could present the case for my return to Ortum as a second doctor who would gradually implement the Kerio-Weiwei project from that base while helping out in the hospital as needed.

After all, I was the one who'd recruited my replacement doctor, and the hospital was not incurring any expenses for his salary or maintenance. I was assured of funds for the project and would not be a burden to the already stretched budget; the work I would do would have the added benefit of increasing the bed occupancy of the hospital and provide field experience for the future community nurse training program. I had all my ducks in a row.

The meeting took place in a corner of a large assembly hall where the group was gathered. Before Sister Felice came to greet me, I noticed she was having a powwow with Sister Maureen, the superior general. Was their conversation about me and my future? I wondered. Somehow, I felt it was.

Even before she greeted me, I could see Sister Felice was nervous. I do not remember which of us opened the conversation regarding my future mission; I only recall that the message was loud and clear. It is seared in my memory.

I was being assigned once again as not only the doctor in charge but also the solo practitioner of Thika Maternity Hospital, a hospital in a busy township where the twenty maternity beds were so in demand that there were often two women to a bed. It had become known, irreverently so, as the Baby Factory. I was replacing Sister Doctor Iris, a specialist in obstetrics, a fellow of the Royal College of Obstetrics and Gynecologists.

In conjunction with my obstetrics practice, I was expected to monitor the activities of one of the sisters in the community. It was an odd assignment, hinted and veiled. As this sister was in the health field, I surmised that she may have had an addiction problem.

That was the last place on God's earth that I'd imagined myself being assigned to. As soon as I recovered my composure,

I voiced my reservations: I did not feel competent and had not had enough experience in obstetrics to accept the onerous position. I reminded her that I had spent the past year, with the full knowledge and blessing of herself and her council, pursuing a different approach to health care.

Was I expected to throw all that hard work and expense to the wind as I spent my days and nights in either the labor unit or the OR? The bottom line was that I realized at that stage of my professional career, I did not have the emotional and psychological makeup for surgical emergencies as were bound to arise in a maternity hospital; there were ethical and even malpractice issues to consider.

I never got around to my spiel as to how I could fit in to the Ortum situation before she lowered the boom: under no circumstances was I going back to West Pokot. What I had learned during my sabbatical was never addressed or acknowledged. She told me that the decision was final and that I should think and pray about it. It was expected that I would be able to return to Kenya and start my new assignment within a few weeks to allow Doctor Iris to go on home leave. If I was unable to accept the assignment, I needed to consult with the superior general.

I was crushed, and for the first time since I'd entered religious life some twenty-four years previously, I found myself uttering, "I cannot do it." I was striking a blow at the core of my vow of obedience, one I'd never thought I would have to make.

To add to the proverbial kicking of someone who was down, she told me that the sisters presently assigned to Ortum did not wish for my return. The reason given was that I had created discord in the community. She offered no specifics, as the information had been given in confidence.

The latter accusation was particularly disturbing. I acknowledge that there were problems in our small Ortum community before I left, and I contributed to them and perhaps created some. In my mind, these disagreements stemmed from my standing up for principles which I thought were warranted, not for personal reasons.

One such ruckus happened after the sister who was working in community development began planning to open a bakery at the market center with a group of local men. The project gained attention when the men commenced felling trees near the river. In addition to making charcoal for the bakery, they were planning to sell charcoal to the local people.

Father Leo objected to the project. He explained that the wheat for the bakery would have to be imported, and there was no good rationale to try to change the diet of the local Pokot people, whose traditional grains were millet, sorghum, and occasionally maize, all served as a gruel or porridge. More problematic, he explained, was that cutting down trees would only add to the erosion in that semiarid terrain.

When we met within our religious community, I voiced my opinion, which was honestly in line with Father Leo's. Members of our community of four, however, believed I was in cahoots with him.

There were other issues whose origins I couldn't put my finger on, but I felt more and more isolated. My relationship with the nursing sister was strained but workable. It was surreal to work in the hospital with someone I felt was undermining my efforts and then have to live and act lovey-dovey with that person in the same house.

As I mentioned earlier, I was more and more convinced that it was difficult to practice as a doctor and still live in the same religious community, especially a small one, as was customary in the mission setup. I think it speaks for itself that out of the seventeen doctors who either entered already graduated or were put through medical school by the congregation, at least six of us left the community.

Even in the Thika situation, there was another obstacle to my acceptance of the assignment: the nursing sister, while competent in labor and delivery practice, gave the message that she was in charge. When I'd been there previously, she'd introduce me by saying, "Meet our little doctor!" She often made medical decisions that were not within her scope of practice, which irked me and made living with her in the community difficult.

Getting back to the aftermath of the meeting with my regional superior in Dublin, I left there shattered and extremely upset. Walking aimlessly along the Clontarf Seafront, I headed toward the bus stop. A little voice suddenly arose from the depths of my consciousness (was it Lucifer himself?) and whispered, *There is only one way to deal with this. I cannot obey this unreasonable command; my vow of obedience is on the line. If I cannot obey, I have no place in religious life. I have to quit; that is the only option. I have to get out right now.*

That defining moment is cemented in my psyche. I can almost mark the spot on the street where I crossed the exit threshold. The decision was extreme, and it shook me to the core. Until that moment, I had been fully committed to the vows I had taken on my profession day.

Somehow, I made it back to base. It was still a rule that we did not enter another sister's bedroom after evening prayer. Well, I didn't care. I knew my friend from Zambia days, Sister Eugene, was in house. I knocked on her door. Although she had already retired, she appreciated how distressed I was and welcomed me in.

As I sat at her bedside, I recounted the events of the day and my plan to leave, perhaps as early as the next day. She was empathetic. She used all of her powers of persuasion to get me to be more rational. We talked for most of the night. In the end, I promised her I would not go AWOL but would take time to think about it; I would make an appointment with the superior general and do nothing rash.

Even though I was calmer by morning, I couldn't stand to meet any members of the community, most of whom were my contemporaries and even friends, all of them enjoying a respite from mission activities at a house of comings and goings in Raheny, on the north side of Dublin.

Where could I go to be alone with my emotions and thoughts? Pondering that question, I got the inspiration to call Sister Vincent at the Holy Ghost College in Kimmage, where she was the nurse in charge of the infirmary and lived with a companion in an apartment on campus. I had known her as a kind soul ever since our time on Leeson Street, where she visited weekly. With no questions asked, she immediately welcomed me to come stay for as long as I wished. By evening's end, I was installed there.

While staying in Kimmage, a suburb on the southern side of Dublin, I had time to think about the enormity of my decision to leave the Holy Rosary Sisters after almost a quarter century and the entirety of my adult life. I would need a dispensation from my vows, which could only come from the pope himself. And then what would I do? I had no job, no money, and no place to live. I certainly could not live with my elderly parents.

I was confused and desperate. The rejection by my own community was overwhelming. I went through the prescribed exercises of prayer and meditation, but I was just going through the motions. I was angry with everyone, even, dare I say it, with God. Nothing could let me believe this assignment was God's will for me, which, as a good religious, I was meant to accept. There had been a shift at the depths of my being, and it seemed I had crossed the point of no return.

I was still in Kimmage when Father Paddy Cullen, who was home on vacation, contacted me. He was anxious to know how the Kerio-Weiwei project was progressing. He took me for a drive into the Wicklow Mountains, and we lunched at the well-known Powerscourt Mansion, on the beautiful landscaped gardens of the estate. I am not sure what spin I put on the progress of the project, but I do know that I did not once hint at the big mess I was in personally. I was too ashamed of myself and my decision. Besides, I did not think he would understand. He always struck me as conservative in his views.

As soon as I could get my act together, I requested an appointment with the superior general, who was still Mother Stanislaus. She had last seen me in action when she made official visitation in Ortum circa 1970.

After some pleasantries, I came to the point and informed her that I wanted to leave the congregation, a decision resulting from my inability to adhere to my vow of obedience as demanded by the recent assignation. I was asking her to initiate proceedings to procure a dispensation from my vows.

I could see by her facial expression that I caught her off guard. She indicated that she was aware there was a problem with my new assignation but was surprised to hear how deeply wounded I was by both the decision and the dictatorial manner with which I felt I'd been treated.

She listened attentively as I poured forth all the reasons for my inability to accept my assignment to Thika Maternity. While she understood my reluctance to practice only obstetrics, her suggestion was for me to take a refresher course in that specialty before I returned to Kenya.

She made it clear that she was not going to interfere with a local decision by the regional superior. I sensed that in spite of her acknowledgment that she appreciated how much work I had put into the health-care plan for West Pokot, my return there was not going to happen.

She, having allowed me to vent and get all that I wanted to say off my chest, was able, through her ingenuity and appeal to the higher echelons of my spirituality and rationality, to get me to reconsider and give the momentous decision some more thought and time. I agreed to the approach but requested I be allowed to work with the government medical services in Kenya. It was not an outrageous request, as quite a few of our medical personnel, such as those in Mzee Kenyatta's Gatundu, were already seconded to the government health services. She was willing to consider this plan but said she had to clear it with the regional superior.

I left the meeting with mixed feelings. I had been embraced with loving kindness and understanding. At the same time, I had a deep sense of uneasiness and guilt that I was again going my way, not God's way, as had been my tenet of faith for so long.

Still adjusting and digesting all that had happened in the preceding weeks, I headed to Clonmel to spend some time with my parents and my sister Breed's family. It was difficult to hide my feelings and my anxiety, but I tried to relax and especially enjoy visits to the ocean with them. In no way would I make them aware of my struggles.

Soon afterward, I was given the all clear to return to Kenya and apply for work in the government health services. My encounter with Sister Felice was cordial, with neither of us referring to all that had gone on in the previous months. There had been some temporary arrangements made that allowed Iris to go on her three-month home leave, the details of which I have erased from memory. I only know the hospital was never left without a doctor during that time.

My application to become an employee of the government health service was approved. They especially welcomed that I had specialized in community and public health. I expected to be sent to a remote district in Kenya where there was difficulty placing Kenyan-born doctors. To everyone's surprise, including my own, I was appointed as the medical officer of health (MOH) for the Kiambu District. My predecessor, a Kenyan, had ended up in prison for some criminal business; I did not inquire about the details.

Kiambu County, as it is known today, abuts Nairobi County all along its northern border. In the 1970s, the area was politically charged, as it was home to the powerful Kikuyu tribe, with the president himself living within its boundaries at Gatundu. Thika, where I would have been working at the maternity hospital, was the largest town in the district.

By that time, Sister Doctor Breed was well established in Gatundu Hospital, which came under my jurisdiction. She had much more medical experience, including surgical interventions, than I had. Ironically, it had been her suggestion that I apply to the master's program at the Johns Hopkins University, but neither she nor I could ever have imagined that I would end up in that position, essentially as her boss. I was tactful. She understood my role and did not resent it. It worked. I am happy to have had her as a lifelong friend.

As MOH, I was responsible for the public health of the district of two million people. I supervised at least ten health centers and was the doctor in charge of the district hospital at Kiambu. The only other doctor stationed at that hundred-bed hospital was a volunteer from the Netherlands. He was a good surgeon and a capable clinician. He did most of the clinical work, and we both took our turns on night call. We decided to split night-call duty so that each of us was on one week, including the weekend, and then off the next.

Clinical officers and midwives did most of the routine diagnosing and treating, so we were only called for complex surgical and obstetrical cases. When it was my night or weekend on call, I still hesitated to perform major surgeries. Luckily, we were able to refer the most serious and complicated cases to Kenyatta National Hospital in Nairobi, ten miles away.

I settled into my new role more confidently than I expected. The environment of the hospital was abuzz with activity: the inpatient beds were full to capacity; the outpatient department was overflowing; and there was a well-organized pharmacy, an adequate laboratory to perform basic tests, and even a working x-ray unit. It was a stark contrast from anything I had previously experienced. Above all else, I did not have to worry whether we had enough money in the kitty to make the payroll.

As I visited the numerous health centers throughout the district, I was impressed by the luscious vegetation and the progressive efforts of the local population, especially the women. I had high hopes of being able to work with the staff of these centers to make them more prevention-oriented and not just purveyors of curative care at a basic level.

Of course, there were day-to-day problems medically and administratively that required tact and good judgment for their solutions in that highly politically charged arena. I had easy access and felt I could rely on good backup from senior officials in the Ministry of Health. I got good feedback when I presented the annual report of the district medical services not only on time but also with a reasonable budget and development plan, all thanks to the skills I had acquired at JHSPH.

One of the perks of the job was free accommodation on the campus of the hospital. I was assigned to a sparsely furnished three-bedroom, one-story house whose origin went back to colonial days. It was in need of repairs and a new coat of paint at the minimum. At least it had interior plumbing and was on the mains for electricity.

The darkly lit living room, with two musty khaki-cushioned fireside chairs and nothing else in the way of furniture, did little to elevate my aesthetic sense. It was spooky at night, but it was my choice, and I had to make the best of it. At least I had an askari for nighttime protection, which was welcome, as I was living in a crime-ridden area, being so near to Nairobi.

I needed a car to get to church, procure groceries, and visit the Holy Rosary community to which I belonged, if at a distance, in Forest Road, Nairobi. I was allowed to use the money from my first few months' salary to buy a brand-new Toyota Corolla.

For the first time ever, I was living alone, but I welcomed it. I was still angry and still felt rejected and victimized by my religious community. I visited the sisters in Nairobi, even my good friend Sister Pauline, as infrequently as possible. The name Ortum was anathema to me. I was determined never again to set foot in West Pokot.

I tried my best to follow a schedule of prayer, although I was unable, due to the demands of the job, to attend daily Mass. On one occasion, a fellow countryman, Father Tom McMahon, stationed in a neighboring parish, brought for treatment a student from the school where he taught, and we struck up a friendship.

As the Irish branch of the Spiritan Fathers, of which my brother was a member, ministered to all the parishes around Kiambu, I had other familiar confreres within easy distance. One of them was Henry's best friend from the seminary days,

Father Paddy Leonard. I have to acknowledge that I felt more at home with them than with Holy Rosary Sisters.

Father Tom invited me to help with the distribution of the Eucharist to the large crowds in his parish, who attended Sunday Mass. I was happy to fulfill that role. Little did I know back then that we were both struggling with our religious beliefs. It was only years later that I learned he had been laicized and was married. We are still friends, if at a distance.

As much as I wanted out of religious life, taking that step, with all that it entailed, was too scary to contemplate. I kept my inner turmoil bottled up and pretended that nothing was amiss. I did not wear my religious habit, but I knew that colleagues and officials in the Ministry of Health were aware of my status.

## CHAPTER 11

# A TURN TO TEACHING

A branch of the Tropical Institute of Amsterdam was conducting an operational research project on the grounds of Kiambu Hospital when I took up duty there as district medical officer of health (MOH). The project was part of an effort to improve the delivery of services to outpatients attending district hospitals and had been requested by the Kenyan government. Since the pronouncement by President Kenyatta some years earlier that all government health services would be free of charge, outpatient services had become overburdened. A deluge of patients flocked to government hospitals, some with serious conditions and others with minor complaints. As a result, the lines were long, and often, patients who were seriously ill had to wait hours to get the care they needed.

In charge of the project was Dr. Leonard C. Vogel. He and his team were using a building with moveable partitions to try various methods to improve triage and the flow through a simulated outpatient facility. Dr. Vogel also happened to be the professor and head of the department of community health at the Nairobi Medical School.

Soon after my first meeting with him, he surprised me by asking if I would be interested in joining his department as a lecturer, or associate professor. I was honored, but I was also torn.

I was only a few months into my position in Kiambu; it would not look good to abandon the position so soon. On the contrary, I was aware that my position as MOH was tenuous, as it was in a convenient location near the center of everything. Finally, I decided I could better serve the long-term interests of health care in Kenya by playing a role in the education of the future generation of indigenous doctors.

I shared the request and my hesitancy with the sisters of my community, all of whom encouraged me to take the position. So with my mind made up, I headed up to Nyeri, the provincial headquarters, a town situated in the foothills of Mount Kenya, where I had an appointment with Dr. Kimani, the provincial medical officer and my immediate boss. I discussed with him the proposal, and to his credit, before I even got around to mentioning any regrets I had of leaving the present position, without hesitation, he encouraged me to take the job.

By April 1, 1974, I found myself ensconced in a spacious office as lecturer in the department of community health at the Nairobi Medical School on a campus across the street from Kenyatta National Hospital, previously known as King George VI Hospital. It was some change from my beloved West Pokot, but I was ready for the challenge.

One of the perks of going with the position was the ability to rent, at a reasonable rate, an apartment owned and maintained by the university. It was convenient to the main campus and within ten minutes' driving distance from the medical school. An affluent suburb, Kilimani was favored by expatriates and had a diverse, educated population. My complex backed up to the Nairobi Arboretum, a well-maintained oasis of green in the city, shaded by specimens of deciduous and evergreen trees and open to the public. It was an idyllic situation.

There were only four apartments in the complex, each called by the exotic-sounding name of *maisonette*, or *townhouse* in today's jargon. In addition to the kitchen and living room—with a sliding door open to a patio overlooking the wooded area—it had two bedrooms and a bathroom upstairs. It was filled with sunshine gleaming through the floor-to-ceiling windows. The hard furnishings, which were of an acceptable standard, came with the lease. I couldn't believe my good fortune. I was in heaven!

Propitiously, Sister Áine'(Gaelic for Anne and pronounced Awn-ye) ni Talbóid (Talbot in English) had just taken up a position as curriculum adviser for primary schools with the Kenyan Institute of Education (KIE) in Nairobi. She and I had been friends since our days in the novitiate many years before. While we were not supposed to cultivate particular friendships, she and I hit it off well and kept contact even when we were stationed in different parts of the developing world. Like my parents, hers had been involved in our war for independence in her native Kerry, Ireland and spoke and wrote in Gaelic as their preferred language.

I invited her to share my spacious residence. Áine, who was an elementary teacher before she joined Holy Rosary Sisters, was sent to Nigeria immediately after profession. She did sentinel work training female teachers in that country before being recognized as a persona non grata after the Biafran War in 1970. After a religious education renewal course in Kampala, Uganda, Áine took up a position as religious adviser to schools in the coastal area around Mombasa until her appointment to KIE.

With this move, at least I was trying to make my way back into the Holy Rosary community. I'm sure Áine sensed my struggle, but she was respectful enough not to probe and was supportive in every way.

Like most residents of our neighborhood, we employed a houseboy. Writing that word more than forty years later makes me cringe, but at the time, many colonial attitudes and practices were still in effect. It was only a decade after Kenya's independence. We found a wonderful man named Joseph, who was of the Luo tribe from the area around Lake Victoria. He was an excellent cook, having been trained in culinary arts by a European settler. He also cleaned the house and did the laundry. We were spoiled.

Each unit in our development had a small one-room house attached for live-in servants, and Joseph stayed in ours. An older man, Joseph was kind, generous, reliable, and loyal. Like my father, he was a man of few words, and he stayed in my employment for the entire duration of my contract. When I eventually left for overseas furlough, Joseph decided to return to his native region not far from where President Barack Obama's father, also a Luo, was born and grew up. I have often regretted that I was not generous enough with a retirement bonus to Joseph. I was still hung up on my vow of poverty and did not feel free to go beyond what was budgeted.

My time in Nairobi was also enriching from a personal perspective. Early on, I had the good fortune to be introduced to a team of senior management from Aer Lingus, now recognized as Irish Airlines. The newly formed Kenyan Airway's directors had recruited these experienced airline executives to help get it functioning efficiently and effectively. A member of that team was Ed Kelleher, at the time Aer Lingus manager at JFK airport in New York. He had attended the same high school in Ireland as my brother-in-law Gerry Griffin. My sister Bernadette had given the Kellehers my telephone number and suggested they contact me on arrival in Nairobi. So began a wonderful friendship with Ed; his wife, Tess; and their daughters.

When the Aer Lingus team arrived in Nairobi, suitable housing for rent was at a premium and difficult to find. There was a rumor abroad that if you were to be successful in finding a nice dwelling, you had to follow a moving van. So with time on my hands, Tess and I took to the road to do just that.

We saw a van exiting a home on a prominent corner on what I believe was then called St. Austin's Road, now James Gichura Road, and pulled into the front yard. Exiting was the crew from Israel who had planned the release of the hostages on the El Al plane that had been hijacked at Entebbe, Uganda, by Idi Amin's forces. We were successful in renting a convenient, architecturally beautiful home, which became a backdrop to many of the elegant parties Tess and Ed hosted during their time in Nairobi.

I was also able to use my contacts to get their two teenage

daughters, Claire and Jane, into the prestigious Loreto Convent Msongari, an all-girls school in Nairobi's upscale Lavington area. Tess invited me to many parties, which got me accustomed to socializing—hobnobbing, if you will—with successful people beyond my network of priests, nuns, academics, and medical personnel. All of this was new to me and helped me transition into the larger real world.

## TAKING TO THE ROAD

In the department of community health, I joined an international group of academics. Five Dutch men, one Canadian, one American, one Iranian, and one Kenyan—that was it. All of them were unique individuals ready to assert their opinions at the least provocation, not always in agreement with the head of the department, so there were some interesting staff meetings. All of it was new to me.

By the time of the new school year in September 1974, we had two new members join the faculty. They were both Kenyans: Dr. Miriam Were, MD, and Dr. Francis Mburu, who had a PhD in social science. Shortly thereafter, with the students on a scheduled break between courses, we faculty members retired to an out-of-town venue for a three-day conference under the direction of a neutral facilitator.

The agenda included ironing out different opinions regarding the curriculum, including the content and objectives of the practical field trip experience. However, we spent most of our energy dealing with complaints from students and other indigenous staff about the tough and overly rigid atmosphere created in the department by expatriate staff and especially issues with Dr. Vogel's micromanagement skills. Being freelancing spirits, some faculty members particularly disliked the requirement that they be present in their offices during regular business hours; they argued that academic freedom should allow more flexibility to engage in community-wide activities or spend time in the medical school library. They held the opinion that as long as they fulfilled their teaching assignments and published the results of their research, they should not have to check in to the department.

The going got heated at times, especially among the volatile men from the Netherlands, and it was good there was an independent facilitator. The bottom line was that while these talented, well-intentioned expatriate academics did a good job in setting up the department, their strict work ethic and Teutonic temperament did not fit in with the more relaxed approach of other members on staff. Dr. Vogel seemed to get the message and did not seek to renew his contract, which was about to expire.

Early in the New Year, Professor F. J. Bennett, MD, took over as head of the department. He was a well-respected community health leader known throughout East Africa. He had been professor of preventive medicine in Makerere, Uganda, and professor of community health at the University of Dar-es-Salaam, Tanzania, before accepting the position in Nairobi.

He brought a completely different management style, tensions dissipated, and the atmosphere changed to one of team building and cooperation. It became a pleasure to come to work.

One by one, the other expatriate men from the Netherlands did not request renewal of contracts, and their places were filled by newly minted Kenyan counterparts. John Bennett served the department well for four years before a Kenyan, Dr. James Kagia, MD, who had studied and obtained an MPH from the Harvard School of Public Health, took over as chair.

The University of Nairobi School of Medicine, a still-new entity that had been founded in 1967, followed the British and European system of education: it offered a six-year post-high-school curriculum, with the first two years dedicated to pre-clinical subjects and the final four devoted to clinical specialties. The department of community health did not get priority in prestige or funding compared to the hospital-based specialties, such as surgery and internal medicine.

For students who were more excited by their newly acquired ability to diagnose and treat in internal medicine, assist in surgical procedures, and deliver babies, one discipline of which they were considering specializing in, community health was way down on the totem pole. They regarded it just as a requirement they had to pass before they could graduate. It was an uphill battle to get them motivated.

The final-year class was divided into three sections that rotated among surgery, obstetrics, and community health. That meant we taught one-third of the class for twelve weeks and then repeated the course twice again in one academic year. During the period students were assigned to our department, we would teach basic public health and take the students on field trips into the rural areas, where they would assess the health needs of the local community, including the nutritional status of children and the general population's need for basic hygienic facilities, such as outdoor latrines and mosquito control.

We tried as much as possible to make the field trips beneficial to the local community as well as to the students. As an example, we would bring students to visit areas where there had been droughts or epidemics, such as cholera. The goal of this hands-on learning experience was to prepare students to deal with similar situations should they become medical officers of health in such a community.

Students who had grown up in an urban setting were boarders for most of their education and had no idea how a majority of their countrymen and countrywomen eked out a living in the rural areas. We worked with the district health services in each area we visited, but the lack of resources, medical supplies, and medicines was frustrating. Again, it was an eye-opener to these elite students to see how 90 percent of their fellow Kenyans lived and suffered.

At least two members of the staff were required to accompany the students on field trips lasting ten days to two weeks. This involved living and eating with them for the duration. Our accommodation was often a dormitory attached to a high school that had been vacated during a school break. At one end of these open dormitories, with a token of privacy provided by a flimsy partition, I would plunk down my belongings and claim my space. The dorms had no ceilings, and the wooden partition separating my bed from my next-door neighbor might as well not have been there. I could hear him breathe and was aware of each time he turned in his bed. Surely an aeon removed from the seclusion of the cloister!

Invariably, there was no indoor plumbing in the dorms. An outdoor faucet attached to the end of a lead pipe standing about two feet off the ground was often the only water supply available for our personal needs. Because we typically set up camp at higher elevations, the mornings were cool, and the water emanating from the faucets was icy cold. To ensure some semblance of privacy, when on one of these field excursions, I would arise early to perform morning ablutions before the students had surfaced. As one can imagine, I appreciated getting home to the soothing waters of a hot tub after two weeks of such rough living.

One memorable morning, I woke up in one of these dormitories to find a bat resting on my exposed left elbow. Not only did I scream, but I bolted for the door. I ended up outside in my night attire, facing the whole dorm of twenty male students, who had gallantly come running out to save me from a horrible fate. An embarrassment, to put it mildly. I explained that bats had always been my biggest bugbear, which restored my dignity and led to a belly laugh afterward.

We occasionally stayed in a local hotel. Although the word evokes the Western sense of a hotel, the Kenyan version is a group of small bedrooms arranged in blocks of about six, on three sides of a quadrangle at the back of a local bar. There were only communal showers and in-ground latrines. I vividly remember one place on the shores of Lake Victoria where the mosquitoes, seeming larger than life and more plentiful than sand grains on the seashore, buzzed around all night outside my bed net, desperate to get a bite of my juicy skin.

While on the field trips, it was our policy as far as possible to share our meals and partake of the same menu as the students. Not having grown up in Kenya, though, I found the diet mostly unpalatable. It was not unusual for the chef in charge to go to the local market in the morning, buy a live goat, have it slaughtered, and dish it up in a stew for the evening meal. I found myself repulsed not only emotionally but also due to the toughness and bland taste of the stew and the accompanying maize porridge. I was unable to get it beyond my lips. The experience was made worse when students would say, "So you don't like our food?" and I got the impression they felt slighted. On subsequent trips, I proclaimed that I was a vegetarian and only ate eggs as my source of animal protein. Thus, I was served fried eggs three times each day.

While the physical aspect of these trips was rugged, the ability to interact in a personal, relaxed way with senior medical students was wonderful and worth the inconvenience. We hoped to instill into their psyche and consciousness genuine concern for the social welfare and health of their less privileged brothers and sisters. We were interacting with bright young men and women who would be the future leaders of Kenya, either in the medical field or even in politics. I was impressed by their idealism and aspirations. The hope was that they would continue to keep these ideals before them in their future careers.

The World Health Organization was sponsoring the medical education of these native-born Kenyan students; otherwise, the majority would never have been able to afford it. About 10 percent of the students were of Indian or other Asian ancestry, and even if their parents were comparatively wealthy, some of them owning big businesses, they qualified for the same free education. Not only did they get top grades in school, but they were also able to get around the regulation that all new graduates, in return for their free medical education, should work for at least two years in a rural government hospital or pay a fine of, I believe, two thousand shillings for noncompliance.

This amount was a pittance for these wealthy students, some of whom came to classes in their Mercedes. It used to roil me up when these students came looking for a testimonial as soon as they graduated so that they could join their thirty-first cousins in the United States or Canada, never again to return to Kenya. It seemed unfair that they were able to take advantage of the system.

While we were on those field trips, the other poorer students would make us aware of the problems they had in being sent to some out-of-the-way stations, such as the lack of good schools for their children and no job opportunities for their educated wives, not to speak of differences in customs and acceptance between one ethnic group and another. Yes, it was sad to witness up close this brain drain in action and how people everywhere can take advantage of a system set up to help the underserved majority.

My area of specialty and teaching was the administration of the health services, which included development of plans, budgeting, and management and supervision of staff in hospitals and health centers. I also lectured on communicable diseases, especially those prevalent in Kenya.

Maybe I was meant to be a teacher after all.

## PROFESSIONAL SUCCESSES

One of our field excursions was to Alupe in western Kenya, where leprosy was still endemic. We were able to see how this disease, caused by the *Mycobacterium leprae* (related to the tuberculosis bacteria), is diagnosed and treated. By that time, patients were being incorporated into the general medical services rather than cordoned off into a leprosarium. Even so, we were able to appreciate the stigma and the community's fear of these patients even after they were declared no longer infectious.

The destructive end results of this devastating disease left the biggest impression on the students and me. We saw the burnt-out cases, meaning that the disease was no longer active, but the stigma was kept alive by the deformities that remained, such as missing digits on hands or toes. Seared into my memory is the image of an elderly man, his whole face disfigured by large nodules, who obviously had had the worst form of the infection, the lepromatous type.

In 1977, there was a severe outbreak of cholera reported from the Kisumu area, adjacent to Lake Victoria. As it was time for one of our field experiences, we made arrangements to set up camp in one of the areas most affected. I was deputed to lead the group of about thirty students. I believe Dr. Mburu, one of our sociologists, was my companion supervisor.

We did not enter into the curative aspects of the outbreak, but it was easy to see the problems of overcrowding in the area hospitals and health centers, neither of which were adequately equipped to deal with the urgency of the situation. The acuteness and the rapidity with which an infected patient deteriorates due to dehydration and electrolyte imbalance necessitates easy access to intravenous fluid replacement. This was not readily available in many of these centers, which was a contributory factor to the high mortality rates.

We did what we could in distributing prophylactic sulfonamides, which I am not sure was effective but was the only option we had available. The students, with the enthusiasm of youth, used all methods of persuasion to get families to build modified latrines and to boil their drinking water. They endorsed the recommendation from the Ministry of Health that the local people change their customary funeral rites, which included touching the deceased body. These were all factors leading to the rapid spread of the disease. While we were aware that our contribution was only a drop in the bucket to solving the crisis, at least we felt we were not just performing a purely academic exercise.

At another time, in that same region on the shores of Lake Victoria, we carried out a nutritional survey of the children under five years of age. We found not only intestinal parasites, anemia, and latent malaria but also a high degree of protein malnutrition leading to the well-described syndrome of kwashiorkor. This condition usually affects children after they are weaned from their mothers' breast, and it is characterized by generalized swelling of limbs, a pot belly due to an enlarged liver, skin changes, and especially sparse copper-colored hair growth. The child is usually extremely irritable. It's a sorry sight to behold.

What struck us about the prevalence of this condition was that the children were born and were being reared on the shores of the largest lake in Africa, which was teeming with fish, a wonderful source of protein. Due to custom and taboo, fish was not a staple of their diet. This brings out how one cannot bring about massive changes in people's health care without taking into consideration the prevalent and contributory economic and cultural influences.

That was the message we tried to get across to the students. Many of the projects they worked on were of superior quality, addressing major issues in the delivery of health care for all. I was able to incorporate some of their findings into a chapter I contributed to a book published by the department, *Community Diagnosis and Health Action: A Manual for Tropical and Rural Areas*, edited by Professor F. J. Bennett, in 1979.

During my tenure in that position, there were at least three strikes by students on the main campus of the University of Nairobi. Each of the strikes resulted in the university being closed, and the students, including those not directly involved, were dispersed and sent home. Invariably, the protest was due to political unrest, even if not involving college students. This completely disrupted the curriculum at the medical school, but the fear that riots might disturb national stability far exceeded the inconvenience.

For those of us on faculty, these strikes were a blessing in disguise, as we were able to use the time to further our research projects, a requirement for renewal of contract or tenure.

As soon as I joined the department, Dr. Vogel offered me an excellent research opportunity: to assess the quality of care for his operational research project in Kiambu. Whenever, at national or international medical conferences, he presented the results of his project, the most dominant criticism was that he was improving quantity at the cost of quality. By the time I actually started on the project about nine months into my job, he was no longer head of the department but had returned to his previous position as chief of research for the Kenya-Netherlands Project for Operations Research into Outpatient Services (KNEPOROS), based at the medical research center adjacent to the medical school.

The task had three principle approaches: to assess the quality of primary care delivered by clinical officers before and after operational improvements were introduced into the outpatient department of a district hospital; to evaluate the quality of the delivery of care in an antenatal clinic when the admission record had the ability to rapidly categorize at-risk factors and there was adequate functional equipment; and to assess the ability of enrolled community nurses to manage child morbidity at an integrated maternal and child health clinic.

For three years, planning and carrying out this project became an all-consuming focus of my energy and intellectual ability. Of course, I still had my classes to teach and my field trips to make. I was advised to submit my project as a work to be awarded a PhD equivalent at my own medical school in Dublin (UCD). Dr. Bennett magnanimously agreed to be my adviser for the research. The deadline for submission was the end of September 1977, so that formed an impetus to get it completed.

By that time, I was living alone in the maisonette after the sisters, in their wisdom, had requested that Áine come join their community on Forest Road. I never understood why that was so, but by that time, I was so alienated from the community that I did not make any effort to have her stay. She was on the regional council, so I assumed the request had something to do with that. Or perhaps she wasn't happy in our situation or needed a more structured community timetable. Who knows? The one constant was that she continued to be my friend.

I carried out the project during working hours at Kiambu Hospital, where I not only knew my way around but also was known to many of the involved personnel and received their full cooperation. The analyzing and tallying of data was a tedious affair, as the era of computer programming was still in its infancy. The vision of the judge in the recount of the votes in the Bush versus Gore presidential election in 2000 holding up the hanging chads captures a picture of how we analyzed data using key sort data or edge-punched cards.

As a major part of the study could not be quantified, I enlisted the help of my good friends and colleagues Dr. Breed O'Keeffe and Dr. Fin O'Callaghan to do a blind and independent audit. Throughout the planning, implementation, and finalizing of the project, my relationship with Dr. Vogel was tentative, to say the best. He could be tough and demanding, tried to unduly influence my protocol and approach, and wanted results faster than I was capable of producing them. I resented his interference to the point that at one time, I decided to quit. However, my interest in the subject won over, and I persevered.

With all the field work done, now came the task of bringing it all together, including an extensive literature search, assembly of tables and graphs, discussions, and conclusions. To accomplish this magnum opus, each evening on my return from the department and while Joseph was preparing my dinner, I would retire to the office upstairs and write and write, every word with a 2H lead pencil and the generous use of an efficient eraser. After just the break to digest my evening meal, it was back to the books until my overwhelmed brain determined it was time to quit.

I made the deadline just barely. I had been fortunate to find an efficient typist, a recently retired administrative assistant, who did a fantastic job not only in deciphering my penciled handwriting but also in dealing with the medical jargon and constructing professional-style tables and graphs. All was done in duplicate with blue carbon paper, the only way to make copies at the time, at least in Nairobi.

Áine and Father Paddy Cullen, who happened to be on a business trip at the propitious time, helped me put it all together in two volumes. We got it bound beautifully. There wasn't time to send it by mail to Dublin in order to meet the deadline, so my friends at Aer Lingus came to the rescue. The original manuscript went overnight as a first-class passenger and was met at Dublin Airport by Tricia Kelleher, a student at Maynooth College, which was quite a distance outside city limits. She graciously delivered it to UCD just before closing on the last day allowed for the acceptance of manuscripts.

Luckily, I didn't have to go to Ireland to defend my dissertation. It passed the litmus test, and with relief and pride, I earned a doctor of medicine degree in June 1978. Relevant summaries were published in the *East African Medical Journal*. By the time I had completed and published my findings, the KNEPOROS project had ended, and members of the team, including Dr.

Vogel, had returned to Amsterdam. We had lost contact, and I only hope he appreciated the outcome and the findings, which endorsed the premise that operational improvements at the basic level of outpatient services need not necessarily be at the cost of quality.

It still gnawed at my inner being that my work on the Kerio-Weiwei project at Johns Hopkins had been for naught, but in my more rational moments, I could realize that the knowledge I'd acquired in Baltimore was not lost. In addition to exposing medical students to the relatively new discipline of community health, I became the medical consultant to the Kenya Catholic Bishops Conference. I worked closely with Sister Joan Devane, a member of the Medical Mission Sisters from the USA who, in her role as medical secretary, represented all Catholic medical facilities with the central government. I was able to contribute my skills and orientation to influence new and ongoing medical establishments to become more community- and prevention-oriented.

As a result of this exposure, Father Jim Barry, medical secretary for the diocese of Kitui in south-central Kenya, requested that I help jump-start a maternal child health program in territory similar to West Pokot. Both he and the Sisters of Mercy, who were planning the clinics, were receptive to my advice. Personally, it gave me great satisfaction to be involved. While I was not around to appreciate its full impact, I understand that when implemented, it was successful. I still treasure a replica of a baobab tree, locally made out of copper wire that Father Jim presented to me in appreciation of my advice and input.

I made some efforts to incorporate myself back into the

Holy Rosary community, but my heart was not in it. It was like the slow and painful dissolution of a marriage or love affair. I would attend meetings of the group, and there were quite a few of those because we had to figure out how to respond to the changing mission environment as well as discuss affairs affecting the community as a whole. At one such regional meeting in Eldoret, the discussion and the views on religious life so expressed, hit a negative vibe in me. I realized I no longer held these tenets. The effect was to open the flood gates and make of me an emotional wreck. I immediately packed my bags and returned to Nairobi. Luckily, I had my own transport.

Significant milestones, such as jubilees, were big events in religious life. I was due to celebrate my silver jubilee, twenty-five years since my first profession, in August 1976. I couldn't contemplate going through a celebration, including publicly renewing my vows before the assembled community and invited guests. It would be hypocritical. Instead, I spent that weekend in solitude at a retreat center in the quiet countryside of Limuru. By deciding not to celebrate the jubilee, I was surely conveying a message to the members of the larger community.

Nonetheless, I was happy to respond to requests from the regional superior to help out in my professional capacity. On two occasions, I agreed to accompany an individual sister who'd suffered an acute mental breakdown, on her flight back to Ireland. The first went smoothly. After getting the patient to the appropriate treatment facility, I returned on the next flight to Nairobi.

The second occasion caused me a lot of stress and anger. In a nutshell, I was asked to accompany the patient to an acute psychiatric hospital in Dublin but was not told the necessary details of her case. The two of us made it safely through London's Heathrow and into Dublin Airport by late evening of the next day, all without incident. Sister was well sedated. At the airport, we were met by two sisters of the general council, an unusual occurrence which signified the seriousness of the situation, who transported us immediately to the hospital.

As the patient wasn't fit to give an appropriate history, the admitting psychiatrist requested I fill him in on details of the case. I could only refer him to the notes in the sealed envelope that had been handed to me on our departure at Nairobi Airport. I had not opened it as it was addressed to the admitting psychiatrist. I was aware that Sister had been treated at the Mater Hospital in Nairobi, and I assumed the contents were a summary of her management.

I visited the patient the next morning before heading to Dublin Airport for my return flight. I was convinced she was severely delusional by the questions she was asking about some procedure that might have been performed on her. I reassured her that none of the upsetting things she was relating were true.

On my return, I discovered the real facts: this poor woman in the midst of an acute psychotic episode had been sexually assaulted and had had a procedure that I assume was most likely a D and C (dilatation and curettage) performed in the hospital. The whole incident was meant to be hush-hush, and I was deliberately not given the full story. When I challenged the regional superior who had not disclosed these important details, her reply was "I didn't think you could keep it a secret." It floored me and took me a long time to get over that affront to my professionalism, This did not help my efforts to rejoin the community.

Another story of those days was interesting and unusual. One morning while in my office, I received a phone call from a priest friend asking if I would meet him in the Intercontinental Hotel, where an American visitor and well-known benefactor of mission projects needed some medical advice and help.

As soon as I could, I got myself downtown, and I was ushered to the penthouse of the hotel, where I was introduced to the gentleman and his teenage son. There, I encountered a tall, well-built man in a complete clerical outfit minus the collar. He was difficult to distinguish from the group of priests surrounding him. The boy seated on one of the beds was not only agitated but also sullen and rude to anyone who tried to interact with him. After brief introductions, the assembled group celebrated Mass—a unique event in a hotel room, I thought. Soon I realized that this was a deeply religious man and that the visiting priests were already beneficiaries of his largesse.

The story went as follows. While the father and his son were visiting a popular national park some distance from Nairobi, the son developed an acute mental episode which required that he be airlifted to a hospital in the city. After he was stabilized, the treating medical team and family members back in the United States decided the teenager should return home as soon as possible. The father did not agree with this line of action as he believed that the boy needed to be exorcized to get rid of his demons. To accomplish this plan he wanted to proceed to Rome, where he was well known in Vatican circles. Fearing the boy would be involuntarily put on a plane, the father took him out of the hospital against medical advice. Hence, he and the whole retinue were holed up in the penthouse of the Intercontinental.

I was asked if I would be willing to accompany the group back to the United States, as the psychiatrist who had treated the boy would not give clearance for him to travel unless he was accompanied by a doctor. Actually, the psychiatrist hoped he would be the chosen one, getting a free ride from London to New York on the famous Concorde. However, it was made clear that he would not be the medical escort.

Soon I discovered that it was a complicated situation. The man's wife back home was using her considerable influence to ensure that there was no stopover in Rome. I tried to steer free of the politics and said I would help recruit a doctor, as I was not free to go myself. I convinced Sister Doctor Iris, who was stationed in Thika, to take up the challenge. She agreed, and within twenty-four hours, all was set for the trip, which was to occur two days hence.

There was more drama the next day, as the whole retinue left the hotel, and no one knew of their whereabouts. We were advised to just show up at the airport in time for the scheduled flight. It took some persuasion to keep Iris involved, but eventually, we arrived at the airport. She had a report from the treating psychiatrist and the prescribed medication in case it was necessary to treat the patient while in transit.

At the Nairobi Airport, when we arrived, there was no sign of the gentleman or the patient. To our surprise, when we approached the check-in counter, a man standing nearby addressed me by name and assured me that the passengers were on their way. This was odd and caused us to wonder what conspiracy was going on. Was this a Secret Service agent or a member of the CIA?

About a quarter of an hour before the scheduled departure, the full retinue arrived, and with them was Archbishop Maurice Otunga of Nairobi, who was soon to be elevated to the status of cardinal. Obviously, this was a VIP as far as the local church was concerned.

The father—still dressed in clerical black, including a jacket with the left shoulder seam ripped wide open, black shoes worn at the heels, and on his head a well-bleached black beret—could easily have been mistaken for a mendicant friar, not the multimillionaire we knew he was. The son was still a passive participant in the whole scenario.

After being introduced to Iris and proceeding with the formal goodbyes, the father turned to me, thanked me for my assistance, put his hand into his inner breast pocket, and, in the dim light of the foyer, handed me an envelope. I was convinced it had to be a check thanking me for my efforts. I got the letdown of my life: inside was a leaflet titled "Devotion to the Sacred Heart of Jesus."

Actually, we had a good chuckle, and the archbishop was appreciative of my efforts to resolve a major dilemma.

To complete the story, Iris had a rough time dealing with the patient but did not need to use any emergency measures or medication. They took the Concorde nonstop from London to JKF Airport, New York. On their arrival in New York, a whole retinue was there to meet the passengers. The father handed Iris her return ticket and literally told her to get lost. She was devastated and, having never been in the USA before, didn't know where to turn.

A priest who had been part of the welcoming group recognized her bewilderment and offered to help. She was able to exchange her ticket for one in coach, which not only covered her return ticket to Nairobi but also allowed a visit to relatives on the West Coast. How the patient fared we never heard. We only hope he received the help he needed.

It seemed that professionally, I was doing well. Inwardly, I was dealing with many demons. The image of myself that kept recurring was that in Isaiah: "smashed like an earthenware pot—so that of the fragments not one shard remains big enough to carry a cinder from the hearth or scoop water from the cistern" (Isaiah 30:14, the Jerusalem Bible).

I was in a long, dark tunnel that seemingly had no exit.

CHAPTER 12

# GLOBAL SOUL SEARCHING

The policy of the University of Nairobi was to award non-Kenyan staff two-year contracts. We were remunerated on the same scale financially as local staff but without benefits, such as retirement pensions. If a Kenyan citizen with similar qualifications but without the same experience applied for a staff position held by an expatriate, he or she would get preference over the expatriate.

This practice was fair enough, but it lent a sense of insecurity to those of us expatriates who wished to renew our contracts. I witnessed a few of my colleagues being held in suspense until almost the last minute, when they were informed that their contracts would not be renewed.

For me, this ambiguity was particularly concerning because I knew in my heart that I wanted to change my lifestyle and make the final break with the Holy Rosary Sisters.

I was considering Kenyan citizenship, but the uncertainty of the future put that on hold. Without assurance that I would be tenured at the medical school or have financial security in my retirement, I considered that I might have to continue my career in another country.

It was worrisome and bewildering. Even though I got assurances from Dr. Kagia and colleagues that I was welcome to stay long term, I knew that the final decision regarding renewal of another contract rested not with the head of our department but with one at a higher administrative level in the university.

By early summer 1980, I was coming toward the end of my third two-year contract, and as was customary in the department, I was encouraged to take a sabbatical to further a research project or get undated on advancements in my chosen specialty.

I decided I would avail of the opportunity, even though I would not be salaried for the duration. There might have been an air of finality as I bade farewell to my fellow colleagues, all of them Kenyans, but I didn't get it. I assumed that my position would be open after my sojourn overseas.

Before I left Kenya for my six-month sabbatical, I thought it prudent to explore other possibilities in the event the medical school did not welcome me back. I considered the possibility that I might be able to be a member of the Flying Doctor Service in Kenya. I had learned they were developing a new preventive health program that they planned to implement in some of the far-flung rural areas they were servicing. I took the risk of meeting with one of the executives of the board of directors and discussed the possibilities. I made no commitment, nor was there an offer on the table. Naively, I assumed my meeting was confidential, but I subsequently learned to my cost that this was not so.

As I should have known I would, within a few months of my departure, receive a letter from Professor Kagia, chastising me for not being more direct. He advised that he had heard of my meeting with the Flying Doctor Services and, as a consequence, would not offer me a new contract if I returned to Kenya. I had messed up. This development was something else to add to the whirlwind of my anxiety.

My contract did include airfare to and from Ireland, including a detour if desired. From the time I had been in the Holy Land in 1969, I had wanted to return, not only to experience that same emotional and spiritual high but also to take time to sort out my future in prayer and solitude.

In order to fulfill my dream, I contacted Father Jean-Pierre Samson, WF, a respected theologian and retreat master, who after years of serving as a missionary in Kenya, was now stationed in Jerusalem. While I personally did not know him well, he was a good friend of many Holy Rosary Sisters. He kindly arranged accommodation for me, not only in a hostel in the center of the Old City of Jerusalem but also for the duration of my twelve-day retreat in Kiryat Ye'arim, some fifteen kilometers away.

Before I left Nairobi, it never occurred to me how important it was to have the exact address of the hostel where I would be staying. I knew Father Pierre planned to meet me at the airport in Tel Aviv and would take me to that address in Jerusalem. On the official immigration customs form to be completed on board prior to landing, I left blank the address of where I would stay while in Israel.

I arrived at the immigration officer's desk. He reviewed my passport and the half-filled-out immigration form. He asked me where I planned to stay while in Israel. I pulled a blank. I wasn't sure. I was being met by a priest friend who was taking me to the hostel of the nuns where I would be staying. A red flag went up.

The immigration officer told me to step aside and I was escorted to a cubicle some distance away. Then started an hour-long interrogation: Where had I been for the previous several years? What had I been doing in Kenya? Why had I come to Israel? On and on it went.

I think they found it the hardest to believe I was a medical doctor, as I was draped from head to toe in black religious garb — so unprofessional looking. I wasn't body-searched, but my carry-on luggage was strewn out in front of me, teased out, and examined item by item. My main concern was that Father was kept waiting all that time, and I had no way of communicating with him.

Eventually, I was able to convince my interrogators that I was bona fide, and they released me. I believe I was within a hair's breadth of being put on a plane back to Nairobi. Being in full religious garb certainly did not help my case.

I next had to retrieve my suitcase, which by then was on its way to the lost-luggage office. That created another excruciating delay. Would my host be still there? What would I do if he had given up and left? Panic gripped me.

When I emerged, I was relieved to see a lone figure

scrutinizing each person who emerged from the inner gates of Ben Gurion International Airport. Father Jean-Pierre had not given up on me. However, I could not blame him for being an unhappy camper. He had no idea what had caused the delay.

I do not know what I would have done had he not stayed the course and waited so patiently. I had no idea where to turn or where I was staying, knew nobody, and had little cash and no credit card. The only option was to continue on the forward journey. One can only imagine how embarrassed and contrite I was.

After we got over the initial stormy encounter and before Jean-Pierre dropped me off at the hostel in the inner city of Jerusalem, he asked if I was interested in joining a group of seminarians and sisters, an international group, going on a pilgrimage to the holy sites around the Sea of Galilee, including Nazareth. There was one seat left on the chartered bus, which I enthusiastically and immediately booked. I couldn't believe my good fortune.

The organization of the pilgrimage was superb, with daily Masses at each of the major shrines in the life of Jesus and prayerful visits to Capernaum, the site of the Beatitudes, the miracle of the loaves and fishes, and the Church of the Rock (or the Primacy of Peter), to mention just a few. While I reverently entered into the reliving of the Gospels at each of these sacred spots, the emotional response of awe and wonder that I remembered from before never occurred. I guess I was expecting too much. As we parted company in Old Jerusalem, I was grateful to my pleasant companions who'd allowed me to journey with them on that educational and faith-filled pilgrimage.

I was now ready for my time in the desert.

I was to spend my retreat in Kiryat Ye'arim, which is mentioned in the Old Testament as the place where King David rested the Ark of the Covenant for twenty years before it was brought back to Jerusalem. It is about six miles (or ten kilometers) from Jerusalem. At neighboring Abu Gosh on the Arab side is the Shrine of Our Lady of the Covenant, a center for prayer and retreats maintained by the Sisters of St. Joseph. To that welcoming center I retired to be alone with my God and my inner self.

I was embraced by the loving hospitality of the sisters. At least two of them claimed Palestine as their birthplace. The convent had the atmosphere of a Middle Ages monastery; the grounds were well landscaped and lovingly attended to by the sisters, and they incorporated the land's fresh fruit and vegetables into our delicious meals.

Taking my first tentative steps outside the walls, I could absorb the wonderful view: the Judean hills to the west and a vast expanse almost reaching the coast to the east. The panorama after dark was even more spectacular as I gazed down on the lights of the Holy City, Jerusalem. I had come to a special place, and I hoped that over the next several days, I could get closer to God and sort out my conflicted emotions and aspirations.

During my daily walks, the only other humans I encountered were young mothers in long, flowing skirts, their heads covered in kerchiefs, walking with their young children in strollers and speaking English with an American accent.

This seemed odd in time and place. Then I discovered that there was nearby a new Jewish community originating from

Yeshiva Telz in the United States, a conservative group getting back to the strict observance of the Talmud. I was impressed. These young women were giving up all the comforts of home to live out their rigorous faith on this isolated mountaintop. Conversely, by virtue of my vow of poverty, I should have been more detached from worldly goods. Here I was now moving towards a life with more earthly pleasures.

I spent the next sixteen days prayerfully trying to sort out my future. Father Jean-Pierre had provided texts and themes from scripture, from both the Old Testament and the New Testament, which I prayerfully read, meditated on, and applied to my spiritual life as I experienced it. I spent that part of the retreat in complete solitude except to attend daily Mass in the sisters' chapel.

My notes speak of a fervor and faith in God that I had not previously experienced—one I wish I could muster up today. I wrote of anguish, searching, openness to seek God's will regarding my future, and prayer to overcome the negative emotions clouding my vision. In the notes is a real struggle between doing God's will and following my own stubborn one—my desire for independence, my self-determination, and my still-strong commitment to spend my life and my talents serving the poor and the less fortunate wherever I was called. A recurrent theme was the importance of good human relations and how much easier it is to see the good in the stranger than in those with whom we live.

At the conclusion of the first eight days, I started a directed retreat under the guidance of Father Pierre Roulens, WF. During a retreat of this kind, one is in solitary confinement except for pre-arranged meetings with a specified spiritual director. Every other day, I journeyed by local bus to Father Pierre's headquarters at the Melkite Seminary in Jerusalem to recount my progress and the results of my reflections on the chosen scripture readings he had prescribed..

Again, I took copious notes. There are daily entries of my reflections on the life of Jesus and the Beatitudes, some so insightful that I believe it was only by the grace of God that they came to mind. I could easily make another retreat on the same reflections in these golden years!

Except for a break during the mid-day luncheon my days were spent in silence. I shared the meal with an African bishop from Malawi who had been summoned to Rome and, on his way, was spending some time in seclusion. When we broke our silence to enjoy the lovely meals the sisters had prepared, we had interesting discussions.

Pope Paul VI's encyclical *Humana Vitae*, detailing the church's position on birth control and abortion, had been promulgated about one year previously. I had many questions, especially regarding the practicalities of observance of the natural method of family planning by the newly baptized Christians in the developing world.

The bishop was receptive and had quite a progressive attitude regarding the affairs of the church, which gave credibility to a lot of my thinking. He was a breath of fresh air, and while I often wondered why he was being called to the Vatican, I never heard news of him after we parted. Somehow, I believe he might have been a bit too progressive.

I emerged from the desert without any miraculous answer

to my fervent prayer, still grappling with uncertainties and worries. In retrospect, I believe that at that moment in time, I would have been sincerely open to remaining in religious life if I had been able to renew my faith in it and overcome my deep-seated anger at the unjust way I had been treated.

My time in seclusion over, back in Jerusalem, before I took my departure, I was able to revisit some of the sacred places in the Holy City, more through a sense of duty than any spiritual expectation. The commercialization and the squabbling among the various religious factions got to me in a negative way.

I retrospect, I wonder if I adequately thanked the two White Fathers, Jean-Pierre Samson and Louis Roulens, who took such good care of me, giving of their time and energy, despite the fact that I was a stranger to them. That is the essence of how missionaries cared for each other. I imagine both of those men have passed to their reward, and I can only, at this time, say a prayer of gratitude for their hospitality and caring.

After Israel, I enjoyed a stopover in Italy to visit with Eilish and her family before going back in Ireland. I took up residence in our convent in Raheny, and almost immediately set up an appointment with the superior general. Sometime between the completion of the retreat and my arrival in Dublin, I had made up my mind regarding how I was going to proceed.

Sister Margaret, who had been the sister representing the congregation's medical work and who'd had the interview with Bishop John that had decided my fate, was now, by coincidence, the superior general. After preliminary greetings, I got to the point wherein I informed her that my mind was made up — I wanted to leave the congregation and seek a dispensation from my vows. She voiced her surprise and sadness that I had arrived at that decision. However, as was her duty, she informed me that she could not start the process until I had been through spiritual and psychological counseling. As I had just spent nearly one month in prayer and received spiritual advice in the Holy Land, she acknowledged she understood that I had not made my decision without prayerful thought and consideration of the consequences. I was willing to go for a psychological consultation and counseling.

Due to the large number of sisters from various congregations who were in the same predicament as I—desiring to jump over the wall, as we euphemistically called it—the powers that be had set up a process for helping religious men and women ascertain that they were taking this step without any regrets or second-guessing. One of the professionals on the panel participating in this process was a priest with a psychology degree. I have committed his name to oblivion—perhaps designedly!

In due course, I made my way to his office on a street near the famous Christ Church Cathedral, the oldest building in Dublin, which dates back to Norman times and was built sometime after 1028. I do not remember details of my sessions with him. Personality wise, he was uninviting. He was formal and cold and could best be described as bored or even tired. While I did my best to open up to him, I got the impression he did not need to hear any more sob stories.

He relied on the bevy of traditional (scientific) psychological tests, which he put me through. Finally, in my third session, he had come to his conclusion as to what had brought me to the edge of perdition, where I now found myself. I could not believe what I was hearing: my life of prayer was insufficient; I hadn't prayed enough, or something to that effect. He had no further recommendations and no further follow-up.

I was thrown to the wind — bewildered, deflated, and more confused than ever!

Fortunately, I did not have to sit too long with that grim verdict. On arrival that night at our convent in Dublin, one of my sister friends from my Monze days informed me that Father Colm O'Riordan, SJ, now home on leave, had been inquiring about my well-being and whereabouts. This could not have come at a more opportune moment. I needed to talk to and share my feelings with someone I trusted. Yes, in spite of my "not praying enough," the Lord was taking care of me.

I had known Father Colm superficially while I was in Zambia. By strange circumstances, we had renewed acquaintance a short time before I left Kenya. A phone call had come from Sister Doctor Maureen in Monze, requesting my help in getting a seriously ill expatriate volunteer admitted to a hospital in Nairobi for a treatment that was not available in Zambia. I was happy to oblige.

When the patient, a father of four young children, landed at Nairobi airport the next day we had an ambulance on site which took him to the Nairobi Hospital and under the care of a pre-arranged consultant. Father Colm had accompanied the patient from Lusaka. When I offered to take him to one of the rectories attached to a church in town where he could get hospitality, he demurred.

The alternative was, dare I say it, that he could stay in the maisonette with me. To my surprise, he chose the latter, saying he really needed some days of R and R (rest and relaxation). I wasn't overjoyed at the prospect—not that I didn't have suitable accommodation, but my previous experience in dealing with Father Colm had not been that cordial. He held an onerous position as general secretary to the bishops of Zambia, and I had formed an opinion of him as aloof and egoistic and feared I would have nothing in common with him. How wrong I was!

Over the next few days, we celebrated Mass in my living room, prayed together, and shared on a deep spiritual level. He was easy to talk to and non-judgmental. I was still hesitant to share with anyone, even him, all that was gnawing at my inner most being. I felt I didn't need to; I believed that he fully understood and was supportive of me the way I was.

After a few days, when the patient was ready for discharge and put on a plane bound for Ireland, his home country, Father Colm and I parted company. He returned to his position in Lusaka. I continued with life in the medical school, realizing that the odds I would ever encounter him again were not in my favor. It was one of those 'aha' moments—or, as my faith tells me, one of those life-changing spiritual gifts of the Holy Spirit.

Within a day or two of the disconcerting verdict, I got to meet Father Colm in Miltown, headquarters of the Jesuits in Dublin. I spilled out all the beans—all my frustrations, the results of my psychological assessments, my journey of reevaluating religious life, and my deep anxiety and fear at what the future held. He listened patiently, reassuring me that he did not agree with the assessment that I was at this crossroads in my life because I had not prayed enough.

After some further encouraging words and a few moments

of prayer together, I left feeling consoled and determined to continue trying to discern what the future held. We made plans to keep in touch, but unfortunately, Father Colm died a short time later. He never spoke of himself or his health, but I was aware that he had a long-standing cardiac condition. I am grateful to have had the opportunity to avail myself of the counsel of this kind, understanding, spiritual man, if ever so briefly.

## PRACTICING IN IRELAND

There were many fears preventing me from taking the step I knew in my heart I should take — the greatest of which was not being able to support myself outside of religious life. My other big concern was the knowledge that my parents would be distressed and disappointed. They had already found it difficult, a few years previously, to deal with my brother's decision to be laicized from the priesthood.

Although well advanced in years, my parents were living in their own house and doing well health wise. In their adopted hometown of Clonmel, County Tipperary, they lived across a narrow street from my sister Breed and her family. She and her husband, Frank, did an excellent job in caring for them as needed.

Sometime in November of that same year, while visiting my parents in Clonmel, I took my mother for a surgical consultation in an adjoining Tipperary town. To my surprise, I discovered that Mr. Gabriel Hyland (in the British and Irish medical systems, board-certified surgeons are called misters) had been a student on my team when I was an intern in St. Vincent's Hospital, Dublin, many years previously. I remembered him well and was happy to renew his acquaintance. Upon learning that I was trying to break into the medical system in Ireland, he recommended me for a six-month job as a senior house intern at the hospital in Clonmel. He promised to put in a good word for me.

So it happened that I became a senior house officer in internal medicine at St. Joseph's Hospital, Clonmel, in early January 1981.

The hospital, from its site towering over the busy provincial town in south Tipperary, had an interesting history. It had formerly been the Clonmel Union Workhouse, an asylum of last resort for the poor and the mentally ill. In 1924, the Irish Free State had designated it as St. Joseph's Hospital, with the Sisters of Mercy as the administrators. Subsequently, after renovations and extensions, it was designated as the county medical and maternity hospital.

That was its function when I took up duty. I am unable to ascertain its bed capacity at the time, but counting from memory, I would estimate it to be about a hundred, including twenty beds allocated to maternity services. It was what we nowadays would call a primary care hospital, with serious or complicated cases referred to more specialized hospitals in Cork, Kilkenny, or Dublin. All surgical cases were referred to Cashel, some eight miles away, where my friend Gabriel Hyland was the consultant surgeon.

My colleagues Colman Walshe and Matt Corcoran, two young men half my age, were fresh out of internship and medical school and up to date on the latest diagnostic and treatment procedures. My years in the African bush and my specialization in public health had kept me from keeping up with the many developments occurring in modern medicine, so it was a stressful situation to contemplate. However, from the outset, my two colleagues were helpful and understanding of my situation.

Most of the routine work of admissions, treatments, and discharges, except those on the maternity ward, fell on our shoulders. This was all done under the watchful eye of the medical consultant, Dr. Tom Prendergast. The maternity unit was overseen by an experienced obstetrician, and we were only called there in an emergency.

While we had our own areas of responsibility during regular working hours, after everyone went home, our clinical and endurance skills really came to the forefront. Whichever one of us was on call for the week took over full responsibility, not only for emergencies and crises in house but also for whomever arrived via ambulance or walked into emergency department.

The responsibility was awesome, at least for me, as I was rusty in clinical practice, and we had little in the way of backup. We were deputed to call the patient's primary care doctor for consultation only in dire circumstances. Often, our calls were met with a not-so-pleasant attitude on the other end of the telephone.

The week we were on call, we would start off with a full day of regular duties on a Monday, stay in the hospital every week night and through the weekend, and then assume our regular schedules from the Monday until the following Friday at six o'clock in the evening. It was an exhausting schedule, one that left me, the not-so-young one, completely overwrought. But I needed to get myself back into the medical profession in Ireland, and I hoped this six-month breathing space would lead me to a less stressful and more secure position. I was determined to fulfil my duties with the utmost dedication.

The weekends were especially busy and overwhelming. We had to deal with all kinds of acute episodes, from automobile accidents to sudden infant death syndrome (SIDS). Memories of some of those cases are still fresh in my mind. In addition to the difficulties of treating such varied conditions, I often had the sad task of consoling family members when tragedy struck and the patients succumbed to their illness or injuries. I recall one handsome young man who was brought in moribund after a fall from his motor cycle and in spite of our efforts he did not make it. It was heart wrenching trying to console the family in their grief. I may add there was no air ambulance service available.

The good news was that we were a happy bunch and supported each other. Coleman, Matt, and even Dr. Prendergast understood where I had come from and were discreet not to ask me why I had undertaken this junior position or my plans for the future. In truth, I had no idea myself. Coleman was especially empathetic and helpful, having himself spent time as a volunteer in a mission hospital in Asia.

When not on call, I lived at home with my parents and was happy to give Breed, my sister, some respite. She continued to cook the midday meal for all of us. I was able to help with the housework. I could not convince Mother that we should get someone in to do house cleaning. Women of her generation were reluctant to allow strangers into their homes, even when they were unable to take care of household duties themselves. There was a sense of pride that made that a no-no.

To my embarrassment, at eighty-plus years, my mother would climb the steep and narrow staircase, tray in hand, to bring me the luxury of breakfast in bed on the mornings I slept in after an exhausting work schedule. I could not convince her that I could take care of myself. That was Mother—always stubborn in her thoughtfulness.

My parents must have wondered why I was not back on the missions. They never questioned me until one evening Mother, with true maternal intuition, asked, "Are you thinking of leaving the convent?" I was flustered, and not having the heart to say yes, I hedged.

Neither could I bring myself to reveal my struggles to my sister Breed, although we were close. There were many winter nights when we both huddled together beside the blazing fire in her sitting room. I was tempted to talk about what bothered me, but somehow, I couldn't get it out. I didn't think she would understand. After all, she had taken marriage vows and was prepared to see them through the good times and the bad. Why not I? I felt alone, as if I were walking a lonely path to nowhere.

My six months at St. Joseph's were coming to a close, and all the efforts I had made to secure employment in the medical field in Ireland had come to naught. On a visit to one of our convents in Dublin, I had a conversation with a contemporary who had just returned from a religious studies sabbatical at Gonzaga University, a Jesuit-founded institution in Spokane,

Washington. She highly praised the program called CREDO (Continuing Religious Education Development Opportunities Program), which provided a source of renewal in mind and spirit.

CREDO had started as a course mainly for religious men and women experiencing burnout. It was designed to help them reawaken their spiritual life, often during a transition to a new type of ministry. While there were special courses and lectures relevant to updated theology, scripture, and religious vows, attendance was not required, and there were no credits involved. The raisin d'être of the program was for participants to relax in prayer and spiritual connection while experiencing community in a happy, caring way.

In July, I had an appointment with Margaret, the superior general. She recommended that for the next year, I join the community at MSHR headquarters in Blackrock, Dublin. She, along with four other counselors and a secretarial assistant belonged to this community..

Margaret felt I needed the experience of a loving, caring community. My official designation would be the bursar, or community treasurer, with my other duties consisting of hospitality and housekeeping. I appreciated her concern. My pride and independent streak came to the fore, and I balked.

I hesitantly let her know that I was considering other plans and was convinced I needed more spiritual and psychological help. Could I have her permission to attend the CREDO program? While it was late in the academic year to be making an application, she agreed I could apply.

So began another saga down that road to independence of

Marita wanting to do her thing!; a clear indication of how far she had strayed from that day of profession when she surrendered her will and her future to God through the voice of her superiors.

With some guilty vibes, I sent a letter of application to Gonzaga University. Shortly thereafter, I received a reply in the positive.

A few weeks later, I was back in Killeshandra for the annual preached retreat. Many of my contemporaries were there. While I was happy to see them, at the same time, I felt I was not on the same wave length as they were. I was glad we were committed to the rule of silence during those eight days so that I did not have to reveal my inner struggle.

The final day was highlighted by the ceremony of first profession. A few young women were taking their vows of dedication to God and the missionary apostolate, just as I had unreservedly done thirty years previously. It was particularly painful to be present at the ceremony as my journey was now on a different path.

Later that evening, as we held each other in fond embraces before we scattered to the four corners of the world to pursue our various ministries, I had an empty feeling in the pit of my stomach. I knew I would probably never see some of them again. They were all my family, the only ones I knew and loved, and they had shown unconditional love while respecting my individuality.

As the car swept down the avenue, I kept gazing out the window so as to conceal the tears that freely flowed. I was turning my back on the only life I knew, and for the last time, I was looking at the shining white house on the hill. It was surreal.

By strange coincidence, my arrival in New York was just in time to attend my brother, Henry's marriage to his bride, Mary, the beautiful lady he had met in our adopted town of Clonmel. He had already sought laicization from the priesthood, and I was comfortable with his decision. Henceforth, he would serve God's people not only as a family-oriented clinical psychologist but also as a model of Christian marriage in his love for his wife and their two sons.

## REFLECTION AND CONFUSION

I arrived in Spokane just in time for the start of the CREDO program in early September. Our group of approximately one hundred were mostly religious sisters. We were an international group, with members coming from as far away as Australia and New Zealand. There was a large contingent from Canada. While we were housed in a building separate from the college students, we took our meals at the main cafeteria of the university so we could intermingle with the young men and women.

In the dorm, the group was divided into smaller communities according to the floor we lived on. While the rooms had been set up to house two students, we were afforded individual privacy. On the third floor, I was lucky to be in an amicable, supportive group of about thirty sisters, ranging in age from forty to seventy. All were from different backgrounds and different apostolates, many suffering burnout and looking to embrace new ministries.

There was a clear joie de vivre and sense of relaxation among the group. I quickly made friends with individual members, but when it came to being part of the wider community on the floor, I was uncomfortable and wanted to steer clear of getting involved. Was this the crux of my problem and why I held myself aloof?—that I was no longer comfortable living in a community of women, no matter how congenial they were. At least it was proving to be one of them.

There were approximately ten men in the group, either priests or religious brothers. While they participated in communal and liturgical get-togethers, on the whole, they kept to themselves. I can honestly say there was no inappropriate intermingling—no opportunity for gossip!

In my first interview with Dr. Helen Douhan, director of the program, I came clean as to the real motivation for my coming to CREDO: I was at a crossroads in my spiritual and earthly life. She assured me that I was not the first person to join the program with those issues. Answering my request for help in counseling, she recommended an experienced psychiatrist on Gonzaga's faculty. The feedback from previous participants whom he had counseled was positive.

I duly made an appointment with Dr. Mc.A. and found my way to his private office, which was a couple of bus rides from the campus. Each week thereafter, I found myself spilling out my life story. The doctor listened to my disclosures without commenting—that is, until I had recounted, and emotionally relived, the episodes around my community's refusal to allow me return to Ortum after I received my master's degree.

He gently broke his silence to observe, "You must be very angry about all this." For the first time, I could reach down to the inner regions of those pent-up, repressed emotions and admit verbally my anger and my extreme sense of rejection regarding the entire situation.

Up to that moment, I had always held tightly to the belief that expressing anger was a sin. It was an emotion to be banished from consciousness whenever it reared its head. Now I was allowing myself to be comforted by someone who could appreciate that I had reasons to feel the way I did. Feelings of relief came over me, finally freeing me to look at the whole situation more objectively.

As the year of renewal progressed, I entered as much as possible into community events, including outings to interesting places, boat rides on Lake Coeur d'Alene in Idaho, and hikes into the Cascade Mountains, all trips arranged to help participants relax and take time to smell the roses. We even found our way to Nordstrom Rack in downtown Spokane for some bargain shopping. From the beginning, we were told that attending courses on campus was non-obligatory; we were free to pick and choose.

In an attempt to regain some faith in religious life, I signed up to attend a series of lectures on the religious vows, given by one of the Jesuits. Although I dutifully sat there listening to him expound on the theology behind the vows of poverty, obedience, and celibacy, I could not connect on a personal level. I recounted my thoughts and negative reactions during my sessions with Dr. Mc A, all of which he absorbed without comment.

My assigned spiritual director was Sister Mary Garvey, a wonderful woman who was also the co-director of the program. Talking to someone about my prayer and spiritual life was never easy, but I did my best during my weekly sessions to give an account of my progress or lack thereof. She was aware of the struggle I was going through. But the decision had to be mine alone—that was a given.

Before the academic year ended in May, we were encouraged to attend a thirty-day retreat following the exercises of St. Ignatius Loyola, who, in the fifteenth century, was the founder of the Jesuit religious order. To explain, I quote from IgnatianSpirituality.com: "The Spiritual Exercises are a compilation of meditations, prayers and contemplative practices developed by St. Ignatius Loyola to help people deepen their relationship with God. For centuries the Exercises were most commonly given as a 'long retreat' of about 30 days in solitude and silence."

One was only expected to perform this exercise once in a lifetime, and it was not meant to be an exercise in discernment about a future lifestyle.

In spite of being in a state of flux and discerning mode, I embraced this exercise with a sincere desire to deepen my relationship with God. Again, I took copious notes. All of them are personal and speak of a special time in my life when, in response to meditating on the prescribed scriptural texts, I was able to experience some of the joys of contemplation. It was overall a time of peace and tranquility in spite of the odd session of tears of frustration. I placed my destiny in God's hands and earnestly asked to be shown the way of the future.

Upon my completion of the thirty days in the desert, it was difficult to get back to talking about mundane subjects after being on another planet. Even the sound of my own voice was strange.

We had a further summer session of lectures and seminars before the final dispersion and issuance of certificates. The group chose me to be spokeswoman to present Helen Doohan and Mary Garvey with expressions and tokens of gratitude for their leadership. I guess you would call me the valedictorian! I don't know how that happened, but it was a boost to my ego to have the group choose me.

As we disbanded and the participants returned to our home bases, I had to question where mine was. I had no idea how to proceed or to whom I could turn. My student visa was expiring. I had to make some urgent decisions.

At one of my last sessions with Dr. Mc.A., he posed the question "Where do you go from here?" After a little hesitation, I stated that my mind was made up. I would leave the Holy Rosary congregation. I would write a letter to the superior general requesting that she start the process of getting me a dispensation from my vows, a dispensation that I knew could only come from the pope, the representative of God on earth. Seeing the difficult time I had in coming to this decision, Dr. Mc A reassured me that he felt confident it was the appropriate path for me.

I returned to my dorm, and over the space of the next week, I wrote my letter to the superior general. As I could not bring myself to mail it, I brought it with me to my final session with Dr. Mc.A. I read it to him and then asked if he would mail it for me. Needless to say, his response was in the negative. "If you had the courage to write it," he said, "you will have the courage to mail it." But I didn't. It was all too scary. All the same old demons of fear, loneliness, insecurity, and failure gripped me.

I took an overnight bus ride to San Francisco to visit my good friend Father Paddy Cullen, who, by that time, was stationed in Saratoga, near San Jose. I guess actions spoke louder than words as I requested he help me get an extension of my student visa. I was hesitant to tell Father Paddy of my predicament. I didn't think he would understand. I know that was a presumptive and wrong judgment on my part. While he was always ready with an "It will all work out" answer to a difficult situation or dilemma, he stood the test of time and was my friend forever after.

After procuring the extension to my visa and doing some sightseeing on the West Coast, including a visit to Yosemite National Park, I headed back east to visit my family on Long Island. Everyone was in vacation mode, and I tried to put on a good face and hide how unhappy and conflicted I was. Family members must have wondered what I was up to, but no one said anything, as I only experienced an all-embracing love and welcome.

Finally, in my sister's vacation house in Hampton Bays, I could bear the procrastination no longer. In desperation, I took up my pen and, in the most uncharacteristic penmanship, scrawled a plea to Margaret, the superior general, asking for direction regarding what to do next. I don't know what I was expecting her to do, but I had reached the end of my rope and was paralyzed in my inability to take the next step. For a moment in time, I was prepared to obey and do whatever she advised.

Margaret must have sensed the urgency and my desperation. A few days later, I was called to the telephone to receive a long-distance call from the superior general in Dublin. To this day, I have no idea how she got my sister's phone number. It would have required some detective work.

Her directive was that I should not return to Ireland. Instead, I should proceed to our convent in Villanova, near Philadelphia. I would be involved in promotional work until further decisions were made.

The Villanova convent, located just behind the main campus of Villanova University, had been the headquarters of the Holy Rosary Sisters since they established a foundation in the United States in the early 1950s.

The huge convent, built during the '50s to accommodate the large number of aspirants applying to become missionary sisters, was by that time, due to various factors in the intervening years, no longer needed and was an immense burden for its upkeep. Luckily, the Augustinian Fathers, who sponsor the university, were interested and bought it to become their regional headquarters. By the time I joined them, the sisters were staying in the gatehouse of the estate until they could find new accommodations.

In Villanova, Sister Nancy, the regional superior, Philomena who was one of the founding members of the congregation and Mike and Terry all gave me a warm, sisterly welcome. They were careful not to pry or ask any questions I was unwilling to volunteer.

In addition to writing letters of thanks to our benefactors, my main responsibility was to take my turn preaching in churches about the needs of third-world countries and especially the work we were doing in Africa and Brazil—for which, of course, we needed financial support. To get to these appointed venues, which ranged as far as two or three states away, I needed a US driver's license and had to get used to driving on the right side of the road, not to mention navigating multilane highways with high-speed traffic.

I had never imagined myself standing at the front of a large congregation in a church to deliver a homily that incorporated an appeal for the missions. Although I was having difficulty with my commitment to religious life, I was still very much committed to my missionary vocation. I tried during the Sunday Masses to incorporate the scripture readings with the spiritual and economic needs of the developing world. Some of the feedback, supported by monetary contributions, helped allay my innate shyness and reluctance to stand up there and speak. In retrospect, I often wonder how I did it!

The first order of business on arrival in Villanova was that I should clear up all legalities regarding my residence in the United States. While I was not seeking the coveted green card of permanent residence at the time, I needed documentation to allow me to engage in promotional work for an NGO (non-governmental organization), such as the MSHRs. This I readily procured from the immigration office, dressed in my full religious garb. I was now armed with legal residence status, even if it was limited in its scope.

During the summer of the next year, we moved to a vacated convent attached to a parish near City Line in Philadelphia. I was commissioned to spearhead the move, which allowed me to dabble in the interior decorating of the new residence, something that appealed to my aesthetic sense. There was no central air, and only the living room had an air-conditioning unit in the window. When we couldn't tolerate the heat and humidity for another minute, we four new residents would converge on that room and fall on the floor to cool down. My first taste of the dog days of August in an East Coast city was worse than anything I had experienced in Africa.

## A BUD OF BRANCHING OUT

With the wisdom that comes with age and the advantage of an objective eye, I needed to come to terms with the fact that just as I loved my biological family, Holy Rosary was a family as well. In spite of my wanderings in mind and spirit, the sisters provided a home I could always come back to and received me with open arms.

Although I had been barred from returning to Ortum in 1973, the congregation had honored a host of nontraditional requests from me: to work for the government and University of Nairobi in Kenya; to live with my family in Clonmel while I tried to restart my medical career after Kenya; and to spend months in Spokane, seeking spiritual renewal. They'd also found a place for me in the U.S. community when I reached out in pain and confusion after I couldn't go through with my plan to leave. Whenever I was sick in body or emotion, I always had guidance from superiors with good intentions—even if I didn't always agree—and sisters who would take care of me.

Yet the part of me that wanted to be free would not rest quietly. I yearned to return to medicine and make a living on my own. Now in the United States, I had no idea where to turn and knew no one in the medical profession in the area.

While visiting family in New York in late summer 1981, following the lead of my niece Marie, I started looking for work. Marie had graduated from college in June and was job seeking, so I joined her and resorted to help-wanted ads in the *New York Times*, surely a strange place to look for a medical position. I was surprised to see a listing for a position that I thought suited my qualifications. A Catholic hospital in Paterson, New Jersey, sought an experienced medical director to oversee the emergency department. The duties included responsibility for the employees' health department. A master's in public health was a requirement. I submitted an application.

Within days, I was called for an interview. I somehow prevailed on my brother Thomas (Mausie) to take me to this event. Mausie picked me up in his automobile and I duly appeared before a search committee of physicians and other senior administrative personnel in the boardroom of St. Joseph's Hospital in Paterson, New Jersey, a far-distant replica of the hospital of the same name in Clonmel, County Tipperary.

I cannot remember most of the questions or why they thought I was qualified to fill the position. One committee member said they were looking for someone who was boarded in preventative medicine. I believe he was indirectly trying to give me a message of my unsuitability. Although I wasn't yet licensed to practice medicine in New Jersey—or anywhere in the United States, for that matter—I replied naively, "No problem. I can get that." I guess the best word to describe my boldness at the time was the Yiddish *chutzpah*, which refers to courage bordering on arrogance

After the interview, I presented myself at the licensing board of medicine in the New Jersey capital of Trenton to obtain a license to practice medicine in that state. I learned that the fact that I was licensed in Ireland, Kenya, and Zambia was of no consequence. I had to take and pass the FLEX (Federation Licensing Exam), better known as the ECFMG (Examination for the Certification of Foreign Medical Graduates), including a test in the English language. I had ten days to submit all documentation to prove that I already had been through medical school and was licensed. This task involved some expedited maneuvers, but I got all of the information submitted in time.

It was now mid-September, and the examination was scheduled for the first week in December. Luckily, I was offered a nice, quiet domicile in which to study without any distractions or interruption. It was in the living quarters of a nursing home in downtown Philadelphia, where a group of the sisters were on staff.

It had now been thirty years since I'd studied anatomy, physiology, chemistry, pathology, and the other subjects on the test. Except for attending daily Mass and having my meals, I spent every waking hour reviewing the medical school curriculum until the neurons in my brain could no longer absorb another detail.

When the exam days arrived, I joined the hundreds of international candidates hoping to get licensed to practice medicine in the state of New Jersey. It struck me how many candidates were from the developing world, where I knew their services were badly needed. It made me sad to see with my own eyes evidence of the well-documented brain drain from those countries.

After two full days of answering multiple-choice questions in the various disciplines, we spent the last day making hypothetical management decisions based on patient case studies. We could not proceed to the next decision until we answered the previous one correctly. For each attempt, points were deducted. My previous experience in clinical medicine served me well in that exercise.

Each candidate had to pass the written test before being allowed to take the English language test, so I was happy when I was given clearance to proceed. Obviously, the test was designed for potential physicians whose native language was not English, but everyone had to be treated equally. I passed the English conversation test with flying colors.

Being approved by the Federation of Examining Boards was essential for a foreign graduate to practice medicine in any state of the Union, although each state had its own licensing board, and there was not always reciprocity. I was elated when I received news that I'd been accepted as a fully licensed medical practitioner in the state of New Jersey.

With that news came a letter stating that I was not accepted for the position at St. Joseph's Hospital in Paterson. It took some time, but I eventually realized my lucky stars. I would have been completely out of my depth and competency as the leader of a team of personnel in the emergency center in urban Paterson, a trauma center kept busy by the crashes on surrounding highways and the violence in neighborhoods riddled with poverty and crime.

My entrée into medical practice in the States came through a chance encounter with an ex–Holy Rosary Sister I had known since our days together in medical school in Dublin. By that time, Gloria, a native of Mississippi, was a pediatrician practicing in Pottstown, some distance from Philadelphia. She still kept contact with friends in Holy Rosary.

While I was still awaiting the results of the FLEX, she invited me to join her in her solo practice, hoping I could hold the fort while she spent several months sorting out family matters in her hometown down south. She also thought I might be interested in specializing in pediatrics. I was happy to get clinical experience, but as I was not yet licensed to practice in the state of Pennsylvania, I was only shadowing her as she made her daily inpatient rounds and treated children in the office. It was soon evident that caring for sick children was not my forte.

I was at a loss as to how I could tell her that this was not working out. That was when providence and Gloria's nurse intervened. Probably from the sick children we were treating in the office, I picked up a bug and ended up with a debilitating case of pneumonia. The nurse, God bless her, realizing the awkward position I was in, offered to take me back to the loving care of the MSHRs in their living quarters attached to St. Ignatius Nursing Home, the place of refuge I'd lived in while

I crammed for the licensing exam. Gloria wasn't pleased, and unfortunately, so ended our friendship.

Before I had totally conquered the effects of pneumonia, I had a blessed respite from career concerns when our parents visited New York to participate in the festivities for St. Patrick's Day. Our mother had been to the States previously, but this was the first visit for our eighty-four year old father, and also his first plane flight. Even though I still did not feel well, I was not going to miss the opportunity to join my sister Bernadette and brother Henry to welcome them at JFK Airport as they arrived in New York. Father enjoyed and took in stride his first transatlantic flight.

My parents spent some time watching the world's largest St. Patrick's Day parade on Fifth Avenue from the grandstand with celebrities of the Irish diaspora. As a special treat and to make sure they wouldn't have to weather New York's March chill for the duration of the six-hour parade, we booked a room for them in the legendary Plaza Hotel. The guest room was a bit cramped as all of squeezed in, not only to enjoy the view of the parade but to serve an impromptu party for our own parade of family and guests. We had a blast.

I recovered from pneumonia and could no longer avoid my own dilemmas. Although I was armed with the licensing requirements to practice medicine in the United States, I didn't have immigration clearance, the famous green card granting permanent residence in the country and the permission to engage in gainful employment—in my case, to earn a living in the practice of medicine.

There were two routes open to me in order to be approved

for permanent residency, either through my sister, who was already a naturalized citizen, or as a change in my status with the MSHRs. The former approach was known to have a long backlog and wait list, so I decided to take the bull by the horns and go the route of the latter.

On the day after Labor Day, one year after my arrival in Philadelphia, I headed to the immigration office and took my place in line. There was a restriction in awarding residency to foreign medical graduates, especially those seeking entrance from the developing world, because of the aforementioned brain drain, but I decided I was not going to lie if asked whether I planned to practice medicine.

As I watched how the different officials greeted and related to applicants before taking them aside for interviews, I kept saying to myself, *I hope I don't get that lady.* (Yes, I hate to admit it, but the not-so-nice officials were female.) There was only one man working the admissions desk, and he seemed pleasant and respectful. I wondered whether it was random fate or the good Lord helping me when he was the one who beckoned me to come forward.

He led me into an interior office and questioned me extensively with regard to my family background and my previous personal and professional experience, but he never asked the critical question that might have disqualified me. After the grilling, the kind gentleman informed me that I would be granted permanent residence, and a green card would be forthcoming in the mail. I'd cleared another hurdle!

# IN REMEMBRANCE OF
MY IRISH TWIN

Recounting Mausie's help in driving me to my interview reminds me that I have not made mention of my brother or his family since the time we bade farewell many years before in Dublin. Upon his arrival to the United States, he took up residence with Aunt Annie's family in Fort Lee, New Jersey, where he found employment with Grand Union Supermarket Company. He fell in love and married Mary O'Sullivan, who hailed from Kerry. They settled in Newton, in northern New Jersey. They had four offspring: one girl, Geraldine, and three sons, Thomas, John, and Kevin.

On my visits to the New York area, I included visits to Thomas and Mary. I was always welcome in their home. Mausie, as we continued to affectionately call him, was reticent, and it was hard to know what he was really thinking. He was definitely a man of few words, but when he expressed his insights, they hit the nail on the head. He was renowned for his work ethic and his ability, for several years, to make a sixty-mile round trip to his job, through rain, snow, or sunshine, without ever a complaint. The company recognized his devotion to duty, and he rose through the ranks of its management departments.

Fast-forward several years, and he was enjoying his retirement, when, with great sadness, we had to say a sudden and unexpected farewell on the Labor Day weekend of 2007. He suffered a massive hemorrhage from a ruptured abdominal aortic aneurysm. He died as he had lived: quietly and humbly. May he rest in peace! My Irish twin, hopefully one day we will celebrate our combined birthdays together in heaven.

CHAPTER 13

# REHABILITATION

My patience was wearing thin. Even with the credentials to practice medicine in the United States, I was beginning to believe I would never find an opportunity to do so. Without success I had tried for a few positions in my specialty of preventive medicine. I was wondering whether I should return to Ireland or go to the United Kingdom to find a job.

Out of the blue, a lead came from an unexpected quarter. A chaplain at one of the Catholic hospitals in the city was a frequent visitor to our convent. He was a Spiritan priest who previously had worked with our sisters in Nigeria. On this particular day I happened to be the only person free to visit with him. In the course of conversation, I told him of my difficulty in getting established in a medical practice in the United States. He generously offered to speak with one of his doctor friends to see if he could help.

A few days later, I received a phone call from Dr. Boyle, the chief of the rehabilitation department at Fitzgerald Mercy

Hospital and a physiatrist, a specialty I had never previously encountered. The equivalent in the British and Irish medical systems would be a rheumatologist. When I found my way to the hospital the next day, Dr. Boyle, whose ancestors had come from county Donegal, was welcoming and supportive. He suggested I come on board as an observer to see if I would like physiatry, the profession that specializes in physical medicine and rehabilitation (PM&R). I accepted the offer, but because I was not yet licensed in Pennsylvania, over the next several weeks, I acted essentially as an aide, even transporting patients to the gym from their hospital beds.

Even though I had not been aware that PM&R was a recognized medical specialty, it fit into my thinking within the discipline of community health. Rehabilitation is regarded as the third degree of prevention and intervention in the public health field. A primary intervention is the prevention of disease or injury, a secondary reduces the impact of a disease or injury, and a third-degree intervention aims to restore as much function as possible and improve the quality of life for the person after a catastrophic injury or illness.

I liked especially the team approach whereby doctors, psychologists, physical and occupational therapists, and speech pathologists all worked together to restore function to patients after catastrophic events, such as stroke or traumatic brain injury. Besides, I was happy to be back in a medical environment.

Dr. Boyle's associate, Dr. Jim Bonner, had just completed his residency after attending medical school in Dublin, and immediately, we established a bond. Jim performed most of the clinical work in the twenty-bed inpatient unit at the hospital.

Seeing my enthusiasm for the work, he suggested I do a residency in PM&R. He had recently graduated from this residency program at the University of Pennsylvania and offered to call the director of the program to see if there might be a place for me at a future intake.

My initial reaction was "No way!" I couldn't spend four more years in training for a new specialty at this stage of my life. But I gave it some thought, factoring in my new status as a permanent US resident, and took Jim up on his offer.

## TWO STEPS FORWARD AND ONE STEP BACK

Shortly afterward, I met with Dr. Stoner, the director of the residency program, and was accepted right away because fortunately for me, someone had just dropped out after only a few months as a resident. I would start on November 1, a few weeks away. I was ecstatic but more than a little apprehensive.

The residency program was affiliated with several medical centers in the greater Philadelphia area, and we rotated for three-month stints through each of them. One afternoon per week, we attended lectures and tutorials on the campus of the hospital of the University of Pennsylvania (HUP). That was when we met the other residents and recounted our experiences, some good and some not so.

While I could have been a mother to most of my colleagues, they made me feel well accepted. They also knew my background and were not intimidated by my knowledge and experience. In fact, they appreciated when I wasn't afraid to represent our needs or gripes at the weekly meetings with Dr. Stoner.

My first residency assignment was at the acute rehabilitation unit at HUP in central Philadelphia. What a rude awakening that was! From my gentle introduction to physiatry at the Fitzgerald Mercy Hospital, I was thrown into the deep end—directly involved in patient care. I was expected to admit and discharge patients, read CT scans (still an unfamiliar technology to me), and replace urinary and gastric tubes. The latter are feeding tubes inserted through the abdominal wall directly into the stomach. I was scared stiff, but I gave it my all and received a lot of support from the other residents and the nursing staff.

On January 2, 1984, I started a new rotation at the Sacred Heart Hospital in Norristown, in the suburbs of Philadelphia and nearer to where I was living. It was a less intense environment, which suited me fine.

There I encountered two doctors who would play significant roles in my new career. Dr. Frank Bonner, an older brother of Jim, was the director of the rehabilitation department. All five of the Bonner siblings had specialized in PM&R, following in the footsteps of their father, who had been one of the founding members of the specialty. Frank, a fellow graduate of University College Dublin, immediately took me under his wing.

Frank's associate, Dr. Wilma Kellerman, like myself, had started a second residency later in her career and understood my circumstances. She was in charge of the twenty-bed inpatient unit, so I worked closely with her. I needed to be on the floor by seven o'clock each morning in order to have the laboratory and all other test results ready for the rounds that started at seven thirty. The fifteen-minute drive through snow and ice in the dead of winter was scary to contemplate and stressful to accomplish, but nothing was going to stop me in my ambition to succeed. I persevered and got a good report at the end of the three-month rotation.

Frank initiated me into the technique of electrodiagnosis, which included nerve conduction studies (NCS) and electromyography (EMG). These tests assess how well a patient's peripheral nerves and muscles are working. NCS measures how fast nerves can contract muscles after stimulation with a small electric shock (e.g., a delay of the median nerve at the wrist might signify that the patient has carpal tunnel syndrome). EMG measures the electrical activity in muscles when at rest and when they contract. Abnormalities might indicate neuromuscular disease (e.g., amyotrophic lateral sclerosis [ALS], colloquially known as Lou Gehrig's disease).

The tests are not pleasant for patients because they involve putting electrodes, some on the skin and others by needle, into the muscles and stimulating them to get them to contract. Accurately interpreting the findings of the EMG requires a good knowledge of anatomy, and I found that the grinding we got in medical school served me well in that respect. The onus of making a correct diagnosis was awesome, and it had to be approved by the consultant before finalization.

My next rotation was in Princeton, New Jersey, a commute of more than one hour each way on the busy Pennsylvania Turnpike. The inpatient unit was attached to the acute-care hospital adjacent to the university campus but not actually on it. I sometimes had to pinch myself when I realized I was practicing in the shadows of such a famous college.

I spent one of the summers at Seashore House, a facility for the rehabilitation of children on the boardwalk of Atlantic City, New Jersey. When asked by the director of scheduling if I would like to take that rotation for the summer months, I thought it would be a plumb assignment to be so near the ocean. After I had agreed, I found out that the majority of my colleagues had turned down the rotation because they did not want to spend the summer months at a facility with a very intensive schedule.

Children with chronic illnesses or disabilities, such as cerebral palsy, muscular dystrophy, chronic asthma, and cystic fibrosis, were admitted to the hospital for a period of approximately two weeks to give respite to parents who took care of them at home for the rest of the year. This made the hospital a revolving door. Mike Spady, my fellow resident, and I were admitting and discharging up to ten patients per day. To add to the intensity of the rotation, either Mike or I had to take turns staying within the four walls of the hospital for twenty-four hours at a time to address emergencies—and there were plenty. The most urgent and nerve-racking emergency was treating a child with the onset of an acute asthmatic attack.

Because I was never off duty at the same time as Mike, there wasn't much to do all by myself, and our domicile was anything but enticing, even though we were right on the boardwalk at the beach. In my few visits to the casinos, I played the twenty-five-cent slot machines but, predictably, rarely came out a winner. Gambling was not in my genes, but there were few other diversions.

To my surprise, the three and a half years of the residency passed quickly enough. After its completion, we sat for the first part of the board examination, a written test. It was such a relief a few weeks later to open the envelope from the examining board and find I had passed. That was in June 1986.

The next step was to practice for one year, where we were essentially subspecializing under the guidance of a fully credentialed consultant. After that, the final requirement for full accreditation and fellowship of the American Academy of Physical Medicine and Rehabilitation (AAPM&R) was to take and pass an oral test. AAPM&R accreditation was a necessary qualification for professional status and a prerequisite for a consulting position in any major clinical setting.

My last few months of the residency were an anxious time, as I was not only preparing for the examination but also deciding on the type of work I wanted to do and at what location. Dr. Frank Bonner encouraged me to take a fellowship at the Graduate Hospital in downtown Philadelphia, where he also was the medical director of rehabilitation. Taking that fellowship meant I would have opportunity to become more efficient in EMG practice. I accepted, knowing I still had to figure out what my long-term plans were. Frank Bonner kept assuring me that he would take care of me if I joined his practice, but he didn't clearly indicate how.

Meanwhile, I had become eligible to sit for the final examination to be boarded in my original specialty of preventative medicine. My experience teaching in the department of community health in Kenya was accepted in lieu of a residency. I decided to take a shot at the written test before my eligibility period expired. I did some review of the subject matter, and on one cold winter day, I landed in some city in the Midwest, I believe it was Minneapolis, where I found the venue and did the best I could answering the multiple-choice questions. It was good news and a boost to my ego when I received a letter a few weeks later indicating that I had passed and would become a fellow of the American Board of Public Health and General Preventive Medicine.

## FINAL DECISION

Although I was doing well professionally, my inner life was still one of turmoil. No matter how I tried, I did not seem to fit into the Holy Rosary community—in spite of the fact that I could not have been in a more understanding, supportive group.

By the 1980s, each of us in the community had embraced individualism to some extent. We had jobs inside and outside the convent and took turns preparing the evening meal, which was one of the few exercises we agreed to attend in common. We also had regular meetings to discuss finances and other housekeeping issues. As is to be expected in any group of independent-minded women, we had differences in point of view, and these created mostly minor stresses. At least we were respectful of each other's point of view.

The straw that broke the camel's back for me happened at one of the annual regional meetings, which must have been sometime in the autumn of 1985. I expressed some of my negative sentiments and opinions, especially as to what the future looked like for the survival of the status quo for us sisters and missionaries. When the discussion got around to how we could be proactive in recruiting new aspirants, my lack of faith in the institution was particularly evident. While at the meeting, there was no challenge to my comments, afterward, one of the participants approached me and said my negativism had upset the group.

I knew I had to take action; the only option was to leave. However, though it is hard to believe, I still needed reassurance.

Over the years since I left Spokane, Dr. Mc.A. and I had exchanged Christmas greetings, so I knew he was now living and practicing in Baltimore. I made contact with him, and he kindly agreed to see me one Saturday morning at his home. I rehashed a lot of what we'd discussed five years earlier. After listening patiently, he eventually said, "I don't understand. What is holding you back?"

I couldn't explain either, but after a moment's reflection, I muttered, "This is it. I am doing it."

It so happened that the evening after I finally said, "This is it," I was boarding a plane to visit my father in Ireland. He had suffered a stroke several days after falling and sustaining injuries that included broken ribs. He survived the acute episode. I would have liked to stay longer than the one-week leave of absence the director of the residency program gave me, but duty called. I felt bad about leaving the care of both my parents, now well into their eighties, to my sister Breed and her husband, Frank, but I felt compelled to follow the new opportunities afforded me.

Still vacilating and to ease the transition, I requested from

Sister Margaret, the superior general, an absence of one year of from the community, a not-unusual request under the circumstances. This was granted.

During my leave of absence, I would be living on my own in a rented apartment and have time to reflect on the future. Any dealings I had with Holy Rosary would be directly with the superior general and not with the local community.

As soon as it was confirmed that all was in order, I informed the sisters in the community I was living with of my decision. There were tears and good wishes all around, although I don't think any of them were surprised at what I had to tell them. Within the next few days, with the help of Sister Mike, the current regional superior, I found the essentials to set up house. The community purchased a good used car for me.

When the day of departure came, it was a painful exit for me. I really loved these women and many others who had been part of my family for nearly forty years. But I had to do what I had to do—at last!

I moved to a high-rise apartment building near King of Prussia, on the outskirts of Philadelphia. While I felt a great sense of relief, it also felt weird. Inside my home, I was at peace, but just shopping for myself at the supermarket evoked a feeling of self-consciousness, as if other shoppers might notice that I was a lost soul. My imagination was running wild.

In my building, everybody minded his or her own business, although we were cordial if we encountered one another in the hallway, the communal laundry, or the outdoor pool area. I was reserved and timid, afraid of letting people know my background and what I was going through. This, of course, did not help me with socialization. Even though I had lived alone before and had adapted to many changes in living arrangements, I had difficulty feeling comfortable in a secular lifestyle after so many years in the protected world of religious life.

I wasn't tempted to retreat back into the convent. While I am rather vague on timing, I believe I quickly made up my mind that this was it; this was to be my lifestyle for the rest of my life. So I set the wheels in motion for the final break.

The most formidable part of the process was writing a personal letter to the pope. I had to inform him of the reasons for my request and humbly ask him to grant the dispensation from my perpetual vows. I penned the letter in my best handwriting and on the finest notepaper available. Following official procedure, I submitted the letter to the superior general to take it from there. This time around, I had no problem mailing the letter.

## EMOTIONAL ENDINGS

Over my years of struggle, my confidante and great friend Sister Áine le Muire was always there for me. By that time, she was living and working in Ireland, and on my visits home, we would meet up and often go on little trips of our own.

As I approached my next emotional hurdle—telling my parents I was leaving the convent—I sought Áine's advice. She knew my parents well and agreed the news would be painful for them. I ultimately decided not to directly inform them;

I would answer any questions truthfully if asked and let the message sink in by osmosis, as it were.

In the meantime, my ninety-two-year-old father wasn't doing well, and he never recovered from the effects of the stroke, even after a stay in a rehabilitation unit. That was particularly difficult for me, seeing as I was now specializing in that field and knew all the possibilities from an aggressive program of therapies. It was particularly difficult to be so far away and not be able to appreciate how he was responding to the therapies at the extended-care facility

On his return home, still with left-side paralysis and unable to walk, he asked Breed whether he would recover the use of his limbs. She gently informed him that the doctors didn't think he would. Father died within a week of that conversation, on May 23, 1986. He was mentally alert up to the end.

I never had to distress my father by telling him of my big decision. At the time of his death, my dispensation had not come through. I must say, however, that I felt somewhat of a hypocrite when meeting my relatives at his funeral. All of them addressed me as Sister. I didn't advise them to the contrary.

On my arrival back in my apartment, there waiting for me was the letter from the superior general with a copy of the indult from Rome, dispensing me from my vows. Margaret wrote a comforting, generous letter, wishing me only the best in my future life. While I had externally broken the final cord that bound me to the Missionary Sisters of the Holy Rosary, interiorly, I was still one of them in love and appreciation.

Over the years since that definitive day, I not only have kept up contact with Áine but also, each time I am in Ireland, have met up with some of my sister friends, especially those I had soldiered with in Kenya when we have shared a meal together. Unfortunately, Sisters Breed and Tina, two of the best, passed to their reward quite a few years back.

On January 27, 2018, I had to face the grim reality that my dearest friend, my *anam cara* (Gaelic equivalent of soul mate), Áine had joined them. The news of her death touched me deeply. I will so much miss visiting with her, such as when in May of this year I attend celebrations to mark the 60th anniversary of our class's graduation from medical school. It will not be the same, not to get to a 'nice' restaurant (of her choice!) and there over a meal and a glass or 'two'! of wine share our deepest thoughts and aspirations. Her oft repeated desire was for me to return to live in the land of my birth. She will be forever in my heart. Ar dheis De go raibh a h'anam (Gaelic equivalent of May she rest in peace)

To continue with the story of the long road to freedom….

After thirteen years of living neither fully as a religious sister nor as a secular woman, my reaction to the indult was one of immense relief. The caged bird was free at last. Interestingly, the card that Margaret, the superior general, sent me, was of a fledgling bird cupped in the palms of two human hands, an image of God's love and care for us that has meant a lot to me: "I have engraved you on the palms of My Hands" (Isaiah 49:16, English Standard Version).

I cannot recall how I informed my siblings or other members of my family of my leaving. In retrospect, I am sorry I wasn't more open with them. I did not try to explain the reasons that got me to that decision. There was an element of silence on their part also. If any one of them had asked why I left, I would willing have explained.

For me, one of the hardest things as I transitioned back into the family fold was to feel I belonged. Not only had my years in the convent distanced me from family, but also, being in boarding school and living with the Misses Maher during my teenage years had added to my estrangement. I am talking about my inner feelings and not in any way implying that I was not fully accepted and supported, not only by my sisters and brothers but also by the next generation of nieces and nephews. They were wonderful.

After my father's death, my sister Breed and her family continued to take care of Mother. I tried to make it home at least once a year to help a little and give Breed some respite. Mother remained in good physical health, although her mental status slowly declined. She was well enough to come to the United States to celebrate her ninetieth birthday and, if I recall, even another subsequent one. Each time, at the end of my visits home, when we were saying goodbye, tears would roll down my face as I related to her that I had to return to the United States, and she would look at me with those appealing blue eyes and whisper, "Will you take me with you?"

It was a great relief to those of us living far away when our sister Eilish came over from Italy with her teenage daughter Rosalind and spent at least one year in Mother's home, helping to care for her. It must have been a big sacrifice for her husband, Orlando, and the other children, all of them barely past their teens.

A phone call from Breed in early February 1997 warned that

Mother's days on earth were drawing to a close. Bernadette and I made it home to be with her for the final hours. Upon our reaching her bedside, while Mother appeared to be comatose, on hearing our voices, she opened her eyes in recognition and indicated that she knew we were there. That was a consolation. She died early the following morning, February 6, in her ninety-seventh year.

I never had to cause her the upset I knew would come from my informing her that I had let her down and was no longer a nun. Knowing how intuitive she was, she probably already had guessed. One thing I knew was that she still loved me.

In an earlier chapter, I referred to the memorable funeral she was accorded, a recognition of her role in the fight for our national freedom. As I have penned above for Áine, I add here for mother, the Gaelic wish, *Ar dheis De go raibh a h'anam* I pray the same for my father of happy memory.

## CHAPTER 14

# THE REAL WORLD

While Dr. Bonner was supportive and offered to take care of me, I could not pin him down on specifics, especially on remuneration. I was not convinced there was a future for me in his practice. I was now in my fifties and had zero dollars in my bank account. I was concerned as to how I could save for retirement. Besides, I was anxious to get out of Philadelphia and make a complete change not only professionally but also in my personal life.

Out of the blue, I got a phone call from a headhunter asking if I would be interested in taking a job in Connecticut. I listened to his spiel and, at the end, decided to go for an interview at the Middlesex Hospital in Middletown, halfway between New Haven and Hartford. For the first time in my life, I had to play hooky in order to get to the interview. I was successful, and they offered me a position as a salaried medical director of the department of rehabilitation, starting in the first week of January 1987.

Frank Bonner was gracious in allowing me to leave the fellowship mid-year.

Thus, I was out on my own in uncharted waters. At least I was nearer to the family in New York and to my niece Siobhan, who was working and living in Connecticut. She helped me find an apartment and introduced me to her future in-laws, dairy farmers in Middletown.

I must admit it was an adjustment, being in a new environment, knowing nobody socially, and being unsure how to get absorbed into my new world. However, a deep peace had come over me, and I had no regrets for my course of action or for the long journey to get there. I still kept in contact with members of the community in Philadelphia. Ties of a lifetime are not easily broken.

Settling into the new position was not as easy as I expected. My predecessor had paid little attention to the department, and as a consequence, the physical therapist who was the manager held full sway and dealt directly with administration. The hospital was anxious to expand service and especially interested in starting a new inpatient unit.

It was my duty to do a feasibility study to assess if this was a viable proposition. I guess I started throwing my weight around, which did not go down well with my manager, so one day she came into my office and asked the rhetorical question, "What have you got to offer the department that I don't have?" That question prompted me to get all of my certificates mounted and framed. They formed quite a display on the wall of my office.

After a few rough weeks, we began to understand each

other and became not only good working partners but also good friends. My management skills were being honed to suit the situation. The medical staff, the majority of whom were in private practice, were not overly supportive of those of us on the hospital payroll. Many of them held the opinion that those of us employed by the hospital were too much under the control of the administration. As I depended on referrals from their practices, I had to tread lightly and sell myself as best as I could, something that got me out of my comfort zone.

As a body, the medical staff were at complete odds with the president of the hospital and were working on getting him ousted. That was an interesting process to witness—a whole medical staff up in arms against this one man and giving full vent to their feelings at staff meetings. Eventually, they succeeded in getting Mr. McWilliams to resign. I was sorry, as I had found him to be approachable, fair, and honorable.

Another concern that kept me busy after hours and on the weekends was getting ready to take the second part of the board exam, a three-hour oral test at the Mayo Clinic in Minnesota. This exam was to take place early in May, five months after I had moved to Connecticut.

While my colleagues had told me that one didn't study intensely for this test, I was not convinced that was so. Every evening after work and on into the night, I read and reread the textbooks. I booked my flight so as to arrive just a few hours before the scheduled time for the exam. On the plane, I continued to review a treatise on electromyography, which included a review of the peripheral nervous system.

Going into the exam, I was a bag of nerves. Per the setup,

one examiner questioned each of us for an hour; a bell sounded; and we passed on to the next examiner. We faced three different examiners for a total of three hours of oral examination.

One of the first questions I was asked to describe was the distributions of the facial nerve, which is the nerve that, through several branches, supplies muscles of expression and other functions around the face. It is one of the most complex of the twelve cranial nerves. My immediate reaction was "Oh, I didn't review that nerve." I froze. I sat there and couldn't answer another question, not only with that examiner but also with the other two. I was devastated and knew in my heart that there was no way I could pass. When the results came a few weeks later, as expected, I had failed.

This was a mighty blow and definitely took my pride down a peg. I would have to wait one year before presenting for the exam again. As that time drew near, my anxiety level was rising to the extent that my brother, the clinical psychologist, noticed and warned that I was on the same road to perdition unless I sought counseling. I did, and besides relaxation exercises, the doctor prescribed anti-anxiety medication. It was difficult to acknowledge that I needed medication, but it worked miracles.

My second time around, I sailed through the three-hour oral examination without batting an eye. What a different experience it was—and what a relief to have it behind me. In due course, my certificate arrived, confirming that I was now a fellow of the American Academy of Physical Medicine and Rehabilitation, dated May 8, 1988.

As an aside, one of the senior staff members I had encountered during the residency rotations had already twice failed the oral part of the board exam purely due to nerves and mental block. She had resigned herself to never becoming a fellow of the Academy. When she learned of my success, she decided to try once more, and she took the antianxiety medication and couldn't wait to tell me the good news that she had passed.

I think especially when one is a mature student, nerves can really get the better hand in an oral test, and this is not indicative of one's knowledge or ability to practice good medicine. Mind you, I am not advocating for widespread use of antianxiety medication. I think there is a place and time to benefit from modern medicine while recognizing the need for caution and knowing that as far as possible, it should be used only as a temporary remedy.

As soon as I was financially able, I started looking to buy a home. My preference was to get a single-family home with an opportunity to do gardening, a hobby I had always enjoyed. However, friends and colleagues advised that as a single woman, I should settle for a condominium. I listened and settled to buy one in Rocky Hill, which was closer to Hartford than the rental apartment where I was living.

I remember well the day I signed on the dotted line and became a homeowner. In my wildest dreams, I could never have imagined owning a piece of ground in the United States of America. Being able to do that within six years of arriving penniless and jobless was something of which only dreams are made.

I wasn't enamored of condo living, but it was good for a start. I still had my heart set on having a home on its own grounds, with the opportunity to exercise my green thumb.

After answering an ad in our local paper, on one walk through the advertised property, I was smitten, especially by the tree-filled backyard overlooking the sixteenth green of the beautiful golf course in Cromwell, where the Hartford Open is played each year. The house, a three-bedroom ranch, needed a lot of work to update it. With the help of a wonderful artisan, David Darley, over time, I was able to transform and decorate it to suit my personal style. I was also able to turn the backyard into a haven of peace and tranquility.

My next-door neighbors, Peter and Sherry Pierson, became good friends. They still are. Peter's father had built the golf course and developed the homes on the street. They had a magnificent home with an extensive view over the lake right through to the clubhouse. I spent many an evening imbibing a glass of wine as we relaxed together and enjoyed the beauty of the idyllic setting. The other residents were also friendly, and I was happy to have a domicile in such a welcoming, caring environment.

It was a proud moment when I became a United States citizen in August 1996. I had delayed applying for this status due to more pressing obligations in my professional career. Prior to approval, it is necessary to take a test demonstrating a good knowledge of how the democratic system of government works, so the task involves some study. Raising one's right hand to take the oath of allegiance to the United States of America is a thrilling emotional experience. Immediately afterward, one is asked to join the political party of one's choice. My choice was to be an independent. It suits my personality.

By then, everything was going well professionally. While

I was the sole practitioner of my specialty in Middletown, we were physically quite close to the well-known Gaylord Rehabilitation Hospital, with its sufficient complement of beds and expertise to take care of the rehabilitation needs of the surrounding communities. I had a good rapport with the physicians there and also with other physiatrists, throughout the state. I took an active role in revitalizing the State Society of Physical Medicine and Rehabilitation and had my turn at being president for one year.

I was able to convince the administration at the hospital that starting an inpatient rehabilitation unit was not feasible, so my practice was confined to seeing outpatients and performing nerve conduction and electromyography examinations. For the latter, I was competing with the neurologists, which, on occasion, created a stressful situation.

I was into my fourth year of practice in Middletown when a new CEO was appointed to the hospital. It soon became clear that he was a hatchet man hired to cut down on expenditure at all levels, including staff reductions. I became one of the first victims. I was told they could no longer afford to employ me as a full-time salaried physician. They said I should consider going into private practice, and they would pay me a stipend to continue as head of the department. The amount of the offered stipend was almost insulting.

This was a scary prospect, to say the least. I had never been in private practice, and for success my specialty depended on referrals from primary care physicians, neurologists, and orthopedists. From experience, I doubted that would be sufficient for me to earn a living, pay my mortgage, and build a sufficient nest egg for retirement.

However, good luck struck again. The physiatrist who practiced at St. Francis Hospital in Hartford had decided on short notice to relocate to North Carolina. He recommended me as a possibility to replace him. This was a well-established rehabilitation department with a twenty-bed inpatient unit in a busy city hospital. It was certified as a first-level trauma unit, which provided a good intake of patients needing intensive rehabilitation.

I interviewed for and was offered the post of medical director of rehabilitation. I would be paid a decent stipend as medical director, but after that, I would be in private practice. This prospect scared me, but at least I had the reassurance that I would have sufficient patient referrals to cover my expenses. The administration was willing to help me get established and offered, at a reasonable rent, office space in the outpatient rehabilitation department in a building adjoining the acute hospital, where a number of the consultants had their offices.

While the responsibility was great, I was pleased and felt at home in a Catholic hospital. Besides being responsible for the overall supervision of the department, I was the physician of record for patients admitted to the inpatient rehabilitation unit. For the first year, I was alone in that role, which meant I had to be available 24-7. I was able to get consultant backup from either the patient's own internist or the specialist who had been involved in the patient's acute care if I requested it. Otherwise, I was fully responsible for the patients' care while they were on the unit. I often found myself in the hospital from seven in the morning until well after eight in the evening. I also had to do rounds and be on call over the weekends.

With the generalized push to cut down on the inpatient days in acute hospitals, we were admitting patients to the rehab unit who were still not fully stabilized and needed constant monitoring. It was a stressful situation, especially as I was not overly confident in my internal medicine skills. It is hard to believe, but for several months during that first year, I never had a day off. As Christmas was approaching, an internist colleague offered to hold down the fort while I made an overnight visit to celebrate with my family in New York.

I was expected to keep the beds fully occupied, which meant promptly answering requests to assess patients in the acute-care hospital. I had the responsibility of deciding their suitability and ability to participate in the vigorous program of the unit. A stumbling block to their admission often revolved around their inability to tolerate three hours of therapy each day. This was especially challenging for patients who had been seriously ill and treated for an extended period in the intensive care unit. Assessing the program tolerance of patients who had suffered severe trauma, including brain injuries, was also difficult. Over the period of one year, we saw the average bed occupancy rise from six to eighteen out of twenty—the result of really hard work.

Around that time, the hospital assimilated into its network the Mount Sinai Hospital, which was scheduled for closure. This hospital, within three miles of St. Francis, had served the needs of a large Jewish population, but when they moved to the suburbs, it did not have sufficient patients to sustain it financially. The uniqueness of the situation—a Catholic and a Jewish hospital amalgamating—received a lot of publicity. To this day, the chief annual fund-raising event for the hospital has been titled a miracle. This autumn, it was "Miracle XXVIII," indicating that it has been more than twenty-eight years since this unique partnership took place.

The long-term plan was to move the inpatient rehabilitation unit at St. Francis to the Mount Sinai campus, where it would unite with a similar-sized unit already functional and become one freestanding rehabilitation hospital. Some, including me, didn't agree with this move, but we had no alternative but to comply and help with arrangements and renovations.

At least there was one immediate benefit from the merger. While plans were being implemented, Dr. Michael Saffir, the director of the Mount Sinai unit, and I, were able to share weekend duties, which meant each of us was off every second weekend, a respite we both sorely needed.

With the help of a consultant, I got the private practice office, including the all-important billing section, up and running smoothly. I was blessed to have found the services of a wonderful young lady, Andrea Sucheki, who became not only manager in chief but also my confidante and support. Now I could relax, especially when reimbursements from insurance companies were sufficient to cover salaries and other expenses. For several years, Andrea served me faithfully, until she decided to go back to school to get her nursing degree. It was hard to part with her, but I was somewhat consoled when she informed me that the manner in which I dealt with patients had inspired her to become a nurse. Andrea was the daughter I never had.

It was obvious I needed help, another doctor to share some of the busy practice. Eventually, I was successful in recruiting a young female physiatrist, Dr. Lisa Bellingham, who had just completed her residency program in another state. It was heavenly having her on board. She took care of the inpatient unit. Unfortunately, in the middle of her one-year contract, she left to take up a position in another city. It was not that we did not get on well—at least I was unaware if there were issues—but another private practice offered her better terms. I was back to square one.

While still the medical director of the St. Francis rehabilitation department, I had my first experience of being sued in a purported malpractice suit. From the word *go*, it was obvious I was an innocent party, but that did not take away from the horrible experience.

To put it succinctly, I was being sued as the physician of record in the acute hospital—the first false accusation. It was alleged that I allowed a patient with a neck injury out of bed to sit on the toilet, when, following an automobile accident, her cervical spine was unstable. The physician of record was actually a neurosurgeon. I had only performed a consultation to assess the patient's suitability for admission to the rehabilitation unit, and I had noted in the chart that she would be accepted when cleared clinically. I had written no orders, nor had I any authorization to do so.

It should have been obvious to anyone reviewing the patient's record that that was the case. My malpractice insurance company's attorney had no problem in extracting the facts from the patient's medical record. Unable to convince the plaintiff's attorney, eventually, my attorney had to present my case before a judge for settlement of the dispute. I was exonerated. That was two long years after the lawsuit was filed.

In the meantime, every year, when reapplying for admitting privileges to the hospital or clearance to treat patients covered by insurance companies, I had to give a substantial explanation in response to "Do you have a malpractice case pending against you? If so, give details." Answering that question would rile me up. It seemed unfair.

As plans for the new hospital were progressing, the administration started recruiting for an overall medical director. From the first day that I interviewed at St. Francis, I was aware that there would be a selection process for this post and that I would be welcome to apply if I was interested. I was conflicted as to whether I wanted to take on that responsibility, which meant moving over to the campus of Mount Sinai about three miles away. It was also made clear that there would be an emphasis on the rehabilitation of patients suffering the results of traumatic brain injuries (TBIs), a subspecialty I was not enthusiastic about. I eventually decided not to apply.

After a national search, Dr. Catherine Bonke was hired as medical director. Due to a childhood disability, she was confined to a wheelchair, which did not stop her from being fully involved with a special interest in the rehabilitation of patients with TBIs. Dr. Saffir and I were appointed as associate medical directors. We took turns in admitting and discharging inpatients as well as being on night and weekend call. At the same time, we both held on to our private practices, mine on the campus of St. Francis, as before. This arrangement meant a lot of commuting back and forth between the two hospitals.

For reasons I never quite understood, it was apparent from day one that the new medical director and I would not hit it off. Without going into details, I'll just say that it became increasingly difficult for me to work in that environment. After much reflection and in consultation with my lawyer, I had no option but to resign as associate medical director.

I duly presented my written resignation to Mr. Paul Stilman, the Vice President of the Rehabilitation Hospital and my immediate boss. He was surprised but did not make any effort to get me to change my mind. He suggested that I inform my colleagues, Catherine and Mike at a meeting with him later that afternoon. Mike was obviously taken aback by the news but it was hard to discern Catherine's reaction. Paul raised the question as to how we should inform the staff of my decision. Without hesitation Catherine suggested a derogatory and I will say sexist solution, one which does not bear repeating in these pages. My reaction in front of these two gentlemen was to be humiliated to the depths of my being. The remark may have been said in jest but I could detect a degree of venom in it. I stood up and in silence left the meeting.

I took myself promptly to the arms of my dear friend Mae Meeney and cried my eyes out. This crying session lasted for a full twenty-four hours. Adding to the pain was the realization that Paul did not comment that the remark was inappropriate or take cognizance of the hard work I had put into the department over the previous several years.

Once again, my livelihood was in jeopardy. With my

resignation came the loss of a substantial part of my income. I was back completely on the St. Francis campus and dependent on referrals from colleagues in order to keep my outpatient practice viable, an anxiety-provocative moment if ever there was one. My only other choice was to retire from practice. I wasn't ready for that either financially or emotionally, so I persevered. It was no surprise when Mike Saffir resigned as associate medical director shortly thereafter. I somehow felt vindicated that it wasn't all my fault.

The real tragedy came several months to a year after we had resigned from our posts as associate medical directors. Two new physiatrists had been hired to replace us. They had just completed their residencies. They were full of enthusiasm but had no administrative experience.

One morning, not too long afterwards while I was in the midst of performing a test on a patient, Mike Saffir called and asked if I was sitting down. He had some tragic news to relate: Dr. Catherine Bonke had passed away. I couldn't believe what I was hearing. I was unaware that she was ill. Neither had she been involved in an automobile accident. The unexpected news led to much speculation, but due to confidentiality, no concrete explanation was ever given as to the cause of her demise.

Shock gripped the campuses of St. Francis and the new Rehabilitation Hospital of Connecticut. Happily, I could find it in my heart to attend her funeral services.

While I never fully understood her animosity toward me, I tried to make peace with it. She often recounted that as a schoolgirl under the tutelage of nuns, she felt she had been treated harshly or perhaps even abused. She might have put me in the same category, seeking some revenge. May she rest in peace, a peace I don't think she had on this earth.

Shortly after my resignation as associate director of the rehabilitation hospital, I was informed that the office I rented in the outpatient department on the St. Francis campus was no longer available to me. At that late stage of my career, I had to search for suitable alternative office space. Luckily, I was able to sublet in the same building, from a hospital-based group of trauma surgeons, a one roomed office with access to common examination cubicles. It was far from ideal, but the rent was within my budget. I felt very alone with high stress levels but I soldiered on.

Relevant to the story at this stage is to say that from the time I left religious life, my main concern was to save for retirement. I was well into my fifties and had nothing put away for a rainy day. It was a scary thought. I was fortunate to meet Eileen Burke in Middletown. I was her first client as she initiated her business as a financial planner. With her help and advice, I was able to build a decent nest egg, which put me more at ease. Within a few years, I had even paid off the mortgage on my home.

Eileen and her husband, Dr. Jerry, became good friends, and introduced me to several of their circle of friends. One of them was Mary "Mae" Meaney, a single lady like myself and one of the most generous souls I have ever encountered. We became best friends and attended many social events together. It was to her that I ran for succor and advice on not only that fateful day but also many times in between. She had had great experience in hospital administration and was an enormous help and confidante. God rest her soul. She died shortly after my move to Florida. I felt compelled to return to Connecticut to attend her funeral and say a final farewell to a dear friend.

Another significant factor in my entry to the real world and the social circle was a linkage with other graduates from our medical school in Ireland. Soon after I left Philadelphia, I was invited back to a meeting of the newly formed American branch of the Medical Graduates of University College Dublin. I arrived at the venue expecting to know no one. Lo and behold, the first person I encountered was a classmate who also lived and practiced in Connecticut, Dr. Eamon Flanagan. That was the beginning of a wonderful friendship. He and his wife, Sheila, lived in the next town, and immediately, I became their guest not only at family gatherings but also at many of the parties they were renowned for hosting.

Under the leadership of Eamon, the branch of the graduates in Connecticut came alive and prospered. We took turns hosting dinner parties in our homes. These were wonderful occasions to bond, reminisce, and enjoy the common experiences of many years ago. There were national meetings also, when we were exposed to a wider bunch of graduates. The realization of how well all the graduates had performed and prospered was awesome and filled me with the utmost pride.

I would be remiss if I did not mention another dear friend, Dr. Pauline Olsen. Pauline is the type of special person one meets perhaps once in a lifetime. She had a background similar to mine: she had been on mission in Korea and had a busy obstetrics and gynecology practice based at St. Francis. She had been lucky to meet and marry a wonderful man named Zenny.

In their beautiful home in Farmington, they were renowned for their amazing hospitality. We would party well into the night, the majority of us of Irish background. Zenny, even though he had Polish ancestors, fit in perfectly with the *craic*. Unfortunately, he had an untimely death when he succumbed to cancer. In her new home, Pauline continued to be the perfect hostess and never forgot to include me in any celebrations she was having. I truly appreciated her friendship and still do, even at a distance.

## SEMIRETIRED

In the medical world of the mid to late 1990s, there were a lot of changes taking place in the delivery and reimbursement of health care, so physicians in solo practice were forming professional corporations (P.C.) or associations. I was one of those affected by changes in policy. My overheads were outpacing my income. I no longer had the support of the Rehabilitation Department. After due consideration I requested and was welcomed to join a multi-specialist group affiliated with St. Francis Hospital, who had amalgamated their individual practices into a P.C. For several reasons I am not at liberty to name the group.

It was strange not to have full control of the financial side of my practice, as everything from billing to banking was done by management personnel employed by the P.C. However, in other ways, it was liberating not to have to get involved in the day-to-day administrative affairs. We seemed to be progressing well, when there was a bombshell.

At an emergency meeting, the president of the board announced that it had been discovered that we were more than $1 million in the red and that the CEO had already been sent packing. We, the partners, either would face bankruptcy or would have to contribute a considerable amount of the fees collected in order to keep the group afloat. We were in disbelief and disarray.

While I contributed my share of the monthly assessment, it soon became clear that this was not a viable situation for me. After all my expenses were paid, there was nothing left for personal income. With some reservations, I decided it was time to quit.

Thus ended my private practice of medicine in the United States of America, a far cry from how I'd started forty years before in the heart of Africa. It was the year 2001.

However, I wasn't completely finished with medical work. Almost immediately, I became a consultant for Social Security Disability Services (DDS), whose Connecticut headquarters were in Hartford and convenient to my home. As a consultant, one contracted for x number of hours in the year. While it was necessary to come to the headquarters to review the files, once one fulfilled the contracted hours, one was generally free to come and go as he or she pleased. For example, one could go on an overseas vacation or could cancel attendance on a snowy day after informing the staff. There was no on-call duty or worry about maintaining an office. We didn't even have to take out personal malpractice insurance. It was necessary to become proficient in computer skills as the records of patients gradually became digitalized. It was an ideal job for semiretirement, a good source of income with the pleasant collegiality of other retired physicians.

During those years, I had the opportunity to visit with my sister Bernadette and her husband, Gerry, as they wintered in their beautiful home in Florida. The heat and sunshine were welcome changes from the harsh winters of the Northeast. Four or five years later, I decided to join them. I would have liked to take up residence in the development they were in, but at the time, that was not feasible. Instead, I bought into a new development some three miles west and had to wait about nine months to have my home built and ready for occupancy. Early in 2007, I moved into my dream home.

This brings me back to the beginning of my story. Over the past several years, Florida has become the mecca for retirement due mostly to its beautiful winter climate. Communities have sprung up exclusively for the over-fifty-five generation, Besides the beautiful homes and the gorgeous landscaping, emphasis is on creating a happy but stimulating retirement.

Soon after taking up residence in my development I was introduced to the game of mah-jongg. This board game, which originated in China had become popular among communities of Jewish women in New York. When they came south, they brought it with them. Four players, with a set of tiles, compete to make combinations of numbers and symbols defined by a card that is changed annually. It keeps the brain cells active, an important factor at this stage of our lives.

While I made some friends, such as my teammates for this game, about one year into my domicile, I realized I was not happy in my new home. It was difficult to put a finger on why that was so, nor will I at this stage try to explain it. Suffice it to say that I learned there is more to living happily ever after than a beautiful home in the most idyllic surroundings.

As one settles into the golden years, it becomes important to maintain social contacts and have a good relationship with friends and family. Otherwise, especially for a single person, it is easy to become isolated and lonely.

I was faced with a dilemma: Where to go next? I seriously considered returning to live in Ireland. I had my niece and namesake busy looking out for suitable property in the suburbs of Dublin. However, there were so many factors, especially financial ones, involved in such a radical uprooting that I could not make up my mind.

While I was still considering my alternatives, the house across the street from where my sister and her husband live, in the development I had initially liked, went on the market, and guess what. That's now my domicile.

I had promised myself that when I retired, I would get a dog. My first was a special guy I named Rafiki (Swahili for "Friend"). I was sad when he succumbed to splenic cancer at age twelve. Then I rescued Brooke from the death chamber. He suffered severe medical and emotional trauma, the result of some human's cruelty and neglect. It is amazing what TLC has done for him. He is now the sweetest companion one could wish for.

When I moved to Florida, I wasn't prepared to completely bid farewell to the practice of medicine. I thought I could continue working part-time for Social Security Disability. I discovered that to do so, I needed to get to Miami, a distance of about forty miles. Due to heavy traffic, the trip would take at least two hours driving each way. I made an exploratory trip to confirm that it was not worth the effort for part-time work.

Then I read an article in the local paper about a clinic in my neighborhood that welcomed volunteer medical personnel to serve uninsured and undocumented patients. I couldn't believe this opportunity was just around the corner from where I lived. I applied and was welcomed to the Caridad Center once I had a medical license for the state of Florida.

Little did I guess how tedious a process obtaining this license would be, just to volunteer at a clinic for poor and uninsured patients. I had to not only go through a criminal background check but also account for every year of my medical career and get the registrar at University College Dublin to send a transcript of my medical education and certification of graduation. This occurred in the year I was celebrating my fiftieth anniversary of graduation. Sometimes bureaucracy seems to go too far. It took one whole year to get the license.

From the day I commenced at this clinic in May 2008, I knew it was the place for me. To be able to work side by side with a group of retired and like-minded colleagues from various specialties and a dedicated staff has been a most rewarding experience. Besides the satisfaction that I was delivering medical care to patients who otherwise would not have access to such, there were other benefits; chief among them was not having to deal with insurance companies and other entities that have to be taken into consideration in private practice.

Over the years on my annual trips to Ireland it was a pleasure to link up with Father Leo when our visits home coincided. He would get me all fired up and have me exclaiming "I have to go and see for myself" as he relayed the progress in West Pokot that had occurred since I left. When I met him in the Summer of 2012, his stories of how the schools had developed, how some Pokot young men were in the seminary studying for the priesthood, how young Pokot women had joined religious congregations and other tales of progress, my mind was made up. "This is it, I am on my way"!.

In Chapter 1, I have documented my experiences and reactions to this gift that I gave myself. Not only was it an amazing experience to witness all the progress, it also completely erased from my psyche any lingering feelings of resentment that I might have had from my sojourn there.

Early in 2017, I realized it was time to completely retire from medical practice. In the two years before I came to this decision, at the invitation of the clinical director at Caridad, I had been involved in the Quality Improvement Program. My interest in that subject had never wavered, not since those days long past when I'd developed my magnum opus, "Quality of Care in the Outpatient Services of a District Hospital in Kenya." My contribution to this important aspect of health-care delivery was a great personal satisfaction and much appreciated by the administrators and the medical staff of the clinic.

It was gratifying when, in May 2016, the Florida Department of Health, Palm Beach County, honored me as their Volunteer of the Year.

## CHAPTER 15

# MUSINGS

Many years ago, I read *Journal of a Soul* by now Saint Pope John XXIII and marveled at how he could commit to writing and present to the world at large, his most intimate thoughts and experiences. He wrote, "My soul is in these pages." In a thousand years I could never have envisaged that I would find myself in circumstances where I would bare my soul as I have in these pages.

Reliving and committing to writing the ups and downs in my life's experience has been cathartic, to say the least. I realize there are certain intimate and painful events I could easily omit, and so be more at ease to publish, what could hopefully be an interesting story. However, that would not be true to my core or fit in with the premise I set out to tell in this story of days of honor and honesty.

One of my objectives in recalling so much of my childhood years was to document the way it was. There has been so much change over the span of my lifetime that I believe it must be hard for millennials to appreciate the wonders of the technological age and how we were able to grow up and prosper with no landline, let alone a cell phone; no electricity; and often no running water or indoor plumbing.

I made a big deal of my thirteen years in the dark tunnel. I can imagine that while reading the book chapter by chapter, the reader must be saying, "Will she ever get on with it? Get out! It is over!" I do not have an adequate explanation. I believe a deep sense of insecurity personally and financially, a fear of the unknown, and a sense of the pain my leaving the convent would inflict on my aged parents, held me back. But at least eventually, I had the courage to take the step. I am convinced there were many more, some of whom I knew personally, who were in a similar mind-set but were unable to make the final break.

As I reflect on what I have documented, it seems my life has been all work and no play, as the saying goes. I am sure many questions arise in the reader's mind about my emotional life, such as "Has she ever been in love?" Let me hasten to answer that question with a resounding yes.

God is love, and I have given my life to care for people and to value and enjoy the wonderful friendships I was privileged to experience throughout my life. Through these friendships, I experienced God and grew in closeness to Him.

The power of the internal drive to connect with and attach to humans, male or female, is amazing. I say "amazing" because my years of religious formation stressed that friendships were obstacles to a life of commitment to God and should be avoided at all costs. Any evidence of a friendship, especially with a person of the opposite sex, suggested either you did not belong in religious life or the relationship had to be broken up, as in my case when I was transferred from Ortum in 1964.

Clearly, relationships—male and female, female and female, male and male—are the only way to experience God in our world. Jesus had close relationships with his apostles, especially St. John, and with Martha, Mary, and Lazarus, whom he loved (see John 11:5 in the Jerusalem Bible).

Pope Saint John Paul II stated in his general audience of February 20, 1980, "The body, and it alone, is capable of making visible what is invisible: the spiritual and the divine. It was created to transfer into the visible reality of the world, the mystery hidden since time immemorial in God." We experience love through our bodies, in conversations, action, respect, loyalty, hugs, and especially friendships.

My heart is not made of stone, and I have always found it easy to be attracted to certain characteristics of the opposite sex. The physical attraction has not been the determining factor as much as sharing the same values and friendship.

I have already referred to how, as a teenager, I fell in love with my handsome, fun-loving cousin Pat. It was my first experience of having a male interested in me as a person, and I guess you could say it was sublimated when we both entered, at almost the same time, religious life.

Then there was the opportunity to date Eamon, the older nephew of my fairy godmothers, Sarah and Annie. I did not have any emotional attraction to Eamon, but perhaps that could have grown, had I not already decided my fate. Even then, I could not imagine myself as a farmer's wife! Don't let me sound elitist. There is nothing more wonderful in this world than being in communication with nature and caring for the earth and God's creatures, big and small, but farming was not for me.

I entered the novitiate just a few weeks after my eighteenth birthday, and if I have any regrets, it is that I never dated before I took that significant step. I can honestly say I had no experience of what one is giving up by taking a vow of celibacy. I was so intent on becoming a missionary that I was prepared to make any sacrifice to get there. We took it for granted that in order to do so, we needed to join a vowed religious congregation. This was more for financial and structural reasons than for the needs of the emerging local church.

In my early years and even as I went through medical school, I was never tempted to enter into any clandestine relationship. I kept an aura of propriety and, I believe, even deterred any male acquaintance from getting too close. I wasn't long on the missions before I felt the full impact of emotions and attraction for the opposite sex. I was in circumstances in which I did not feel much support from the sisters in my community, and the work put me in close contact with a male counterpart, that made me realize that at the core, I was fully human.

Besides Father Leo there have been two other men in my life, both of them missionaries and celibate priests. I offer no apology for my friendship with them.

Father Leo, he has been my hero. I say that with the utmost sincerity. Before I left Ortum in 1972, we had already parted company when he voluntarily went twenty miles farther into the bush to start a new mission center in Sigor. We continued to be friends and still are, fifty eight years later. He continued to minister there, building up the progressive schools and parish for another twenty or so years. He was beloved by the people and lived a humble, frugal lifestyle perhaps not so much appreciated by associates sent to help him. All of this came from a deep spirituality and love of the people he was sent to serve.

While I lived in Nairobi, Father Leo occasionally visited. I was still so angry about the whole Ortum affair that I avoided any conversation or update on progress in West Pokot. On one occasion, he invited me to come to Holy Family Cathedral to attend a meeting of the Catholic Charismatic Renewal Program. While I felt uncomfortable with such demonstrative expressions of faith, such as arms and hands raised heavenward as we implored the Holy Spirit to descend on us, he was fervently a part of it. He has continued to be actively involved with this movement and is not shy to express his deep spirituality and faith in the charismata (Greek for "gifts") of the Holy Spirit.

On my visit to Kenya in 2013, I saw faith in action on his part. A few years before, he had initiated the BobLeo Home for the physically and mentally challenged children of Pokot and surrounding areas. Unlike what happens in the United States or Europe, such children are kept hidden at home, do not go to school, and are seen as burdens on their families.

Instead of taking it easy in retirement, with seed money from the estate of his late brother, Father Bob, who had visited Kenya several times, Father Leo undertook the onerous and complicated project to ensure that these forgotten children receive an education and as far as possible learn a trade or profession so they can live independently as adults.

On the day of my visit, dormitories to house thirty boys and thirty girls were complete, and the assembly and dining hall were under construction, being supervised by this almost ninety-year-old priest. Watching these children with severe limb and body deformities, some of which could have been avoided with proper treatment during the acute phase of their illness or injury, was salutary for me with my background in rehabilitative medicine. I was tempted to volunteer my services, but better judgment prevailed.

As I stood there and saw what was involved in getting this project under way, I wondered what the future held. Was this a crazy idea that Leo had, knowing on the law of averages he was not going to be around to see it self-sustaining? Where would the personnel and the long term maintenance costs come from? These were just some of my questions.

The answer to these questions came shortly afterwards when Father Leo accidentally met up with a group of religious brothers based in Uganda whose special mission is to work with children so challenged. These brothers are now running the home, even though Father Leo, at age ninety-two, is still peripherally involved, especially fund-raising to complete the buildings and for maintenance costs.

Then there is my long-term friend Father Paddy, God rest him. I referred earlier to how I reconnected with him when I was a lonely soul in Baltimore in 1972, and he took me under his wing. I had known him peripherally in Kenya when he was education secretary for the diocese. His job entailed visiting all the Catholic Church–sponsored schools in the area. He was always thoughtful when coming to Ortum and would fill up his VW Beetle with fresh bread, milk, and other delicacies and, of course, most important, our mail bag. Whenever we arrived, seeking hospitality at St. Joseph's Teacher Training College in Kitale, where he resided, he received us with a *céad mile failte* ("a thousand welcomes" in Gaelic).

By the time I arrived, Father Paddy was well established in his ministry in the United States and had become an expert at fund-raising for the missions. As I discussed earlier, his struggles with the duplication of different denominations approaching the same donors or foundations for financial support led him to be a founding member of a consortium of such denominations, known as CODEL. He served as an ambassador for this agency for several years. His travels to assess projects worthy of their approval enabled him to continue contact with fellow missionaries on the ground, which he enjoyed.

He became almost a member of my family. He officiated at the weddings of my two nieces and was the chief celebrant at my brother's funeral. He was my support through all the ups and downs of my career, from that first meeting onward.

Unfortunately, Father Paddy became a victim of Alzheimer's disease. It was sad to see this brilliant man's intellect and memory succumb to the ravages of that condition. I remember some years ago, when I did not realize what was going on, he was visiting and bothering me for attention, and I suggested he read a book written by James Good entitled *Mission to the Turkana*, about a mission in the desert Father Paddy had started in the 1960s. I could not convince him that he knew Father Good, even though I was certain he did. Neither could I convince him that this was a familiar story that should have happy memories for him.

In later years, he had a desire to reenter direct ministry,

which he did in parishes of the diocese of Paterson, New Jersey. Even in retirement, he continued to serve his society by traveling in his Volkswagen for hundreds of miles on weekends to preach in appointed churches on behalf of the spiritual and financial needs of the missions.

In 2011, it became clear he needed supervised care at the society's headquarters in Kiltegan, Ireland. The last time I visited at the care center, which was a few months before he died in November 2014, was sad—he did not know who I was. "But I am Marita," I explained. "No, you are not. I only know one Marita, and she is a doctor. That's not you," he said. He looked at me with a vacant gaze that made me realize the person I'd known was no longer with us. It brought home to me how devastating it must be for families when a loved one, a spouse, father or mother, battling this disease, no longer recognizes them.

Then there is Fintan—no, not Sister Fintan of my medical school days, but Father Fintan. My friendship with him has grown over the years in mutual respect and appreciation. My impressions of Fintan when I first met him way back in the early 1960s was that while he seemed deadly serious and somewhat aloof, there was behind that exterior an independent thinker and free spirit. The first part of my initial impression changed as I got to know him better but especially when I saw him in action at some of the hoolies, as we called them, we missionaries held, such as celebrating our heritage on St. Patrick's Day. Father Fintan would be out on the floor, doing a dramatization of his party piece, "Phil the Fluter's Ball." Yes, he was capable of letting his hair down and was not so serious after all.

If I may speak for him, over time, he came to believe, just as I did, we could best help the poor people we were sent to by getting them to take care of themselves and accomplishing their priorities, not what we assumed were their needs or preferences. Way before it was a household concept, Father Fintan implemented the idea of small Christian communities in the parishes where he was pastor, a movement that is now fully endorsed by the Catholic Hierarchy of East and Central Africa.

Even in retirement, he continued to work with the poor and initiated the St. Vincent de Paul Society in Kitale town. Through the society, if members of the local Christian community see a need to help people poorer than themselves, they provide help, monetary or otherwise, from their own resources and not as a handout from a foreign source.

I have been drawn to Father Fintan for his nonjudgmental attitude, acceptance of me the way I am, and openness to problems in the real world. At times, his methods might not appear to be in full compliance with orthodox teaching, but they are more aligned with the message of the gospel.

He has never been a person to intrude into personal matters unless others volunteer them. While I imagine he knew over the years that I was afloat, so to speak, he never pried for information. I always felt he was there to support my decision, whatever it was.

More recently, especially since my visit to Kenya in 2013, when we had a chance to have good personal (mine) and theological chats, we have renewed our friendship. In fact, after I completed the first version of this memoir, as I felt embarrassed about some of the content, the only person I felt comfortable sharing it with was Father Fintan. His verdict was "This is your story; none of it should be omitted." He expressed no element of surprise or harsh judgment, which attests to the quality of the man. I am blessed to have such a soul mate and also blessed by today's technology to be able to communicate at a distance.

I would be remiss if I concluded this chapter without an appreciation for the St. Patrick Fathers Missionary Society. In these days, when Catholic clergy are often assigned to the doghouse and ubiquitously blamed for the sexual scandal that rocked the church, I can only say I have never encountered any grounds for this accusation among the members of this society who have crossed my path.

I have only the greatest admiration for these men. They have taken on the most difficult missions, even in desert territory, such as Turkana, and in difficult political situations, such as in South Sudan. They have lived frugally yet have been a font of generosity and hospitality, prepared to share even the last slice of bread in the house if a casual visitor knocked at their door. As we used to say (in private, of course!), "We have taken a vow of poverty, but these guys live it." While they are not religious in the technical sense and are masters of their own finances, my experience has been that they have put all their possessions into helping the people to whom they were sent. *Ad multos annos* (May they prosper for many years).

When eventually I was free to enjoy relationships with men or even enter into marriage, I became selective as to whom I might even think of dating. One of my priorities was that whomever I dated must have the same values as I and also be free to marry in church. That excluded divorced men. They did not necessarily have to be Catholic.

As I look back on what I think would have been an ideal situation for me, it would have been to fall in love and marry a fellow Catholic missionary, and the two of us could have continued to serve the poor in our beloved Kenya. But this brings up the issue of celibacy, a discussion I will leave for another day.

I must confess that I made some efforts to find a partner through a dating service. I would sneak a peep at some of the bios of potential suitors, but it was too scary to follow through and indicate that I was interested. I went on a few dates, which never got me anywhere.

There was one man among my circle of friends who was recently widowed, and whom I saw as a possible partner and even a husband. I invited him to escort me to one of the annual the St. Francis Miracles' gala events. This he graciously did but when at my suggestion (yes mine!), that we meet again he demurred and informed me he was not ready for dating, that he was still in love with his wife in the grave. So that ended this possible romance.

There was another attempt to introduce me to a widower. He was the brother-in-law of my dear friend Peggie. This man was expressing his loneliness and interest in finding another partner. He was a prominent lawyer in Washington, DC. It just so happened that at the time, I had planned to attend a medical conference at the headquarters of the Ministry of Health in Bethesda, in the suburbs of Washington. A date was duly set up for Sunday, the day before the conference started.

The gentleman asked if I would like to accompany him to a

picnic at the home of friends in the horse country of Virginia. Come midday, he picked me up at the entrance of the hotel where I was staying, and we proceeded the twenty or so miles to our destination. I socialized well with the hosts and the group of some twenty guests. I will admit that I did not greatly indulge my appetite, even though the food was plentiful and there for the taking.

Around five o'clock, it was time to return to Washington. We ran into a lot of traffic, which slowed our pace. My impression was that we were getting on well, and we were both at ease while chatting with each other.

Unexpectedly, as soon as we reached the door of my hotel, without getting out of the driver's seat, he bade me farewell and wished me a successful stay at the conference. What a letdown! I muttered some words of thanks and disappeared into the hotel lobby. I was crestfallen. I kept saying to myself: *Was I so boring that he was not able even to share a meal with me? We were both hungry, and it would have been my pleasure to treat him and put the expense on my room charge.*

Of course, that wasn't his reason for dumping me; obviously, he didn't feel any chemistry. I had a lonely meal all by myself in the hotel restaurant—an unexpected ending to what I'd thought was a pleasant day. My friend who'd arranged the encounter couldn't wait for me to get back from the conference to ask how the date had gone. She was taken aback, to say the least, when she heard how it had ended. The reports she had heard from her sister's lady friends at the picnic were that I would have been a good match for the gentleman. But it was not to be.

So I had to settle into being single. In some ways, that suits my independent spirit. On the other hand, I believe there is nothing more beautiful in life than having a loving relationship with a human being of the opposite sex. My regret surfaces especially when I see couples show their love in action. Not becoming a mother has not been a sacrifice.

Like so many of my friends, including my sister who enjoy retirement in Florida, I would have liked to have taken up the game of golf, not only for the opportunity for socialization and camaraderie but as a good wholesome exercise. A chronic shoulder injury has prevented me from that. I am happy to catch up with my reading. I have a preference for books that record events in history or stories of real peoples' lives. I read the odd spiritual and philosophical treatise. I have recently been inspired by the writings of the late John O'Donohue especially in his *Anam Cara. A Book of Celtic Wisdom*. I quote some sentences that resonate with me: "Words that would mirror the soul carry the loam of substance and the shadow of the divine" (P 67) and "We are sent into this world to live to the full everything that awakens within us and everything that comes towards us"(P 123)

I must say that I love good prose, the artistry of words and I wish I could write poetry!

As everyone knows over the past fifty years, there have been many nuns *jump over the walls,* and return to secular life and supposedly live happily ever after. I have read the memoirs of a few of them and what interests me is how they found a partner, some in the most unlikely of places. One of these is the recently published book by Adele Azar- Rucquoi entitled "The Nun and the Bum". It raises the issue for me as to how come I was not so lucky? Was it my fault? Was I too busy building up my nest egg and didn't allow providence to take care of me? I guess I will never know.

# EPILOGUE

I close as I began, with the question "What if?" There were so many what-ifs. In my heart, I don't think anything happened by chance; the hand of God or my guardian angel was there guiding me all along. I am in a happy place right now and know I am where I am meant to be. The Swahili phrase *"Hakuna matata"* (There is no problem) not only sounds poetic but also sums up my sentiments.

I appreciate even the hard knocks, as I would never be in this place of peace if I had not gone through the crucible of fire. Through it all, I have learned to be less judgmental and more understanding of human behavior. For example, when a love affair is over, I believe it is over. For my part, once I had crossed that line of commitment to religious life, even after thirteen years of struggle, I was unable to turn back the clock and fall in love with it again.

I am happy to be alive at this time in history, when the emphasis is on implementing the gospel as Jesus taught us, and not in the world in which I grew up, when the focus was on personal perfection and preparing for the next world.

I imagine many of us have our favorite guiding principle from scripture or elsewhere. Mine has been from the prophet

Micah: "This is what Yahweh asks of you: only this, to act justly, to love tenderly and to walk humbly with your God" (Micah 6:8, the Jerusalem Bible).

I still struggle to follow that guiding star, but I believe that God will take care of me for the rest of my days, just as He has in the past.

This anonymous quotation—I cannot remember where I found it—epitomizes my state of well-being:

> Come sit with me ...
> Today may there be peace within
> May you trust that you are exactly where you are meant to be
> May you never forget the infinite possibilities that are born of faith in yourself and others
> May you be content with yourself just the way you are
> Let this knowledge settle into your bones and allow your soul the freedom to sing, dance, praise and love.
> It is there for each and everyone of us.

# ACKNOWLEDGEMENTS

There is one person that deserves priority among the many who have helped to bring this memoir to print. That is my niece, Marie Griffin. Marie took on the task of converting a long tedious rigmarole into the readable manuscript one finds between the covers of this book. Her expertize, her insightfulness and her interest in all things pertaining to Africa, especially Kenya, not only got me to highlight aspects of the story that did not seem worthy of record but made me go beyond my comfort level in documenting the more personal, private moments of my life experience. Even the catchy chapter headings and sub headings are of her creation and testify to her literary genius. Thank you Marie.

When it gets to acknowledging everyone else who have helped me along the way I know not where to start or end. I simply say *Go raibh maith agaibh* (Thank you in Gaelic); *Asante sana* (Thank you in Swahili)

My love and gratitude to my parents and my siblings is unconditional as was their love for me. I especially thank my brother, Henry for his encouragement and expert input into the more difficult emotional aspects of my story.

Nancy Dixon came to the rescue when it seemed I was

getting nowhere due to my lack of knowledge of the intricacies of the electronic era. Not only is she an expert in the technical aspects of e-writing but she has held my hand and calmed my nerves when all seemed lost! Bless you Nancy.

And then there is my friend, Dr. Miriam Were. When I started to think as to who might write a Forward to my story it was an easy choice. Miriam and I soldiered together in the Medical School in Nairobi many years ago and while over the years we have not been in constant communication it was with great joy that we renewed our friendship in 2013 when I revisited Kenya. She does me a great honor by taking time out of her busy and responsible schedule to read the manuscript and write such an insightful Forward. I love you, Miriam.

My debt of gratitude to the Missionary Sisters of the Holy Rosary is boundless. I am what I am by having been one of them. There would be no story otherwise. I love and thank them one and all.

Note: Parts of Chapter One have already been published in *AFRICA*, the publication of the St. Patrick Missionary Fathers, under the title "West Pokot Revisited: Reflections and memories from a Doctor's notebook", Vol 79. No.4, May 2014

CPSIA information can be obtained
at www.ICGtesting.com
Printed in the USA
BVHW030219050920
588203BV00001B/34